GREAT
Anzac
STORIES

GREAT Anzac STORIES

THE MEN AND WOMEN WHO CREATED THE DIGGER LEGEND

GRAHAM SEAL

ALLEN&UNWIN

SYDNEY•MELBOURNE•AUCKLAND•LONDON

First published in 2013
Copyright © Graham Seal 2013

Allen & Unwin
Sydney, Melbourne, Auckland, London

83 Alexander Street
Crows Nest NSW 2065
Australia

Phone: (61 2) 8425 0100
Email: info@allenandunwin.com
Web: www.allenandunwin.com

Cataloguing-in-Publication details are available
from the National Library of Australia
www.trove.nla.gov.au

ISBN 978 1 74331 059 5

Cover photo: Australian War Memorial, Negative Number CAM/68/0144/VN (E00233)
Index by Jon Jermey
Set in 12.5/17 pt Adobe Caslon Pro by Bookhouse, Sydney
Printed and bound in Australia by Griffin Press

10 9 8 7 6 5 4 3 2 1

Contents

Introduction

Since 25 April 1915, Australians have progressively expanded and deepened the significance of Gallipoli, the battles of the western front, Tobruk, Kokoda and Long Tan, in addition to many other engagements in the Middle East, Korea, Malaya, Indonesia, Iraq and Afghanistan. The national community's awareness also encompasses the many peacekeeping operations around the world in which Australian troops have taken part. The death and injury of hundreds of thousands of Australians, together with the resulting grief and ongoing suffering within their families, have left a permanent and profound imprint on the nation. This is recorded in stone, wood and metal on memorials and honour boards in almost every community in the country and in many places abroad.

The term that embodies this combination of sacrifice, duty, loss and meaning is 'Anzac', formed from the telegraphic address of the Australian and New Zealand Army Corps—ANZAC. This 'one little word' has come to resonate many things Australians consider to be profoundly symbolic of their identity: courage, determination, anti-authoritarianism, egalitarianism and a larrikin attitude to the grim realities of war and so, of life and death in general. Whether these characteristics are genuine or not is a question that is often debated. Certainly, the fact that the concept of 'Anzac' has persisted for almost a century and shows every sign of strengthening into the future as a popular focus of national identity, among the young as well as the old, suggests that it has wide support in the community.

Through the decades following World War I, during which Anzac has become an inescapable aspect of our society, innumerable stories have been told about those who contributed to its making. These spoken and written memorials include tales of heroism, suffering and endurance. Perhaps surprisingly to some, Anzac tales are often humorous, for laughter is an essential element in coping with the realities of war and its long aftermath. Many are widely known, in one version or another, and are told and retold in books, newspapers, films and even in schoolrooms. Many other Anzac stories are known only to particular groups or to the inhabitants of particular communities, perhaps only to a family. Whatever their provenance, these stories together make up an intangible web of knowledge about the Australian experience of war and the way we understand it through Anzac. They form a network of shared meaning that is publicly reaffirmed every year on 25 April at memorials around the country and, increasingly, around the world.

It is these stories, told whenever possible in the words of those who were there—at the front line or at home—that appear in *Great Anzac Stories*. At least, a few of them appear. Anzac's long existence and wide appeal has generated a vast body of anecdote, legend, reminiscence and yarn and this book can only represent a small selection of these many tales.

In telling these stories, the book begins with 'Foundations', a selection of accounts from Gallipoli, the western front and the Middle East. This is followed by 'Heroes', which tells of courageous deeds in many of Australia's wars. Home fronts are as important as battlefronts, and a selection of tales from Australia and 'Blighty'—the United Kingdom—next appears here. The large body of digger humour is given due representation under the heading of 'Laughter', followed by a collection of Anzac 'Legends'. The book concludes with a section titled 'Memories', which focuses on the commemoration of war and its consequences for all, at home and at the front.

The concept of 'Anzac' is treated broadly. As well as stories about the army and the original diggers—the largely citizen foot soldiers of the First Australian Imperial Force (AIF)—the book includes those of the Royal Australian Air Force (RAAF) and the Royal Australian Navy (RAN). As well as tales of men at war it includes those of nurses, doctors and even animals. While the 'NZ' in Anzac is often overlooked, there are also a few stories specifically about the Kiwi experience of war and the considerable significance of Anzac in that country.

Anzac is an idea that is a vital element of the Australian consciousness. It has been with us for almost a century, sometimes referred to as 'the spirit of Anzac', or the 'legend of Anzac'. Over that time it has increased and decreased in popularity, with the lowest level of public observance occurring on the Anzac days between the late 1960s and late 1980s. Since then we have seen a strong resurgence of interest in the day and, consequently, the meaning of Anzac itself. This has been particularly marked among young adults, although older Australians have also been flocking to Anzac Day events—especially the Dawn Service—as well as travelling to the various sites of Anzac memory in Britain, Turkey, France, Vietnam, Papua New Guinea and Singapore, to name only some of the more popular destinations for these 'pilgrimages', as they are often called.

This enthusiasm for what some consider to be a glorification of war has generated controversy from time to time, with various groups, including anti-war organisations, voicing their opposition to aspects of Anzac. Arguments that Anzac and its day are about acknowledging sacrifice and remembering those who made it are not accepted by all Australians. Whatever the view taken, though, it is very difficult not to have a position for or against Anzac, so completely does it pervade our society.

This book seeks to present the Anzac stories it contains as straightforwardly as possible, allowing readers to make their own judgements. The stories are left largely to speak for themselves, with only a minimum of explanation and background detail to provide context for today's reader. Spellings, punctuation and other usages have been variously standardised and corrected, except where it is necessary to retain the original to preserve the sense of the quotation. A glossary of military acronyms, specialised terms and slang has also been provided. Military titles, ranks and honours are generally those possessed by the individual at the time of the events witnessed or experienced.

To convey the immediacy of the events as they were experienced, many eyewitness accounts taken from letters, diaries and other contemporary documents have been included. These sources resonate with the attitudes and values of the day, and the emotions of the moment—and they are often rich in Australian 'slanguage', giving them colour and impact, even after many decades. The downside of this is that these accounts sometimes contain terms and represent attitudes that are no longer socially acceptable.

Some pieces written in reflection, after the events they describe, are also included to show the always-developing significance of Anzac, not only in war but also in the periods between them that we call 'peace'.

Acknowledgements

MAUREEN SEAL, JOHN Stephens, Alan Williams and the Fovant Badge Preservation Society, and the staff at Allen & Unwin. A portion of the royalties generated by this book will be donated to Legacy, a volunteer organisation formed by war veterans in 1923 to care for the dependants of deceased Australian servicemen and women—a great Anzac story of its own.

Glossary

THE MILITARY, TECHNICAL and slang terms that sometimes appear in the documents used for this book may not be familiar to most readers. The following list should be helpful.

AB   able bodied seaman

Ack emma   am, the morning

ADS   advanced dressing station

ASC   army service corps

Batman   personal assistant to an officer

Billyjim or Billjim   terms sometimes used for an Australian soldier in World War I

Blanky   euphemism for 'bloody', or any other swear word

Bn, or Bat   Battalion

(the) Boche (sometimes as Bosche)   Germans

CO   commanding officer

DCM   Distinguished Conduct Medal

DSO   Distinguished Service Order

'Eggsers'   28th Battalion AIF, from their battle cry 'Eggs-a-cook'

Enfilade   to fire into a trench or enemy position from a number of sides at once

Minenwerfer   German artillery piece, World War I

MM   military medal

NCO   non-commissioned officer

OC   officer in charge

Pip emma   pm, the afternoon

QMS   quartermaster's store

Sap   a tunnel or trench

TB   torpedo boat

VC   Victoria Cross

WAAC (sometimes as 'Waacs')   Women's Army Auxiliary Corps

Woodbine   derogatory term for the British, derived from the brand name of the cheap cigarettes they usually smoked

WT   wireless telegraph

8 chevaux ou 40 hommes   French for '8 horses or 40 men', a sign commonly stencilled to the side of French rail wagons in which many troops were transported in World War I

Foundations of Anzac

AUSTRALIA'S EXPERIENCE OF World War I, from September 1914 to the armistice of 11 November 1918, is the basis of the Anzac tradition. The high drama of the Dardanelles landings in Turkey on 25 April 1915, and the dogged fighting of the next eight months, meant that Gallipoli (Gelibolou) quickly became the originating location of Anzac and all it has come to stand for. Other events and locations—sometimes not so dramatic or formative, but all contributing to the evolution of the digger—have disappeared from our general knowledge of the war. The fighting in German New Guinea the year before Gallipoli, the importance of the Greek island of Lemnos and the significant role of submarine *AE2* in 1915 have suffered this fate of being largely forgotten. On the western front, meaning the trench lines that ran the breadth of Belgium ('Flanders') and France, further feats of bravery, endurance and sometimes incomprehensible sacrifice burnished the legends of Gallipoli and the digger, in the minds both of the Anzacs themselves and of those waiting and worrying at home in Australia and

New Zealand. Pozières in France and Passchendaele in Belgium are among the places that still draw large numbers of visiting Australians and which are recorded on war memorials around Australia. In the region now known as 'the Middle East', some serious battles were fought, now mostly forgotten, with the exception of Beersheba in 1917. These events, a handful among the many that took place in four years of fighting, are the foundations of Anzac.

Digger

The term 'digger', meaning the rank-and-file Australian foot soldier, is closely tied to the significance of 'Anzac'. Together, these two words have been at the centre of popular ideas about national identity since World War I (1914–18).

The term Anzac is derived from ANZAC, the telegraphic abbreviation of 'Australian and New Zealand Army Corps'. It seems to have become a self-descriptive word in use among members of the First AIF during training in Egypt, perhaps even earlier, and was immediately applied to the beach where the Australian and New Zealand troops first landed at Gallipoli on 25 April 1915. At this time, the soldiers were often referred to as 'Anzacs', sometimes as 'Billjims', with the term 'digger' not becoming an accepted denomination until 1917 on the western front. Nevertheless, the term is commonly employed retrospectively to refer to Australian and New Zealand soldiers who fought from the beginning of World War I.

The image of the digger draws on the nineteenth-century romance and mythology of the Australian bush and its heroes. These include the pioneer, the free selector, the gold prospector or 'digger', the shearer, even the bushranger, as well as many similar characters who feature in bush verse and song, and in the literature and art of writers Andrew 'Banjo' Paterson and Henry Lawson and painter Tom Roberts, among many others. From the 1890s, these archetypal figures were closely associated with popular ideals concerning Australian identity. When the country went to war, most Australians considered that this event represented the emotional 'birth of a nation'. Through the experiences of the AIF, the ideal of the bushman effortlessly morphed into that of the digger. Instead of driving cattle overland, shearing sheep or rounding up herds of brumbies, the bushman now wore a uniform—more or less—and employed his bush skills and nous in excavating 'dugouts' and 'possies', making jam tin bombs, sniping and generally trying to outfox a wily enemy resisting an invasion of its homeland (in the case of Turkey). Even though many members of the First AIF came from the city rather than the country (contrary to a popular and persistent myth), as a body they demonstrated the bushman's independence and ingrained disdain for authority, as well as pursuing—frequently to excess—the masculine pastimes of drinking, fighting and gambling. The digger's symbolic status, rooted in these available traditions of the bush, was immediate and enduring.

With this background it is not surprising that the origins of the term for the Australian infantryman have been the cause of ongoing controversy. It has been argued that the term was derived from the mid-nineteenth-century gold rushes in the eastern colonies, in which the men who hastened to the goldfields to seek their fortunes came to be known as 'diggers'. It has also been suggested that the word originated at Gallipoli, because the Anzacs who landed there were quickly compelled by the

Turkish resistance to 'dig in'; they were famously commanded by General Sir Ian Hamilton to 'dig, dig, dig'. New Zealand variations of the story include the suggestion that it came from the local term 'gum diggers' for fossickers of the fossilised resin of kauri trees. Another claim has been made for the origin of the term among members of the 3rd Division's 11th Brigade, training and digging on England's Salisbury Plain in September and October 1916.

There are numerous other folkloric accounts that claim to pinpoint the origins of the word. The only certainty is that Australian troops did not begin to call themselves 'diggers'—or to be called so by others—until at least early 1917, two years after the Anzac landings at Gallipoli. From the moment the term first appeared it was, and continues to be, frequently debated in letters to the editors of newspapers and within the ranks of ex-service associations around the country.

Writing in 1944, Lieutenant Colonel C. Dennis Horne gave this version:

Just before the last war I was employed in the PWD Tasmanian Railway Construction Branch. In one of the day-labour gangs a typical old bowyanged navy (ex-N.Z. gum digger), Digger Cowley, always greeted you with 'Good-day, digger.' The timekeeper on these works, W H Sandy and I drifted to World War I.

After Gallipoli we went to France. On a typical grey sloppy Flanders morn, early 1917, Captain Sandy (now Lt-Col Sandy, DSO), and I were plodding through Poperhinge near the original Toc H building [a comforts facility in the Belgian town of Poperinghe]. I was surprised and impressed by 'old Sandy's' greeting to each passing lad—'Good-day, digger.' Like magic the term became mass-produced. From every estaminet, urged by the vin rouge or vin blanc plonk, oozed the expression, 'Good-day, dig', or, more slangishly, 'How's she, dig.'

I often think of 'old Sandy', that cheerful unorthodox soldier with the persistent bubble in his Adam's apple, and I feel that many, knowing him, will say: 'Well, now you come to think of it, he is just the likeliest old b—— in the first AIF to have been the originator of "digger." '

A Major T. A. Connor responded to this version.

I must join issue with Lt-Col Horne on the origin and application of the word 'digger' in the first AIF. At least two years prior to 1917 this greeting was in general use, and I submit that its origin may be traced to the later days at Gallipoli.

Following the unsuccessful battles of early August 1915, the bulk of the Australian forces was engaged in constructing and improving trenches. The 7th Brigade (2 Division) was on Cheshire Ridge, The Apex and Durrant's Post, and it was a general source of merriment to other units to inquire of our boys their 'present occupation', to which the reply was generally 'Digging, digging, always b—— well digging.' My own battalion (27 battalion) became well known as the '3 D's' ('Dellman's Dugout Diggers') to which we added the then popular 'dinkum', and so caused the battalion to be known as 'Dellman's Dinkum Dugout Diggers.'

I suggest that the greeting 'digger' originated at this time and not, as suggested by Lt-Col Horne, in the early part of 1917.

The controversy continues today.

First to fall

The first Australian engagements—and casualties—of World War I took place not in 1915 at Gallipoli but during the year before in what was then known as German New Guinea. In September 1914 a combined Australian Naval and Military Expeditionary Force attacked German forces and wireless installations at and near Herbertshöhe (now Kokopo, East New Britain province in Papua New Guinea). These installations were considered dangerous because they formed the communications hub for Germany's East Asian Cruising Squadron. A month or so after the engagement, First Class petty officer C. Hoffman wrote home to Rockhampton in Queensland about his experiences, giving an on-the-ground account of the fighting.

You know that we left Rocky and everything was a whisper. When Max Jeffries and myself reached Brisbane we were ordered to Sydney by the same train that brought us from Rocky, along with over fifty Queenslanders bound for Sydney. Still everything done in a whisper. When we got to Sydney there was no secret about it. All along the line the people were at the stations to give us a cheer, right up to 2 am. We were a queer looking crowd, only one third of the boys in uniform. On arriving in Sydney we were run to Edgecliff. Some were fitted out with uniform and boots, and webbing gear similar to the soldiers. I was not fitted with clothes until we were at sea in the *Berrima*. We had a fine passage right through. We anchored ten days in the Palm Islands, going on shore in the ship's boats, skirmishing and rifle practice. There were about 500 naval reserves and over 1200 soldiers with two machine guns.

. . . When we arrived off here at 7 am on the 11th we had orders to go on shore for the great ceremonial as the Germans had surrendered, but we very soon found out that they had not. The Governor said that he could not surrender and the navals were landed. The run to the wireless station, called Kabakaul, about six miles from the landing, was a dangerous piece of work. It was one open road with thick jungle on both sides, with a trench across the road which was mined in places. We lost the best naval officer of the expedition, Lieutenant Commander Elwell, a real 'toff', Captain Pockley of the Army Medical Corps, another 'toff', and four of our reserves, all AB's, along with three other reserves wounded.

Landing parties from the destroyers also landed and did good work. We also had one naval officer, Lieutenant Bowen, wounded, but he has since rejoined. Our boys fought like tigers; no holding them back. The Germans themselves did not do much damage. They cocktailed [failed to fight]. The native armed police did most of the damage. They were posted in trees. We got a number of German officers and non coms, also thirty-six native police besides those that were sent to the boneyard. The two officers that were shot, also the AB's, were shot with soft-nosed bullets, the lead standing out about a quarter of inch above the nickel. Some of the nickel bullets were filed like a cross over the point of the bullet, and others were sharp-pointed. There would be no chance of living if any of them went through you. The bullet-holes in Lieutenant Elwell and Captain Pockley on the one side were very small, but where they came out you could drop a billiard ball in.

After the wireless was taken we had to look for the Governor, forty Germans, and 200 armed native police in another part of the island. The *Encounter* shelled in the direction where the force was supposed to be, about six miles in a straight line, and that put the fear of God and old England into their hearts. They had retreated to another place. We had been in the bush all day, and just about dusk located them up a bit of a mountain. Two shots from our field gun into the ridge and out came a white flag with word that the Governor and his troops would surrender. On the Thursday the Governor came in and surrendered on condition that they got full honours of war.

On the Monday it was a grand sight to see the Germans coming in with their black police. Their drilling was something lovely, just like a piece of machinery. Three days after the battle I was made a first-class petty officer for services, and two days later was appointed master of native police. I took charge of the police when they surrendered and disarmed them. They were armed with 1912 and 1913 Mauser rifles and jagged bayonets. They are a fine body of boys, I have got them into shape with the English words of command. They have no time for the Germans on account of the Germans ill-treating them. When the Germans started getting away from us the niggers started to talk amongst themselves, and the only way for the Germans to save their own skins was by surrendering themselves and the black police as well. They fed them up like fitting [fighting] cocks and got the ball cartridges away from them, and gave them dummy ones instead.

The Germans had another wireless station about thirty-two miles from here, and the road to it was a beauty. It was simply a pass in places and if they had put up a fight in this direction there would have been very few of us left to tell the tale. There were places where it would have been almost impossible to get at them, but thanks to the native police the Germans threw in the towel.

Another twenty-six blacks and whites arrived from New Guinea as reinforcements and walked across the island. We intercepted these, and they surrendered. All the ships lay up in Rabaul, the capital, which is on Simpson Haven, about fourteen miles from here. The soldiers are in garrison there with the exception of about two companies, which are in New Guinea, and twenty-eight naval reserves and four companies of naval reserves are stationed here at Herbertshohe. I take my armed police into the bush and am away two and three days at a time. I am not a bit afraid. They swear by me and say, 'Hoffman, he good feller master. You no make him cross.' The other natives on the island take some watching; but they all say they are 'English—German no good.' In all the southern papers, we get here there is nothing in them about the forces bound for England; not a word about our boys being boiled up under the Equator, and never a murmur from the papers. The soldiers that have accompanied us here have never fired a shot yet, and are not likely to.

Things are quiet here. It is simply garrison work. I get plenty to do. I have to look after the native police and natives, and I have a lively time hunting up the German planters for ill-treating natives on their plantations. I have got Max Jeffries in the office here with me now, so don't wonder at Max forgetting his English when he returns. He is getting quite a big chap, and is filling out fast and has helped to keep up the name of the Bulldog Breed and Sons of the Sea.

How are all the boys in Rocky? We should have had fifty at least from Rocky. Some of the lads from Victoria are not eighteen years of age. I would like to tell you a lot more, but enough said for the present. I see by the southern papers that Lieutenant Commander Elwell and Captain Pockley were killed at

Rabaul in Simpson Haven, and that they were bayoneted with jagged bayonets. That is incorrect. The fight took place between Kabakaul and Bitapaka, where the wireless station was situated, as none know better than the Australian Naval Reserves. Kabakaul is between Cape Gazelle and Point Liaison.

Now I think I have said enough for once. With kind regards to you and yours from Max and myself. Hoping you are all well. Give our chin-chin to all Rocky, and tell them we came out to win and win we did. With the best of good-wishes for dear old Rocky.

Australia's first submarine, *AE1*, was part of this operation but was lost at sea with all hands—and has not yet been found. These events, occurring immediately to Australia's north, took place before the formation of the Australian and New Zealand Army Corps, which is perhaps one reason they have not received the same attention as Gallipoli. But the attitude and approach to the fighting give a hint of what would develop into the Anzac tradition.

The forgotten island

The story of Anzac is founded on events that took place on Gallipoli from dawn 25 April 1915 to dawn 20 December 1915. Forgotten in this chronology is the Greek island of Lemnos, around 130 kilometres from the fighting on the Turkish mainland. While the island is fairly well known for its role as a hospital base for Gallipoli casualties, Lemnos was the point at which the various Allied forces assembled prior to the 25 April landings. It was also the place to which many soldiers were taken after the evacuation of Gallipoli and was effectively the main support base for the entire campaign. Even twenty years later, A. H. Edmonds of the 1st AIF vividly recalled the scene of the combined landing force assembled in Mudros harbour, on Lemnos.

Those members of the A.I.F. who saw Lemnos can never forget the wonderful concentration of shipping which sprawled over the spacious harbour of Mudros. Everything that could float seemed to be there, from the world's largest battleships and liners down to the tiny torpedo boats and trawlers. Flags of all the Allied nations fluttered in the breeze. Freakish-looking craft not seen before by Australian eyes helped to swell this floating world . . .

This was the start of what was to be a close and ongoing relationship between the British, Australian, New Zealand, French, Newfoundland (Canada) and Indian forces and the islanders of Lemnos. The island, especially around Mudros, rapidly became an extensive military complex of hospitals, rest camps and associated administrative facilities essential for the medical and recreational support of the troops. Cemeteries were also laid out. Lemnos had originally been planned as the main base for the campaign, although this was moved to Alexandria in Egypt, over 1000 kilometres away, due to a perceived lack of facilities. However, as the campaign progressed, Lemnos became increasingly important for its proximity to the fighting, as the official war correspondent Charles (C. E. W.) Bean noted: '. . . this splendid harbour sixty miles from the Peninsula, though nominally never more than an "intermediate" base, inevitably became an important centre . . .'

Just before the various waves of the landing forces sailed from Lemnos to the shores of Gallipoli, Lance Corporal Archibald Barwick, 1st Battalion AIF, noted in his diary:

The day before the fleet sailed we were all drawn up and General Birdwood spoke to us to be careful with our water, food and ammunition and told us that the eyes of the whole world would be on us, to see how we fought. They must have been cock sure of breaking right through, for they told us that there would be no haggling in the villages we were to pass through as all the prices would be fixed. We were paid on the 22nd with notes which had Turkish writing on them.

Barwick also described the scene aboard his ship as the troops prepared to land the following morning.

The fleet . . . picked up their anchors and slowly steamed out of the harbour and what a mass of ships there was as we slowly steamed out of Lemnos. We could hear the warships belting away at the forts as we went along. We got a certain distance out and anchored for the night. We were then given each man 300 rounds of ammunition and his rations for 3 days. That night everyone was as happy as they could possibly be. We had our mandolins, guitars, banjos etc going for all they were worth. Nobody thought of what was going to happen on the morrow. And so we went to bed about 10 o'clock with everything ready for an instant move.

With his comrades, Barwick returned to Lemnos for a well-earned rest in September.

We were landed about 11 o'clock that morning and some of the chaps were that weak that a motor ambulance fetched them round to the camp. As we passed the hospital the Drs and nurses came out and had a look at us and I heard one nurse say 'poor fellows they look more fit for the hospital than anything else' and she was right. Half of them knocked up before they got round to the camp. On the way over we had to cross a long arm of the sea, a sort of backwater. It was a short cut so you can bet we went across it though it was up to our thighs in places.

Arrived at Sarpry [Sarpi] camp thoroughly knocked up, and were detailed off to the tents. How glad we were to throw our packs and rifles off and to get outside and buy some grapes and figs. The grapes were very plentiful and cheap you can buy enough for three as you could eat . . . Everyone gorged themselves with fruit for you know we were fruit hungry and it was a sort of craving we had on us. Needless to say we paid pretty dearly for it the next day didn't our stomachs ache and roll. Eggs also were plentiful and we used to get any amount of them and cook them for our tea.

All that afternoon the boys kept straggling home one by one for some of them had to have a dozen spells before they could get round. Needless to say we slept soundly that night, for we were away from the sound of the guns for the first time for many months, and we missed them but in the right way. The next morning we had a good breakfast and had the day to ourselves. The first thing we done as you might guess was to have a good clean up wash and shave. There was no roll call that day. Some of us washed our clothes over at the well. There was a bonzer spring there and we made full use of it. A day after this we were all issued with new clothes and felt like new men. The lousy clothes were all burnt and we were clean once more.

As well as the luxury of being clean and louse-free, the troops were able to enjoy entertainment on Lemnos.

The New Zealand Band gave several fine concerts at which the nurses on Lemnos Island attended. What a relief and pleasure it was to see the girls of our land after six months of roughing it at Anzac. They made the place look quite bright with their pretty uniforms. They were bricks to stick at Mudros like they did for I can tell you they had some rough times there. They even had to live on bully beef and biscuits at times and time after time their tents would be blown down in a raging rain storm and they would turn to help and put them up again in the pouring rain. Their first thought was for the sick and wounded men and they looked after them splendidly. One cannot praise our nurses too highly. They were bonzer girls.

On the 21st the 1st Division gave a concert. All the items were rendered by members who came with the first contingent. It was a great success, there were thousands there and the Dean of Sydney presided. There were a lot of naval men present. Just before the concert opened about 20 nurses came in and didn't they get a reception. It must have been several minutes before the uproar died down. At this concert the Maoris gave their war cry. They took a lot of coaxing to get them on the platform but once there they were right. Their war cry is a most unearthly row and no wonder it frightened the Turks the first time they heard it on 'Sari Bair' during the great battle there. The concert ended up by singing 'Boys of the 1st Brigade' and thus a most enjoyable evening ended.

But the grim reality of what the Gallipoli campaign truly meant only sank in at roll call.

In the afternoon we had the first proper Battalion roll call since we left Egypt and it was sad to see the few of the old original men that were left. Only a handful it seemed . . . a lot of them were in hospitals crippled, some were back in Australia and between 200 and 300 were lying in their graves at Anzac. The majority of them were splendid fellows too.

Barwick returned to Gallipoli with the 1st Brigade and survived the campaign, coming back to Lemnos once again with many other evacuees. They celebrated Christmas 1915 in a relaxed but also sombre mood.

We received our Xmas billies on the 22nd and very good they were. On the outside of the billy cans they had a kangaroo with his feet on Anzac and underneath were the words 'This bit of the world belongs to us'. That caused many a laugh for we had sneaked away from it . . .

The war entered a new and more disastrous phase on the western front and, while Gallipoli itself remained in popular memory, Lemnos faded into the forgotten past. However, many soldiers, nurses and doctors who experienced Lemnos did not forget, as evidenced by their published recollections and in the names of repatriation hospitals and related facilities around Australia.

Since 2001, Anzac Day commemorations have been held on the island, and a stone memorial was erected there in 2002.

The silent Anzac

In April 1915, one of Australia's first submarines, *AE2*, carried out what was originally thought to be an impossible mission and made an important contribution to the Gallipoli landings of 25 April 1915. While preparations were being made to land troops at Gallipoli, the Allied navies were trying to penetrate the 'Narrows': the sea passage through the treacherous and heavily fortified Straits of Marmara. If successful, this strategy would allow the Allied fleet into the Sea of Marmara to threaten Constantinople (present-day Istanbul), and so force the Turks to scale back their confrontation with Russian forces in the area between the Black Sea and the Caspian Sea known as Caucasus.

Under the command of Lieutenant Henry Stoker, the *AE2* first attempted to force a passage on 24 April, but failed due to a broken hydroplane or underwater wing. The submarine was forced to return to base for repairs. But on the fateful morning of 25 April, Stoker and his crew of thirty-one took their 55-metre metal container into the treacherous and heavily mined Narrows. Crewman Albert Knaggs told the story in his diary.

April 25th At 2 am slipped from HMS *Swiftsure*, proceeded up the Dardanelles and dived at 4 am but not until we were fired upon by the enemy. After diving we proceeded at a depth varying from 70 to 90 feet, came up to 20 feet periodically to take headings. This day was also the day of the great landings on the peninsula. 6 am the captain informed us we were through the worst part of the narrows and he came up to twenty feet to have a look around and saw a Turkish Battleship at Chanak. The bow tube was loaded and we made to attack her, when a minelayer steamed across our bows. The captain immediately fired the torpedo at her as she was apparently dropping mines for us to run into. The torpedo hit its mark and sank her (*Feihh i Shevist*) [the name of the Turkish ship]. Our orders were to sink everything at Chanek [Chanak], and found it very difficult to maneouvre the boat, it being very narrow. Immediately on firing the torpedo we went down to 90ft. We heard the report of the explosion and was just complimenting ourselves when we came from 90ft to 8ft. We were half out of the water and on the shore right under the forts. Fire was opened on us from all sides, the captain said the sea was one mass of foam caused by the shells fired at us but luckily we were not hit, but we could hear inside the boat the shrapnel dropping on us like a lot of stones.

During this time the motors were doing their best, first going ahead then astern the propellors cutting into the ground but the captain said the boat had to come off whether the propellors got damaged or not. With this he sped up the motors to their speed limit which brought us safely off and down to 90ft again. As we came off the ground we turned making for the entrance for Gallipoli and Sea of Marmara, but did not turn sharply enough as we had to turn up against a 4 knot tide and consequently we ran up on the opposite bank and showed ourselves when another fusillade of shells were fired at us with no effect.

We were soon off to 90ft again where we settled on a bank and remained there from about 7.30 am to 5 pm. Being Sunday prayers were read then with the exception of two watchkeepers the remainder of the crew had an opportunity to get some sleep if their nerves would let them. About every quarter of an hour we could hear a boat passing overhead on the lookout for us. Early in the afternoon something dropped or banked against our starboard side forward which made everybody on the alert expecting something serious to happen.

The hands had been lying down by their diving stations so we were all ready for emergency. About 5.30 pm things became quiet overhead so the captain thought it was time to make a move. We went astern and slipped down a big incline, the diving gauge showed a bent needle at 100 signifying we were deeper than 100ft but knew no more. Then the captain had a rather hard job to get the boat up but after doing everything he possibly could he eventually brought her safely to 20ft and proceeded alongside Chanek Harbour and broke surface at 10.30 pm in a little bay and commenced charging up batteries until 3.30 am.

April 26th The night was dark which favoured us as our batteries were nearly exhausted. A strict lookout was kept on deck and boats could be seen passing up and down the channel. Dived at 4 am and proceeded towards Gallipoli where we fired a beam torpedo at a Turkish Battleship but missed. The sea was so smooth all the time it was impossible to show our periscope without being seen and when we did, everything movable got on the move. Some to get out of our way, others such as TBs [torpedo boats] came after us.

After being hotly pursued we managed to reach the Sea of Marmara safe where we broke surface and hoisted the White Ensign while we were cruising around charging up batteries. At dusk we proceeded down towards Gallipoli and communicated by Wireless Telegraph with our fleet that the attempt to force the narrows had been carried out successfully. We were interrupted by Destroyers scouring the coast for us as they probably heard our wireless but they could not interpret it as it was in code, and they fired on us at short range but we were soon down under where we remained for the night.

April 27th Broke surface at daybreak and proceeded to Gallipoli making several attacks but had no hits on account of torpedoes running too deep. The chase was picked up again and could not remain on the surface very long during the day.

When it was dusk we proceeded to make WT reports to our friends on the other side of the peninsula. The Enemy torpedo craft crept up upon us again and fired but missed as usual. Down under again we remained for another night.

April 28th Broke surface daybreak and cruised around charging up batteries in the vicinity of Marmora [Marmara] Island waiting for transports to come round the coast but nothing turned up. That night we found new lodgings.

April 29th Broke surface at daybreak proceeded to Gallipoli making more attacks on transports crowded with troops which were guarded by Destroyers. We sank one transport and was chased and worried all that day. Towards the end of the afternoon we got back to the Sea of Marmara and charged up batteries. While thus steaming along HM Submarine broke surface about a mile off our port bow. We immediately steamed close up to her showing the White Ensign. Her captain then told us how she had come straight through as far as Gallipoli where she had made an attack but did not know if she secured a hit. Made arrangements for meeting next day then proceeded to the bottom for rest of the night.

April 30th Broke surface and proceeded to meet *E14* [a British submarine] and then we were going to Constantinople to see if there was anything doing. *E14* was sighted on the horizon coming from Gallipoli as she had been communicating with the fleet the night before, on nearing *E14* we saw she was being chased by TBP and two gunboats.

E14 dived and we continued to draw the enemy on while *E14* maneouvred for an attack. When we was getting too near we dived and then the boat got into difficulties and unmanageable, exposing ourselves frequently. At one time the Capt gave orders to take her down and she broke surface. Then came the worst experience we have had and it was by the captain's presence of mind that the crew lives.

Came to the surface again, more water was let into the tanks and down we went again nose first this time (as we had been going up and down all ways previous to this) with what seemed a terrible speed and at an awful angle. Everything that was not a fixture went sliding forward. It was about noon and the dinners etc in the cooking process flew here and there mingling with other various articles. Everyone had to hang on to his station or else we should have found ourselves with the other things mentioned. The captain quietly gave the order Full Speed Astern and if ever our motors had a trial it was then for we fairly shot out of the water on reaching the surface stern first.

By this time a torpedo boat was on top of us firing for all she was worth, also one of their Gunboats but from a much further distance. The 2nd Capt reported that the TB appeared to be making ready to ram us. Under we went and found that we were holed in the after end of the engine room and that the pressure was too great to remain under much longer as the water was coming in with great force. We were absolutely crippled, all being sorry that we had to give in, broke surface and surrendered. Capt ordered all hands on deck and when we gained the bridge a Gunboat was still firing at us but his shots were falling short. The torpedo boat got in the line of fire and, blowing her siren while her signalman waved his flag, the firing ceased. Then the TB lowered a boat to take us off in which there was a German Officer but she could only take five hands so we had to swim for it. When we got onboard the TB we saw that her torpedo tubes were empty and a German sailor who could speak English told us they had both been fired at us but missed, also that one of the Gunboats had fired one with the same result, which was lucky for us.

Before leaving the boat the captain opened up a couple of tanks to ensure the boat sinking, which she did a few minutes after leaving her. Aboard the TB the officers were kept in the after cabin while we were in the forward mess deck. While our clothes were being dried on deck the TB proceeded to Gallipoli and made fast alongside a hospital ship, while we were interviewed by General Liman von Sanders who was in command of the Peninsula.

As Knaggs recorded, *AE2* had grounded twice in the shallows and was under fire from Turkish guns. The crew got the boat off, though she was too damaged to fight further. But, as Stoker later wrote, 'I considered my chief duty was to prove the passage through the straits to be possible, I decided to continue on my course'.

When they broke through the Narrows, *AE2* had signalled her success on the experimental 'wireless telegraph' or radio equipment they carried. They were unable to receive a reply but continued to transmit in the desperate hope that the message would be received. It was. The news that an Australian submarine had penetrated the Dardanelles and torpedoed a Turkish warship provided a much-needed morale boost in the midst of the faltering Gallipoli landings when campaign commander General Sir Ian Hamilton received the message in the grim early morning hours of 25 April. Instead of agreeing with the shore commanders' recommendation that the landing forces withdraw, Hamilton informed them of *AE2*'s success and urged them 'to dig yourselves right in and stick it out'.

As a result of these actions, the Turks were forced to reorganise their supply lines to the Gallipoli Peninsula, transporting their ammunition, reinforcements and supplies by the much slower overland route. This provided significant relief for the hard-pressed land forces on Gallipoli.

Stoker and his men became prisoners and were held until the end of the war. While two Victoria Crosses and other decorations were awarded to British submarines, *AE2*'s achievement remained largely ignored. Stoker apparently never complained about this, although in his autobiography he dryly noted that the results of the campaign in the Dardanelles for the submarine commanders '...was death for one; three and a half years of the living death for another; and Victoria Crosses for the other two'.

Henry Stoker would eventually be awarded a Distinguished Service Order, be promoted to commander after the war and go on to a notable show business career as an actor, writer and producer. But the gallantry and unprecedented achievement of *AE2*—and the long imprisonement of the men—were forgotten as the horrors of the western front unfolded. Albert Knaggs himself did not survive the experience. He died of dysentery in October 1916.

The first day on Gallipoli

On 8 May 1915, the *Sydney Morning Herald* carried a report of the Gallipoli landings by the English journalist Ashmead Bartlett. Under the multiple headlines

AUSTRALASIANS
GLORIOUS ENTRY INTO WAR.
HISTORIC CHARGE.
BRILLIANT FEAT AT GABA TEPE.

Bartlett observed the landings from aboard a warship and his report was the first to reach Australia. At this early stage of the fighting only 142 Australians and New Zealanders had been killed.

It required splendid skill, organisation, and leadership to get the huge Armada under weigh from Mudros Bay without accident. The warships and transports were divided into five divisions. Never before has an attempt been made to land so large a force in the face of a well-prepared enemy.

At 2 o'clock on April 24 the flagship of the division conveying the Australasians passed down the long line of slowly-moving transports, amid tremendous cheering, being played out of the bay by the French warships. At 4 o'clock the ship's company and troops assembled to hear the Admiral's proclamation to the combined forces. This was followed by the last Service Before Battle, in which the chaplain uttered a prayer for victory, and called a divine blessing on the expedition, all standing with uncovered and bowed heads.

RESTING FOR THE ORDEAL.

At dusk all lights were put out, and the troops rested for the ordeal at dawn. It was a beautiful, calm night, with a bright half moon. By 1 o'clock in the morning the ships reached the rendezvous five miles from the landing place, and the soldiers were aroused and served with their last hot meal.

The Australians who were about to go into action for the first time under trying circumstances, were cheerful, quiet, and confident, showing no sign of nerves or excitement. As the moon waned the boats were swung out, the Australians received their last instructions, and men who six months ago were living peaceful civilian lives began to disembark on a strange, unknown shore in a strange land to attack an enemy of different race.

Each boat was in charge of a midshipman, others were loaded with great rapidity, in absolute silence, and without a hitch. The covering force was towed ashore by ships' pinnaces. More of the Australians' brigade were carried aboard the destroyers, which were to go close inshore as soon as the covering force landed.

TENSE MOMENTS.

At 3 it was quite dark, and a start was made shorewards, amid suppressed excitement. Would the enemy be surprised or on the alert?

At 4 o'clock three battleships, line abreast and four cables apart, arrived 2500 yards from the shore, with their guns manned and searchlights made ready. Very slowly boats in tow like twelve great snakes, moved in-shore. Each edged towards each other in order to reach the beach four cables apart. The battleships moved slowly in after them, until the water shallowed.

Every eye was fixed on the grim line of hills in front, menacing in the gloom, the mysteries of which those in the boats were about to solve. Not a sound was heard nor a light seen, and it appeared as if the enemy was surprised. In our nervy state the stars often were mistaken for lights ashore.

THE ALARM.

The progress of the boats was slow, and dawn rapidly was breaking. At 4.50 the enemy showed an alarm light which flashed for ten minutes and disappeared. The boats appeared almost on the beach, and seven destroyers glided noiselessly inshore.

At 4.53 came a sharp burst of rifle fire from the beach. The sound relieved the prolonged suspense, which had become almost intolerable. The fire lasted a few minutes, and then a faint British cheer came over the waters, telling that the first position had been won. At 5.30 the fire was intensified, and by the sound we could tell our men were firing. The firing lasted twenty five minutes and then died down somewhat.

The boats returned, and a pinnace came alongside with two recumbent figures on deck and a small midshipman cheerfully waving his hand, with a shot through his stomach. Three wounded in the first burst of musketry.

A TERRIBLE FUSILLADE.

The boats had almost reached the beach when a party of Turks entrenched ashore opened a terrible fusillade with rifles and a Maxim. Fortunately most of the bullets went high. The Australians rose to the occasion. They did not wait for orders or for the boats to reach the beach, but sprang into the sea, formed a sort of rough line, and rushed the enemy's trenches. Their magazines were uncharged, so they just went in with cold steel.

It was over in a minute. The Turks in the first trench either were bayoneted or ran away, and the Maxim was captured.

Then the Australians found themselves facing an almost perpendicular cliff of loose sandstones, covered with thick shrubbery. Somewhere about half way up the enemy had a second trench, strongly held, from which poured a terrible fire on the troops below and the boats pulling back to the destroyers for a second landing party.

A TOUGH PROPOSITION.

Here was a tough proposition to tackle in the darkness, but those colonials were practical above all else and went about it in a practical way. They stopped a few minutes to pull themselves together, get rid of their packs, and charge their rifle magazines. Then this race of athletes proceeded to scale the cliff without responding to the enemy's fire. They lost some men, but didn't worry, and in less than a quarter of an hour the Turks were out of their second position, and either bayoneted or fleeing.

As daylight came it was seen that the landing had been effected rather further north of Gaba Tepe than originally was intended, at a point where the cliffs rise very sheer. The error was a blessing in disguise, because there was no places down which the enemy could fire, and the broken ground afforded good cover for troops once they had passed the forty yards of flat beach.

The country in the vicinity of the landing is formidable and forbidding. To the sea it presents a steep front, broken into innumerable ridges, bluffs, valleys, and sandpits. Rising to a height of several hundred feet the surface is bare, crumbly sandstone, with thick shrubbery about six feet in height, which is ideal for snipers, as the Australasians soon found to their cost. On the other hand, the Australasians proved themselves adepts at this kind of warfare.

CASUALTIES IN BOATS.

In the early part of the day heavy casualties were suffered in the boats conveying troops from the destroyers, tugs, and transports. The enemy's sharpshooters, hidden everywhere, concentrated their fire on the boats. When close in, at least three boats broke away from their tow and drifted down the coast without control, being sniped at the whole way, and steadily losing men.

The work of disembarking proceeded mechanically under a point-blank fire. The moment the boats touched the beach the troops jumped ashore and doubled for cover; but the gallant boat crews had to pull in and out under a galling fire from hundreds of points.

All through the 25th this went on, the boats landing troops, ammunition, and stores. When it was daylight the warships endeavoured to support them by heavy fire from secondary armaments; but not knowing the enemy's position this support was more moral than real.

SPLENDIDLY CARRIED OUT.

When the sun had fully risen we could see that the Australasians had actually established themselves on the ridge, and were trying to work their way northward along it. The fighting was so confused and occurred on such broken ground that it was difficult to follow exactly what happened on the 25th; but the covering force's task was so splendidly carried out that it allowed the disembarkation of the remainder to proceed uninterruptedly, except for the never-ceasing sniping. But then the Australians, whose blood was up, instead of entrenching, rushed northwards and eastwards, searching for fresh enemies to bayonet. It was difficult country in which to entrench. They therefore preferred to advance.

AUSTRALASIANS IN TROUBLE.

The Turks had only had a weak force actually holding the beach, and had relied on the difficult ground and their snipers to delay the advance until reinforcements came. Some of the Australasians who pushed inland were counter attacked and almost outflanked by oncoming reserves. They had to fall back after suffering heavy losses.

The Turks continued to counter attack the whole afternoon; but the Australasians did not yield a foot on the main ridge. Reinforcements poured up from the beach, but the Turks enfiladed the beach with two field guns from Gaba Tepe. This shrapnel fire was incessant and deadly. The warships vainly for some hours tried to silence them.

The majority of the heavy casualties during the day were from shrapnel, which swept the beach and ridge where the Australasians were established. Later in the day the guns were silenced or forced to withdraw, and the cruiser moving close inshore plastered Gaba Tepe with a hail of shell.

PRESSURE BY ENEMY.

Towards dusk the attacks became more vigorous, the enemy being supported by powerful artillery inland, which the ships' guns were powerless to deal with. The pressure on the Australasians became heavier and their line had to be contracted.

General Birdwood and his staff landed in the afternoon and devoted their energies to securing the position so as to hold firm until next morning, when they hoped to get field guns into position.

Some idea of the difficulty can be gathered when it is remembered that every round of ammunition and all the water and stores had to be landed on a narrow beach, and carried up pathless hills, through a valley several hundred feet high, to the firing line. The whole mass of troops was concentrated in a very small area, and was unable to reply, though exposed to relentless and incessant shrapnel fire, which swept every yard of the ground. Fortunately much of it was badly aimed, and burst too high.

HEROISM OF WOUNDED.

A serious problem was the getting of the wounded from the shore. All those unable to hobble had to be carried from the hills on a stretcher, and then hastily dressed and carried to the boats. Boat parties worked unceasingly the entire day and night.

The courage displayed by these wounded Australians will never be forgotten. Hastily placed in trawlers and lighters' boats, they were towed to the ships. In spite of their sufferings they cheered the ship from which they had set out in the morning. In fact, I have never seen anything like these wounded Australians in war before.

Though many were shot to bits, without hope of recovery, their cheers resounded throughout the night. You could see in the midst of the mass of suffering humanity arms waving in greeting to the crews of the warships. They were happy because they knew they had been tried for the first time, and had not been found wanting.

A WORTHY FEAT.

For fifteen mortal hours they occupied the heights under incessant shell fire, without the moral or material support of a single gun ashore, and subjected the whole time to a violent counter attack, by a brave enemy, skilfully led, with snipers deliberately picking off every officer who endeavoured to give a command or lead the men.

There has been no finer feat in this war than this sudden landing in the dark and the storming of the heights, and above all, the holding on whilst reinforcements were landing. These raw colonial troops in these desperate hours proved worthy to fight side by side with the heroes of Mons, the Aisne, Ypres, and Neuve Chapelle . . .

It would be another week before Australia heard from the official war correspondent, Charles Bean, who took part in the landing. His account had been held up by military red tape but it confirmed the glory admired by Bartlett at a distance and ended with a few paragraphs under the heading 'Imperishable Fame':

B ut when all is said, the feat which will go down in history is that first Sunday's fighting when three Australian Brigades stormed, in face of a heavy fire, tier after tier of cliffs and mountains, apparently as impregnable as Govett's Leap. The sailors who saw the Third Brigade go up those heights and over successive summits like whirligig with wild cheers, and with bayonets flashing, speak of it with tears of enthusiasm in their eyes. New Zealanders are just as generous in their appreciation. It is hard to distinguish between the work of the brigades. They all fought fiercely and suffered heavily; but considering that performed last Sunday, it is a feat which is fit to rank beside the battle of the heights of Abraham.

I believe that the British at Cape Helles fought a tremendous fight. Of Australia it may be said that Australian infantry, and especially the Third Brigade, have made a name which will never die. Around me as I write, guns of half a dozen warships are shaking the hills. The evening is a quiet one. From the ridges above comes the continuous rattle of musketry. As no bullets are whistling overhead, the firing must be by our men. The issue cannot be in doubt, but one knows that even if it were, nothing would take away from the Australian and New Zealand infantry the fame of last Sunday's fighting.

Talk about go!

While Bartlett had the advantage of viewing much of the battle-front from a distant vantage point and Bean was able to roam from place to place compiling his reports, Private F. H. Richardson had a more restricted but more intense experience both on the sea and on the shore. Around June 1915, from an Egyptian hospital, he wrote about it to his sister in Unley (in Adelaide, South Australia). Richardson landed with one of the first waves and was wounded, but he was anxious to return to the fighting.

I am going to put in for a discharge so if there are any troops leaving for Gallipoli next week I may be chosen to go back to the front with the next lot. We are sick of being here in Egypt. You may think it's only kid but every jack one of us are the same.

We want to get back to see how our own mates are faring. As for fear, well you don't have time to think of it. Of course it makes a man shrink away when the shrapnel starts bursting all round and kicking up the dust all over you but their artillery is nothing to ours. Between our land batteries and gunboats the enemy must have had an awful time. We had a rather ticklish job with their big guns for a little while, but our warships have been dealing old Harry to them, and I think by now they must have most of the Turks' guns silenced.

We have good trenches now. It is rotten luck to get hit. Only about one in every ten that get hit is killed, so you see we have a pretty good gamble. You ask if I am really glad that I came to the front. Our company was chosen to be the landing party for our battalion at Gallipoli. I can assure you that there was not a prouder man than yours truly, although we had the toughest job of any. I never felt more pleased in my life than when we steamed out of Lemnos Island for Gallipoli on the battleship *Prince of Wales*. It would have made anyone's heart glad to be there to see the sight. All the warboats sailed in a line, twisting and turning like a huge snake as they followed the leader. Then came the battleships, and then the torpedo destroyers and torpedo boats. We cruised about till nearly morning. About 1.30 a.m. we had a good hot meal, and then got ready to get into the boats to go ashore. The rowing boats were towed by motor boats.

All went well until we got near the shore, all packed in the boat like sardines. All of a sudden we heard a single rifle shot, and silence for about half a minute (which seemed like an hour). Then hell was let loose, and hundreds of shots from machine guns and every other sort of gun began to pepper us. We all ducked our heads as low as we could, and kept quiet. Then the motor boats cast off so that we could run our boats aground, but we had to row a good way and with 40 men in one of those big ship's boats it is no light job to pull with only four oars. Some of our poor boys never landed. The bullets were like hailstones. When the boats did run aground we all had to jump out in the water, and I, being in the stern of the boat, jumped into the deepest water, with a box of ammunition. I was in water up to my armpits. I nearly fell over three times, but we got ashore all right, put the ammunition away on the beach, and then joined in the charge.

Talk about go! We did go. We could only just see the enemy, as it was only break of day. You ought to have heard the cheer when they gave us the word to charge. You could have heard it for miles if you could have stopped to listen. Some were saying (or roaring), 'Come on, Australia!' and others 'Australia for ever!' and some 'Come on, boys!' and 'Give it to 'em, boys!' but the funniest part of it was hearing chaps talking to themselves, or at least at the Turks, and calling them all the Saturday night bar fight words ever heard. It was good game running along and shooting as fast as ever you could go, but I nearly lost my rifle the first shot. I forgot to put it close to my shoulder, and it kicked nearly out of my hands.

I got rather a late start when they began to entrench, as I stayed behind to help another chap to give a lift to a wounded man out of the range of the lead pills. I hadn't got a hole big enough to hide a bottle of West End when they counter-attacked us, but I kept pegging away with my old entrenching tool every chance I got, and I finished up by getting a fairly snug place, though I used to get stiff as a board lying in the one position. I made it large enough to kneel up and fire at last. Then, when we did get a spell (which was five minutes at the most) I would have a lie down and next time I would sit down, and the next time I would kneel up, so my positions were varied. Anyhow, our trenches are all right now, as we got the shovels to work. We are all happy as Larry, as we are doing so well. There were some most awfully sad sights the first week, but it may never be so bad again.

The landing

This recollected account of the landing, written 'By a Man of the Tenth' (A. R. Perry), appeared in *The Anzac Book* (1915), a collection of writing and drawing by the men at Gallipoli. It provides a more crafted account of the attack from the memory of a soldier who took part in it.

'Come on, lads, have a good hot supper—there's business doing.' So spoke No. 10 Platoon Sergeant of the 10th Australian Battalion to his men, lying about all sorts of odd corners aboard the battleship *Prince of Wales*, in the first hour on the morning of April 25th, 1915. The ship, or her company, had provided a hot stew of bully beef, and the lads set to and took what proved, alas to many, their last real meal together. They laugh and joke as though picnicking. Then a voice: 'Fall in!' comes ringing down the ladderway from the deck above. The boys swing their rifles, silently make their way on deck, and stand in grim black masses. All lights are out, and only harsh, low commands break the silence. 'This way No. 9 –No. 10– C company.' Almost blindly we grope our way to the ladder leading to the huge barge below, which is already half full of silent, grim men, who seem to realise that at last, after eight months of hard, solid training in Australia, Egypt and Lemnos Island, they are now to be called upon to carry out the object of it all.

'Full up, sir,' whispers the midshipman in the barge.

'Cast off and drift astern,' says the ship's officer in charge of the embarkation. Slowly we drift astern, until the boat stops with a jerk, and twang goes the hawser that couples the boats and barges together. Silently the boats are filled with men, and silently drop astern of the big ship, until, all being filled, the order is given to the small steamboats: 'Full steam ahead.' Away we go, racing and bounding, dipping and rolling, now in a straight line, now in a half circle, on through the night.

The moon has just about sunk below the horizon. Looking back, we can see the battleship coming on slowly in our rear, ready to cover our attack. All at once our pinnace gives a great start forward, and away we go for land just discernible one hundred yards away on our left.

Then—crack-crack! Ping-ping! Zip-zip! Trenches full of rifles upon the shore and surrounding hills open on us, and machine guns, hidden in gullies or redoubts, increase the murderous hail. Oars are splintered, boats are perforated. A sharp moan, a low gurgling cry, tells of a comrade hit. Boats ground in four or five feet of water owing to the human weight contained in them. We scramble out, struggle to the shore, and, rushing across the beach, take cover under a low sandbank.

'Here, take off my pack, and I'll take off yours.' We help one another to lift the heavy, water-soaked packs off. 'Hurry up, there,' says our sergeant. 'Fix bayonets.' Click! And the bayonets are fixed. 'Forward!' And away we scramble up the hills in front. Up, up we go, stumbling in holes and ruts. With a ringing cheer we charge the steep hill, pulling ourselves up by roots and branches of trees; at times digging our bayonets into the ground, and pushing ourselves up to a foothold, until topping the hill, we found the enemy had made themselves very scarce. What had caused them to fly from a position from which they should have driven us back into the sea every time? A few scattered Turks showing in the distance we instantly fired on. Some fell to rise no more; other fell wounded and, crawling into the low bushes, sniped our lads in plenty, cunningly hidden in the heart of the low green shrubs. They accounted for a lot of our boys in the first few days, but gradually were rooted out. Over the hill we dashed, and down into what is now called 'Shrapnel Gully,' and up the other hillside, until, on reaching the top, we found that some of the lads of the 3rd Brigade had commenced to dig in. We skirted round to the plateau at the head of the gully, and took up our line of defence.

As soon as it was light enough to see, the guns on Gaba Tepe, on our right, and two batteries away on our left opened up a murderous hail of shrapnel on our landing parties. The battleships and cruisers were continuously covering the landing of troops, broadsides going into the batteries situated in tunnels in the distant hillside. All this while the seamen from the different ships were gallantly rowing and managing the boats carrying the landing parties. Not one man that is left of the original brigade will hear a word against our gallant seamen. England may well be proud of them and all true Australians are proud to call them comrades.

Se-ee-e-e . . . bang . . . swish! The front firing line was now being baptized by its first shrapnel. Zir-zir . . . Zip-zip! Machine-guns, situated on each front, flank and centre, opened on our front line. Thousands of bullets began flying round and over us, sometimes barely missing. Now and then one heard a low gurgling moan, and, turning, one saw near at hand some chum, who only a few seconds before had been laughing and joking, now lying gasping, with his life blood soaking down into the red clay and sand. 'Five rounds rapid at the scrub in front,' comes the command of our subaltern. Then an order down the line: 'Fix bayonets!' Fatal order—was it not, perhaps, some officer of the enemy who shouted it? (for they say such things were done). Out flash a thousand bayonets, scintillating in the sunlight like a thousand mirrors, signalling our position to the batteries away on our left and front. We put in another five rounds rapid at the scrub in front. Then, bang-swish! Bang-swish! Bang-swish! And over our line, and front, and rear, such a hellish fire of lyddite and shrapnel that one wonders how anyone could live amidst such a hail of death-dealing lead and shell. 'Ah, got me!' says one lad on my left, and he shakes his arms. A bullet had passed through the biceps of his left arm, missed his chest by an inch, passed through the right forearm, and finally struck the lad between him and me a bruising blow on the wrist. The man next him—a man from the 9th Battalion—started to bind up his wounds, as he was bleeding freely. All the time shrapnel was hailing down on us. 'Oh-h!' comes from directly behind me, and looking around, I see poor little Lieutenant B——, of C Company, has been badly wounded. From both hips to his ankle blood is oozing through pants and puttees, and he painfully drags himself to the rear. With every pull he moans cruelly. I raise him to his feet, and at a very slow pace start to help him to shelter. But, alas! I have only got him about fifty yards from the firing line when again, bang-swish! And we are both peppered by shrapnel and shell. My rifle-butt was broken off to the trigger-guard, and I received a smashing blow that laid my cheek on my shoulder. The last I remembered was poor Lieutenant B—— groaning again as we both sank to the ground.

When I came to I found myself in Shrapnel Gully, with an A.M.C. [Army Medical Corps] man holding me down. I was still clasping my half-rifle. Dozens of men and officers, both Australians and New Zealanders (who had landed a little later in the day), were coming down wounded, some slightly some badly, with arms in slings or shot through the leg, and using their rifles for crutches. Shrapnel Gully was still under shrapnel and snipers' fire. Two or three platoon mates and myself slowly moved down to the beach, where we found the Australian Army Service Corps busily engaged landing stores and water amid shrapnel fire from Gaba Tepe. As soon as a load of stores was landed, the wounded were carried aboard the empty barges, and taken to the hospital ships and troopships standing out off-shore. After going to ten different boats, we came at last to the troopship *Seang Choon*, which had the 14th Australian Battalion aboard. They were to disembark the next morning, but owing to so many of us being wounded, they had to land straightaway.

And so, after twelve hours' hard fighting, I was aboard a troopship again—wounded. But I would not have missed it for all the money in the world.

Parables of Anzac

At the end of the Dardanelles campaign, official war correspondent Charles Bean edited *The Anzac Book*, a compilation of verse, prose and art by Gallipoli troops that became a bestseller, with many Australian homes having a copy on otherwise sparsely populated bookshelves. It portrayed the Anzac troops who would later be named 'diggers' largely in their own words and images. Under the heading 'Parables of Anzac', a couple of yarns gave a glimpse of casual digger humour.

From Shell Green
From a Correspondent in Australian Field Artillery, 'Sea View,' Bolton's Knoll, near Shell Green.

> I was looking out front the entrance of my dug-out, thinking how peaceful everything was, when Johnny Turk opened on our trenches. Shells were bursting, and fragments scattered all about Shell Green. Just at this time some new reinforcements were eagerly collecting spent fuses and shells as mementoes. While this fusillade was on, men were walking about the Green just as usual, when one was hit by a falling fuse. Out rushed one of the reinforcement chaps, and when he saw that the man was not hurt he asked: 'Want the fuse, mate?'
>
> The other looked at him calmly. 'What do you think I stopped it for?' he asked.

Another parable highlights the potential perils of using the crude periscopes the Anzacs invented to safely observe the enemy from below the parapet of the trench.

Bill Blankson was a real hard case, happy-go-lucky, regardless of danger. Bill was out on sapping for over a fortnight, and at the end of that time had a growth of stubble that would have brought a flush of pride to his dirty face if he had seen it. But he hadn't seen it—one does not carry a looking-glass when sapping.

At the end of the fortnight he was taken off sapping and put on observing. Anyone who has used a periscope knows that unless the periscope is held well up before the eyes, instead of the landscape, one sees only one's own visage reflected in the lower glass.

Bill did not hold the periscope up far enough, and what he saw in it was a dark, dirty face with a wild growth of black stubble glaring straight back at him. He dropped the periscope, grabbed his rifle, and scrambled up the parapet, fully intending to finish the Turk who had dared to look down the other end of his periscope.

He had mistaken his own reflection for a Turk's.

Silence of the guns

In late May 1915 a truce was called between the warring sides on Gallipoli to bury the dead and rescue any wounded from no man's land. Folklore has it that the blindfolded Turkish officer who came into the Anzac camp to parley was Mustafa Kemal Atatürk, destined to be the first president of the Republic of Turkey. It was also rumoured that General Birdwood had taken part in the fraternisation between the Anzacs and the Turks dressed as a private soldier. Unlikely though these tales are to be true, they suggest the psychological importance of the event to both sides when, after a month spent killing each other, they suddenly smoked cigarettes together, talked and swapped mementos—and then went back to killing each other. Military orthodoxies on both sides were strongly against any kind of fraternisation, fearing that it would make the men soft and less aggressive towards the enemy. But on Gallipoli, war was such a new experience for most of the combatants—and the stench of the unburied dead was so nauseating for Turks and Anzacs alike—that these considerations were, briefly, put aside.

Aubrey Herbert, a member of the Irish Guards, who spoke fluent Turkish, acted as interpreter for the Anzacs during the truce. He published his recollections in 1919.

We were at the rendezvous on the beach at 6.30. Heavy rain soaked us to the skin. At 7.30 we met the Turks, Miralai Izzedin, a pleasant, rather sharp, little man; Arif, the son of Achmet Pasha, who gave me a card, 'Sculpteur et Peintre,' and 'Etudiant de Poesie.' I saw Sahib and had a few words with him but he did not come with us. Fahreddin Bey came later. We walked from the sea and passed immediately up the hill, through a field of tall corn filled with poppies, then another cornfield; then the fearful smell of death began as we came upon scattered bodies. We mounted over a plateau and down through gullies filled with thyme, where there lay about 4000 Turkish dead. It was indescribable. One was grateful for the rain and the grey sky. A Turkish Red Crescent man came and gave me some antiseptic wool with scent on it, and this they renewed frequently. There were two wounded crying in that multitude of silence. The Turks were distressed, and Skeen strained a point to let them send water to the first wounded man, who must have been a sniper crawling home. I walked over to the second, who lay with a high circle of dead that made a mound round him, and gave him a drink from my water-bottle, but Skeen called me to come on and I had to leave the bottle. Later a Turk gave it back to me. The Turkish captain with me said: 'At this spectacle even the most gentle must feel savage, and the most savage must weep.' The dead fill acres of ground, mostly killed in the one big attack, but some recently. They fill the myrtle-grown gullies. One saw the result of machine-gun fire very clearly; entire companies annihilated—not wounded, but killed, their heads doubled under them with the impetus of their rush and both hands clasping their bayonets. It was as if God had breathed in their faces, as 'the Assyrian came down like the wolf on the fold.'

The burying was finished some time before the end. There were certain tricks to both sides. Our men and the Turks began fraternizing, exchanging badges, etc. I had to keep them apart. At 4 o'clock the Turks came to me for orders. I do not believe this could have happened anywhere else. I retired their troops and ours, walking along the line. At 4.17 I retired the white-flag men, making them shake hands with our men. Then I came to the upper end. About a dozen Turks came out. I chaffed them, and said that they would shoot me the next day. They said, in a horrified chorus: 'God forbid!' The Albanians laughed and cheered, and said: 'We will never shoot you.' Then the Australians began coming up, and said: 'Good-bye old chap; good luck!' And the Turks said: 'Oghur Ola gule gule gedejekseniz, gule gule gelejekseniz' ('Smiling may you go and smiling come again'). Then I told them all to get into their trenches, and unthinkingly went up to the Turkish trench and got a deep salaam from it. I told them that neither side would fire for twenty-five minutes after they had got into the trenches. One Turk was seen out away on our left, but there was nothing to be done, and I think he was all right. A couple of the rifles had gone off about twenty minutes before the end but Potts and I went hurriedly to and fro seeing it was all right. At last we dropped into our trenches, glad that the strain was over. I walked back with Temperley. I got some raw whisky for the infection in my throat, and iodine for where the barbed wire had torn my feet. There was a hush over the Peninsula.

Furphy

'Furphy' was—and often still is—Australian slang for a rumour. It arose from the trade name of water and sanitation carts used in Egypt, around which the troops would gather to swap gossip. And there was plenty of it. Wars are always hotbeds of hearsay and speculation, sharpened by a lack of official information. Soldiers naturally speculate about what they don't know, think they know or would rather not know. From a morale and discipline perspective, rumours can be dangerous because they can negatively affect the will to fight. Officers at Gallipoli were especially worried about furphies in the relatively confined area in which the troops lived and fought. This story, contributed to *The Anzac Book* by 'QED' (probably from the Latin for 'which was to be proved'), treats the problem humorously and also gives a feel for how small a space was actually occupied by the Anzacs.

It was the colonel who propounded the theory first, on hearing some rumour more optimistic than reliable. 'These furphies are the very devil,' he said.

Now, I had a theory about Furphy. I was waiting for an opportunity of following it up, and it came this way:

I was on the beach one day when a friend met me and asked if I had heard the latest dinkum. On learning that I hadn't, he informed me that Greece had declared war on Turkey, and was going to land 100,000 men within the next few days on the

Peninsula. I inquired for the source, and he said he got it from the beach towards the left. I asked what the man was like. That sort of puzzled him. He said he was a tall man—no, he thought he was only middle height or perhaps a bit on the small side. His hair was dark—no, now that he thought a bit, he fancied it was fair. In fact, the more he tried to describe him the less could he remember him. 'He's my Moses,' I said, and hurried off in the direction he had gone.

Passing through the sap to Shrapnel Gully, I met another friend.

'Heard the latest?' he inquired. I said 'No.'

'Four Italian staff officers seen on the beach today,' he said breathlessly.

'Two hundred thousand Italian troops being sent here.'

'Who told you?' I asked.

'Fellow just going into White's Valley.'

'What was he like?' I inquired excitedly.

'An ordinary fellow—not tall, and not short.'

'His hair?'

'Well, it wasn't dark—yes, it was—no, I don't know.'

'How did he walk?'

'I never noticed,' he said; 'in fact, he didn't seem to walk at all.'

I left him standing, and got down the sap and over into White's Valley in a record time, and bumped into another acquaintance.

'Heard the news?' he said.

'No.'

'Why, three hundred thousand Italians have landed at Helles, and Achi Baba is to be taken tonight.'

I asked who the informant was, and he began to flounder into contradictions. I rushed off, knowing that I was well on the track of Furphy.

In Victoria Gully I heard that Roumania had declared war, and 400,000 troops were marching through Bulgaria to Constantinople.

'Who told you? What was he like?' I gasped at the teller.

'Just a bloke,' was the answer, ''E 'ad two legs, two arms and a 'ead, two eyes.'—Then he added in a puzzled fashion: 'But, dammit did 'e?'

I didn't wait any longer, but was off again. At Shell Green I heard that a man—just a feller, rather—had told them that the Russians surrounded and captured Hindenburg's army, and that 500,000 Russians were to make a landing in Turkey. The Russian officers were here already. The man who had seen them had just passed five minutes before, I wasn't far from Furphy now.

At Chatham's Post they were buzzing with excitement over the news that 600,000 French were going to be landed between Kaba Tepe and Helles.

I asked if they thought it was true, and they assured me that they had heard it from a man who looked as if he knew. No two descriptions of him, however, agreed. I was getting closer to Furphy.

I hurried along the trenches as fast as I could, but got no information till near Lone Pine, where I heard that a big mob of Turks was expected to surrender that night. It was said they should not face the prospect of the coming landing of the whole Italian army. Besides, they were short of food and water, they were being badly treated by their officers, and their guns had hardly any ammunition left. A 75 just then knocked a portion of parapet over me. I remarked that anyone could see the information was right about Abdul being short of ammunition, but where did the information come from?'

'A fellow that just went by,' they said; 'looked like a staff officer.'

Getting near Steele's Post, I saw in front of me a man with an indescribable gait. He seemed to float along instead of walk. It was Furphy!

I hurried, but seemed to make no gain on him. I began to run. Near Courtney's Post I was twenty yards from him, and called to a man to stop him. My quarry brushed past, I put on a spurt, I was within about five yards of him when, all of a sudden, he sank into the earth. As his head disappeared he smiled an oily grimace at me.

I noticed that there were small horns behind his ears.

Leaving Gallipoli

Despite the insistence of Winston Churchill, the first lord of admiralty, and General Sir Ian Hamilton that the campaign could be won, the decision was made by Hamilton's replacement, General Charles Monro, to withdraw from Gallipoli. The evacuation of the Anzacs from the peninsula took place on the night and morning of 20–21 December 1915. Machine gunner Cedric McKail, 28th Battalion, wrote home to his mother from Tel-el-Kebir a month after the evacuation. As well as describing his withdrawal he also writes about the aftermath of the fatal charge of the Light Horse at the Nek in early August.

We got another mail yesterday and I received your letter and papers. It's A1 being certain of a letter from home by every mail. It is nearly 11 months since I left home for Blackboy [Blackboy Hill depot], though it seems much longer. The days on the peninsula seemed to pass wonderfully quickly; even now I can hardly realise that we were there over three months. Of course, every day was much the same as the previous one, and Sunday didn't exist, so there was nothing to mark the passing of the weeks. As you remarked in your letter, it does seem hard that all those poor fellows should have been killed in taking the bit of country we had, and then for us to have to give it up, but the fact that very few lives were lost in the evacuation is something to be thankful for. Had there been some blunder, or if the Turks had managed to get a spy into our trenches, as they had often done previously, very few would have got off with a whole skin.

During the last days it gave one an eerie feeling to think that a paltry handful of men were holding back thousands of the enemy, and our trenches seemed quite deserted after all the crowd had gone. On the last night, in all the trenches close to the Turks, we tore up blankets and put them on the ground so that they would not hear any unusual noise while we shifted guns, ammunition, etc., and we all wore socks over our boots. As you will have read long before this it was a complete bluff, and even when we exploded an enormous mine between the trenches, instead of taking it for an evacuation, they thought we were attacking, and opened a [sic] fire with rifles and machine guns, that made us feel very thankful that we were not. The rifle shots merged into one continuous roar as Jacko got the full strength of his supports to work, and the air above us was full of the whistling and cracking of bullets so that you could hardly hear yourself speak. The Turks must have been as thick as ants to put up such a fire, and must have had dozens of machine guns.

The part of the trenches we evacuated, known as Russell's Top, was the place where the Light Horse got cut up in that charge. There was a ridge about 30 yards wide connecting our trenches and the Turks. Along all the rest of the front is a deep gully, so that the Nek as this ridge was called, was the only place where a charge could be made. The Turks had all their machine guns trained on this spot, besides searching it with rifle fire right through the night, and continually dropping bombs on it. The scrub, which is dense all over the hills, is cut right away here with the fire, and the place is covered with the bodies of those who dropped in the charge of the Light Horse. Even in death they got no rest, as bombs which dropped short of our trenches were continually blowing the bodies into the air. I remember one day a clenched hand was blown right over our trench. Sometimes with a land wind blowing the stench was vile. What it must have been a few days after that charge, one can imagine.

We are looking like a lot of scare-crows as we have had no new issue of clothes yet, and are wearing those we left Gallipoli in, but expect a new rig-out any day. I shall be glad of the steel shaving mirror you are sending, as I have broken enough looking glasses in my pack to give me bad luck for life . . .

At Pozières

The action known to Australians as 'Pozières' was fought in France from July to August 1916 and was part of the battle of the Somme. Captain Norman Malcolm of Adelaide wrote home about the Pozières he and his men went through.

I went over with the first line on August 8, after leading the battalion on to the tape line—I had reconnoitred the position the day previously. We had a terrific barrage, said to be the heaviest ever put up—all high explosive with instantaneous fuses and it cut everything to pieces. It was a very foggy morning, and this, with the smoke of the bombardment, made it impossible to see further than 8 to 10 yards. Consequently, although we started in line, it was only a matter of minutes before we were in a column of lumps, having only the faintest idea of direction. However, we collected what men we could and pushed on, sometimes getting into our own barrage, and at other times losing it completely. Still, the fog saved us many casualties, and we had only to collect our souvenirs and get forward. Our division reached its objective, which was about three miles, up to time [on time]. During the advance we took innumerable prisoners and a tremendous amount of booty, including several headquarters, and batteries of field artillery. Soon after reaching our objective, a corps of cavalry passed through our ranks, followed by another lot of our infantry divisions, while tanks cleared the front, and armoured cars whizzed along every road, shooting everything on sight.

By night we had pushed Fritz back about 10 miles, taking thousands of prisoners, two trains loaded with Huns returning from leave, an armoured train with 11in. guns on board, and enormous quantities of stores of every description. Next afternoon our division again attacked with the aid of tanks, but without a barrage. We went another three to four miles, taking a corps headquarters in our sector, but unfortunately my company got pretty badly mauled. We went rather further than we intended, and our tanks ran into a 5.9-in. battery, and got blown to pieces at point blank range. We were close behind, and they fired at us with open sights, while machine guns raked us from either flank (we were in a direct line between a village and a big chateau, both full of machine guns). We stuck it out, but it was a warm corner, and I was not sorry when darkness came and we were able to collect our wounded and get a better position.

Our boys are fine; to see them advance across open country without the least cover and all the time under heavy fire both from artillery of all calibre and hundreds of machine guns, without a single falter, was well worth seeing. They are without doubt the best storm troops in France.

After 10 days solid fighting we had a few days rest, and then again went into the line, this time reaching our objective—Peronne—after a rather heavy time. I reached the river opposite Peronne with out serious loss, but as Fritz had blown up all the bridges, was unable to cross and follow him up. The river and canal here are several hundred yards across, so we occupied some old French 1916 trenches and waited until another brigade crossed further up and took Mont St. Quentin. During these two days we were shelled continuously day and night—mostly by heavy stuff at long range. We had a pretty rotten time, for every shell contains gas of one sort or another. However, after the fall of Mont St. Quentin we evacuated this position under fire from the opposite bank, and, crossing the river further up, again attacked up the Canal du Nord on the morning of September 2.

We hopped off at 5.30 a.m., but Fritz was holding the position in some force, and we got it in the neck. After going a few hundred yards he put down a terrific barrage just in front of us, while his machine guns were as thick as flies in summer. We had just dived into the barrage when I got my issue. The shells were about as thick as hailstones and I got too near one, with the result that I got one piece through my face, entering the top lip, knocking out a couple of teeth, and coming out under the left ear. At the same time another chunk went through my knee, just missing the cap. Of course, I did not take much further interest in the scrap, but getting back to a trench just in the rear I was picked up by our stretcher bearers, and finally carried out about two miles by four Fritz prisoners.

In hospital I saw a photo of you and some of the light horse boys in *The Observer*. I am glad to know that you are still going strong and carrying on the good work. Give my kind regards to any of the old hands who are left at Mitcham.

From a different perspective in the chain of command, Private Andrew Clancey wrote to his sister about his Pozières experience. He was in a hospital in 'Blighty', the soldiers' name for England.

I am very comfortable, and my wounds are getting on splendidly. I got shrapnel in both legs, just above the knees. The piece went right through the right leg, but there is still a small piece behind the left knee, which I expect they will take out in a few days. My flesh is very healthy, and the doctors and nurses are very pleased with the way the wounds are healing.

This is the home of Lord Lucas, and is a beautiful place. The doctor tells me there are some very fine stock here—prize pigs and cattle, worth over £1000. I am anxious to get out and see them. Lord Lucas is on active service in Egypt, and has given this place as a hospital while the war lasts. It is not a purely military hospital. The doctor living here is a civilian, but military doctors visit on certain days. The place is very clean, and the food fairly good. My next door neighbour is a Canadian; and 'Shure,' 'He's some kid,' 'Believe me'—his expressions keep me smiling. I guess he's a hard snap.

We were at Pozieres and did not really know there was a war on till we got there. It was a dreadful place, and a sight I will never forget. Pozieres had been taken by our first division and some of the Tommies, and there were dead Germans and English lying everywhere. With such a serious business going on burying them was out of the question just then. I will try to give you a description of what we went through.

On July 28th at 7.30 p.m. a party of us were called to carry bombs, bags and water to the battalion who were charging that night. From the dump to the firing line—about a mile—was enfiladed by German artillery fire, and as the communication trench was shallow they could see us moving through, and peppered us properly. We had several of the party killed and a lot wounded. We had to make six trips in, and after the first trip it was left to me to take charge of our party. Thank goodness I had plenty of nerve, and got great credit from the men and officers for my work, and it was reported to the battalion officer next day when we returned. We had three officers with us but they stayed behind to look after the dump . . . we had to make our way in and out over dead bodies and pass other crowds going in and out. We were hung up in the trenches at midnight for hours, while a big bombardment and a charge were on, and I could see waves of our men charging over the ridge. We were in again three times early next morning, and the sight was dreadful. The trenches were almost level, and the dead were lying everywhere. We found one of the lads from my section and buried him in a shell hole. His name is Charlie Carter from Pomborneit, and he was my section bomber. It seems wonderful how any of us came out alive. They call it the night of horrors, and a good name, too.

The next night we went into the trenches, and the shell-fire was worse than it had been the night before. As the lads had advanced 300 yards and dug in on the previous night, we had to go over the open right to the new line. The shells were bursting everywhere, and you would think it was impossible for anybody to live. However, with the exception of about ten casualties, we got into the trenches all right and were fairly comfortable for the night. At daybreak we moved further along the trenches to where they were not so deep. Fritz kept putting in his shells, and kept us busy dressing and sending away the wounded. We were very fortunate and had but few deaths. Our sergeant was wounded going into the trenches, and I had to act as platoon sergeant. I had some miraculous escapes from death.

When I left only 17 of our platoon remained out of 50. On the last night I was out in 'no man's land' with a party preparing communication trenches to charge from, and as Fritz did not see us we had a good time. The last job I did was to bury an Australian officer, whom we found lying out in the front. After that I was about to have a sleep when a shell burst over me and cracked me in both legs. It was 3 a.m. on August 1st.

We did all that was asked of us

The battle known as 3rd Ypres began as an attempt by the British and their allies to conduct a decisive offensive against the Germans in Flanders (modern-day Belgium). The action began on 31 July 1917 and ended with the conclusion of the grim events at Passchendaele in early November. On 19 October 1917 Lance Corporal W. H. Murray wrote a letter about his experience of the fighting still going on to take the strategically vital ridge and village of Passchendaele. The sometimes upbeat tone of the letter cannot hide the horrors of the battle.

After leaving camp we sneaked up through Ypres in parties of about 50 men and camped in the mud on the frontier side of what was once the fine town of that name. It is now simply a heap of ruined buildings, and fine old churches and other structures famous for their beauty have been blown to pieces, and even tomb stones and graves have been shelled with the rest, while all along the roads are holes in which a man can stand without being seen. We lay in the rain in our mudhole camp all the first day without any shelter, but within a couple of hours the lads had unearthed galvanised iron, wood, etc., from some adjacent vacated trenches and had erected quite a little town, and were under shelter, even though they had to enter their dwellings on their hands and knees. Our tents arrived at evening and the office staff was then fixed up. We remained here for two full days just about two miles from Fritz, and as soon as he picked up our position he hurled shells at us and tried to bomb us and the big guns around us from his planes.

On the evening of the second day we prepared to move into the line where we were to make a push on Passchendaele Ridge and capture the village of the same name. We moved out in the dark in single file and moved along the famous Ypres-Menin road, which was filled with traffic of all descriptions. How vehicles of all sorts move up and down the road, which is simply a continuation of shell holes, is wonderful. Soon we left the main road to travel along a long boggy winding road (or track) over, through, and around shell holes. That trip must have taken us at least two hours. At both ends of the track Fritz showered high explosive shells on us, while in the middle he pumped gas shells into us.

Eventually we reached the jumping-off point and lay under a bank. Fritz knew where we were, under the bank of a sunken road, and pumped the shells into us. At 5.45 a.m. our guns opened up with a barrage. When I heard the rattle and roar and saw the flashes behind me I felt like crying. I knew that the boys were going forward in the semi-darkness. Scores of our guns were buried in the mud and useless, while it was impossible to get ammunition to others, and they could not fire a shot. The guns were too far back and could not be got up closer owing to the bad state of the ground. Scores of Fritz's strong points contained machine-guns. These strong points are made of very strong concrete and are proof against anything but very powerful and big shells.

During the early hours of the morning we got into the village and up on to the desired ridge, but, as the troops operating on our right and left were unable to advance with us, we had to retire to within 300 yards of our starting point in the afternoon. All night long the strafing continued while we lay in shell holes in the slush, mud, and rain, though during the evening I wandered about, looking for our company headquarters, with whom I should have been, and how all the shells, machine-gun and snipers' bullets missed me I do not know. One cut the leather over my big toe, but that was all. Two of our officers had been wounded close to me, and had gone to the rear to the dressing station so that I had to find the next in command and attach myself to him.

Mud! Don't mention it. Time after time I went in up to my hips and was never in less than to the tops of my boots. This is the kind of ground on which we advanced. After digging a hole in this mud for protection it would fill with water in an hour and then fall in. Eventually I found a small dry place under a bank, and spent the rest of the night there in my soaked, and mud-caked clothes, and even dozed for a couple of hours. Very shortly after awakening, Fritz dropped a shell within 6ft. of my 'possy,' and up I went and came down with the mud and slush which buried me, but, though half dazed, I dragged myself out of the mire and shifted. Altogether I was blown out three times, and buried to my armpits once.

Next morning things quietened down considerably, and both Fritz and our chaps brought in their wounded and buried the dead. We brought in some Tommies who had been lying wounded in shellholes, left by their own chaps when Fritz pushed them back a few days before.

On the second morning we formed and consolidated our new line, and at about 10 a.m. Frank and I ran into one another while going over to a party which had arrived with food and ammunition for us. I can tell you it was a relief to both of us when we met. Two brothers being in the same crowd in a stunt like this is a great strain on both! In the evening we were relieved by fresh troops. Altogether I think our prisoners for the brigade numbered about 600. When our barrage opened and they knew that we were advancing the Huns simply threw away everything and ran to us with their hands up. They go straight to the rear without any escort, too. In fact, scores of them did fine work in carrying and assisting our wounded to the dressing stations. Some of them were wounded, and had their wounds attended to when an opportunity offered.

At 5 p.m., just before being relieved, Frank and two others and myself took a wounded man from No Man's Land out on a stretcher, but could not leave him at any dressing station as there were no carrying parties to take him on, and leaving him would mean that he would remain there in the cold until next day. In the end we carried him 4½ miles, to a motor ambulance, and then crawled on to our old mud camp, which we reached at midnight. I was never so close to physical exhaustion before. I am certain that without exaggeration I was bogged to the hips 50 times at least, and crawling out of that alone knocks it out of a chap. We got hot stew and tea when we got to camp, and just lay down where we could and knew nothing. Fritz bombed and shelled us all the way out of the line, and all night and next day, but we only stirred out for meals and did not worry at all.

Next morning we moved away and picked up motor lorries three miles from Ypres, and were brought back and turned into our old billets. When I returned to mine I found Frank, and five others waiting for me. We were the only six left out of the 17 who left here like a happy family three weeks ago. Three of the others are dead, and the remaining eight wounded. The Frenchy's wife bustled in to see us next morning before we were out of bed, but when she found that only six of us were left, she and a friend of hers went away in tears. Shortly after she returned with a jug of steaming coffee and rum, and gave us each a cupful in bed.

We are out of danger again now, but our stunt was hell while it lasted. Fritz knew we were going in and had picked troops and every thing prepared for our reception, which was a hot one. But not all his preparation could have stopped us. The nature of the ground hampered us; so the stunt was only partially successful. We did all that was asked of us.

The charge at Beersheba

The famous charge against the Turkish defences of Beersheba (now in southern Israel) during the Sinai and Palestine campaign was the culmination of a lengthy and complicated operation. Two attacks had already failed in late September 1917 and an attempt was made to outflank the enemy at dawn on 31 October. The battle was not going well by the afternoon, at which point the commander of the Desert Mounted Corps, Lieutenant General Harry Chauvel, ordered the 4th Light Horse Brigade to charge. Light horsemen fixed bayonets to their rifles and used them like lances in a wild ride towards the Turkish defences. The suddenness and speed of the charge allowed the Light Horse to sweep through the enemy defences before they could accurately aim their artillery, forcing their subsequent withdrawal into Palestine.

Eighteen-year-old Trooper Jack Margrie of the 11th Light Horse gave his account of the fall of Beersheba in a letter home. He was wounded in the foot—his 'issue of lead', as he put it. His letter had been censored by army authorities to conceal military details that might assist the enemy.

You will have read in my previous letters all about our big stunt up to the time I received my issue of lead; but you will be interested to hear fuller particulars of how Beersheba fell into our hands. After riding hard for three days on a wide flank movement—get out your map of Palestine—we eventually arrived in position five miles east of the town at dawn on 1st November. The Camel Corps constituted our extreme right flank and established communication with the Sheriff of Mecca and his guerilla army. On their left was the –th brigade, to which my regiment belongs; then came the –rd, –nd and –at brigades in succession, the –at being s.s.w. of the town. On the s.w. of our objective were the brigades who were linked up with the right flank of the Infantry, who occupied the whole line from this point to Gaza.

The attack began at dawn and lasted all day, the Turks putting up a stubborn resistance to our fire, both artillery and small guns replying shot for shot. At last, about sunset, General——— our Brigadier, got tired of such slow business. If 'Jacko' (the Turks) got a chance to bring up reinforcements and supplies under cover of darkness, he would never be shifted, so our General sent forward the order: 'The brigades acting as cavalry will move forward and take the position at the gallop.' Then wasn't there a wild hullabaloo. Imagine about 2,000 men strung out abreast, standing up in their stirrups or crouching low in their saddles, in proportion to the amount of stomach they had for the game, and galloping madly down on the little Jackos, who threw away their rifles and gear as they ran—in utter astonishment at finding that the men they had always treated as mounted infantry were prepared to be cavalry if the need arose.

Good Lord, wasn't there a scatter. One of our men had his horse shot under him, and just then espied a Turkish officer, who had been hiding in a deep dug-out, and finding the place too hot tried to get away on a superb white Arab stallion. After him went our 'Billyjim' and, succeeding in cutting him off, grabbed the reins and yelled out—'Get off this animal, you.' The fellow wanted to argue the point and received a rifle butt over his head for his pains. Into the saddle jumped 'Billyjim', happy in the possession of the best mount in the troop, if not the whole regiment.

Well, we hardly fired a shot, but just galloped and galloped until we got right into the town. Then the —st and —nd brigades took up the pursuit and we left to enjoy the fruits of our labours. We fed and watered our horses, put our posts on for the night, and then slept. Sleep had practically been an unknown quantity to us during the previous four days. Next day we went on foraging and got all sorts of tucker-grain and 'tibbin' (chaff) for our horses, Turkish bread, fowls, biscuits, Australian bully beef (which tastes like horse flesh or worse), and all sorts of eatables and souvenirs for ourselves. I feel that I cannot do justice to Beersheba on paper, but hope to re-tell the tale some day, soon, in the dear old home land.

Heroes of Anzac

THE COLLECTIVE ANZAC hero is the 'digger', originally the volunteer citizen-soldier of the First AIF and the ANZAC Corps who saw the war as an unpleasant but necessary job that had to be done and so went and did it. The digger was impatient with official discipline, rank and drill and was more than a handful when on leave, but he fought fiercely and efficiently, if in an unorthodox style. This image of the Anzac hero, of course, leaves out nurses, sailors, aviators and a range of other brave people who saw it as a duty to serve their country. The digger is undoubtedly the idealised human symbol of Anzac but, as in the ancient mythologies of Greece, Rome and other cultures, Anzac has many individual heroes and heroines.

They just poured into the wards all day

Nurses arrived at the front during World War I by various routes—some through official military arrangements, some through charities and some by private means. With an ethos derived from Florence Nightingale's ideals and teachings, developed through her Crimean War experience, nurses were ready to serve. Sister Tucker from Launceston in Tasmania wrote home about her time on hospital ship HMS *Sicilia*, the first to begin taking off the wounded from Gallipoli. She and the medical staff accompanying her had a relatively pleasant voyage from Alexandria in Egypt to Lemnos, though the situation changed dramatically soon after their arrival in Mudros harbour.

We see masts and funnels by the score all round, but do not know whether our troops are landed or are still on them. We had a very nice trip here, after waiting at Alexandria for three or four days for orders. Most of the crew are Indians—also the doctors, orderlies, dressers, waiters, and stewards. The colonel and medical officers are from India; but, of course, are Imperial men. Colonel Bird and his son are Australians, and we have 12 nurses. We have the honour to be the first hospital ship to enter the Dardanelles. We are equipped to take 400 patients. The boat is fitted with five large wards, with a couple of officers' wards, special wards, and a nice little theatre. One night at sea was fairly rough; but everybody was able to appear at meals—of course, we were very keen to do so, as we were chosen on account of being good sailors. The French uniform is a pale blue flannel material, with long coats, and blue or scarlet caps. We do not think they look so nice as our men. Perhaps it's conceit on our part, but we are so proud of being Australians when we see our troops marching by.

April 29—We returned to Alexandria yesterday, after three weeks. We spent the day unloading our patients, and are to sail again at 6 p.m. When waiting in the harbour at Lemnos, four of us nurses were ordered to transfer to the hospital ship *Gascon*. We left Lemnos on Saturday evening, and early on Sunday morning came to the Dardanelles. About 2 a.m. the first shot was fired. We were right up in the firing line—several gunboats were behind us, firing right over us. Several shots from the boats splashed very near to us. About 9 a.m. the first patients were brought on board. It was awful to see them, some with scarcely any clothes on, blood pouring in all directions, some limping . . . others with an arm bandaged. Several died as they came across in the boats to us. It was absolutely grand to see how 'game' they were. I felt just proud of being an Australian, and owning them. They just poured into the wards all day. My ward holds 96—and I was responsible for about 40 on deck. I had three orderlies and a sergeant-major to assist. The dock was just lined with patients lying on mattresses—530 patients—though our boat is only fitted up for 400. You can imagine how we all worked until we got to Alexandria again—early on Thursday morning. Now we are making bandages—dressing, splints, etc. ready for the next patients.

Landing the patients was a pathetic sight. Hardly any of them had shirts. They were so blood-stained and torn they had to be thrown overboard. Others had their coats and trousers split, and hurriedly sewn over. Some were minus a boot; very many minus socks. It took hours getting the stretcher cases off. We started at 9 a.m. The last was landed at 4.30. One day we had six to bury at sea; another day several . . .

After a few months medical supplies and water became scarce on Lemnos, as this doctor described to relatives in Adelaide.

I must say that the men we brought from Australia have turned out grand fellows, and one could not wish for better nursing orderlies, nor find more conscientious and hard-working fellows. I am helping to look after 1100 patients, as we have taken over No. 2 Australian Hospital. All the nurses have been ashore (from the transports) for three days, and have to sleep in tents, so it is rather rough on them. There is a limited supply of water, so I expect they find life rather rough and dirty, but it gives them an idea of how things are run in a camp hospital. One night I had to admit patients from 10.30 p.m. to 1 p.m., and as I had started at 5 o'clock and been on my feet all day I was rather tired. We start at 9 o'clock doing the cases, and generally finish about 10 p.m. We commence to operate at 7.30 p.m. For my first seven days at Mudros I had 60 patients to look after, and could generally manage to finish by lunch, as the greater number were suffering from diarrhoea. This complaint has been troublesome lately, three-fourths of our patients having been complaining of it. They are a jolly fine crowd, and are always ready to see a joke.

Mudros has altered beyond recognition since our first arrival. There are numerous hospitals around the bay . . . We are frightfully short of beds. Many of the men are accommodated on mattresses on the floors, and are as comfortable there as on beds, although the insect life is simply dreadful. I was showing a naval doctor around one day and he asked me about the livestock. I asked one patient, and when he pulled back the blankets to show how numerous they were, one of the Australian wits at the end of the ward cried out, 'Company, form fours.'

The water problem has been solved to a certain extent. Water is brought to a certain spot every day in barges and thence carted by the two or three water-carts attached to each hospital. Unfortunately we have been unable to obtain reinforcements, and have had to take a man from the Evacuation depot at Mudros to help. Practically none had done any nursing or medical work, so you can understand our position. Still the raw material is turning out well, and without such assistance it would be impossible to carry on. We are also frightfully short of instruments, and have to do what we can with the few things we have. Of course, we have the instruments in the theatre, but one cannot send an orderly 250 yards every time, and, again, the instruments there are in use most of the day and evening. There is a disease prevalent here characterised by 'tripexia,' dirty tongue and loss of appetite. It is like typhoid, but certainly is not true typhoid fever.

The X-ray cases are all seen at night time, so we manage to look at these between the operations, and while the orderlies are cleaning the theatre. The majority of the operations are small, such as looking for and extracting bullets and pieces of shell and cartridge casings. These take more finding than one would imagine. We take off a fair number of fingers and extract numerous shrapnel bullets.

Everyone was as cheerful as possible

In July 1915, Dr Brennan wrote home, praising the heroism of the troops on Gallipoli, from the landings onwards. Brennan had been in the first wave of the landings and had himself performed acts of gallantry, which he does not mention in his letter, preferring to praise the men who served with him. The letter also records the moment at which the Anzacs realised that they were too far north of their prescribed landing point.

On the day of departure from the island (Saturday, April 24) half our battalion embarked on destroyers and were taken to H.M.S. *London*, and started out, all the battleships and cruisers in line, the transports (with the remainder of the troops) following, and the destroyers buzzing about like bees. The *Queen Elizabeth* went on ahead. We cruised about the Aegean Sea all the afternoon, and at dark started slowly up the Gulf of Saros. The officers of the *London* were awfully good to us; they gave up their beds to us and fed us up like fighting cocks. If you ever hear anyone saying anything derogatory about the Navy in future just plug him and explain it's from me. They really are the finest lot of men I have ever met.

After a few hours sleep we were called at 12.30 a.m., and had another feed. By this time we were just in sight of land, and the night was glorious; but as the moonlight was so bright we had to keep well away from the land. About 1.30 a.m. we embarked in boats which were towed by the battleships' packet boats on the opposite side of the ships from the land, so that only the battleships could be seen, and then started slowly in diagonally towards the part of the shore where we were to land. Of course, there were no lights, and the silence was absolute, except for an occasional low-voiced order from a naval officer. By this time the moon had gone down, and we had just an hour before dawn. Then all at once the battleships stopped, and we turned half-right and started hell for leather for the shore—six packet boats (off three battleships), each towing four or five big pinnace launches and cutters. Our tow was on the extreme left. A few hundred yards behind us came seven or eight destroyers packed with the remaining companies of our battalions, which they had collected off the transports; then behind them again came the transports carrying the troops of the other brigades waiting until we were landed for the picket boats and destroyers to return and land them.

The land loomed closer and closer, and there was still no sign of the enemy having discovered us, but all at once it struck me that the look of the land ahead of us was distinctly different from what it should have been by the maps which were issued to us: the hills were steep right to the beach, instead of the ground gradually sloping as we were told. Evidently others made the same discovery, for presently I heard a navy chap say in a drawlly way 'I believe we're A Mile Too Far North.' But it was too late to mend the error—dawn was just breaking—so after turning still further north for a couple of hundred yards about quite close to the shore we made straight on. Just as the picket boat cast off and we were lowering the oars to pull in the last 40 or 50 yards a single rifle shot rang out in the stillness, and everyone jumped about a foot off his seat. But we all soon got over the jumping business, as within about five seconds the fire opened from the whole hill in front of us, and then a machine gun opened fire.

I was in the second boat of the tow, and being a fairly light boat we ran well into the beach. The first boat of the tow was a big pinnace, and having 50 men on board she grounded a fair distance out, and when the troops got out they were up to their shoulders in water; we were only up to our waists. There were only a few casualties in our boats—the machine gun didn't get into it—but there were more in others especially those who didn't get rowing while they still had way on [forward motion] from the picket boat. As you can imagine, there was no time wasted in getting out of the boats and across the beach (only about 15 yards wide), to the shelter of the bank; but even there we found we were not safe, as they were enfilading us from a bit of a cape about 200 yards to the south, so we had to crawl round until we found a little depression in the bank. Of course, all this was a matter of seconds. Soon there were a good number of men ashore. I heard an officer sing out 'Fix bayonets, lads and up we go' and with a yell they started up the hill, which was very steep. They had to crawl up on hands and knees: more men were coming all the time, following the others up. Suddenly the shrapnel started. They were firing from a battery on the Gaba Tepe, a cape about 1½ miles south of us, and at once the battleships opened in return, and the din was tremendous. There seemed to be shrapnel bursting over and all round the boats. I was busy dressing all kinds of bullet wounds. An engineer was shot through the chest just beside me, and died in a few minutes. Suddenly there was a cheer from the top of the hill; our boys had captured the machine gun and driven the Turks out of their trenches. All this time there was not a rifle fired by our side. Coming ashore the rifles were not even loaded. I followed them up, dressing the wounded and leaving them to be picked up by bearers.

As soon as our fellows got the First Hill they got the Turks on the run and kept them going, down the other side of the hill they went, and up the next—very stiff climb; a hill or a ridge rather about 400ft. high. The whole country is covered with low scrub, and in the rush forward lots of the Turks lay down under bushes and sniped our men off after they had passed them. They crossed a plateau 100 yards wide, and followed down another dip into a big gully with a creek in it, where we found five tents, evidently having been occupied by supports for the trenches. There were a lot of wounded Turks about, but as there were so many of our wounded I hadn't much time to look at them. Besides, they had no field dressings like our men carry. I gave some morphine to a few of them, but most of them spat it out.

Everyone was as cheerful as possible in spite of everything. Coming up the first hill I heard one fellow say (the bullets were very thick at the time), 'If they're not careful they'll fire one shot too many, and the bullets will chock [collide] in the air'. On the plateau I met my A.M.C. sergeant, and it was very fortunate, as two can do better than one, especially with fractures and bad haemorrhage cases. We fixed a couple of shattered legs, and went on down into the big gully, along that for a bit, and then up on to the top of the main ridge which our fellows had just taken. The first wounded man up there that I struck was Peck, our adjutant; he had a bullet through the shoulder. It had just missed the bone.

Our men had gone on still further, but by this time (about 10 a.m.) the Turks were reinforced strongly. Although during the morning and early afternoon some of our sections got out more than a mile further, they had all eventually to fall back to the main ridge. During the later afternoon this position got very warm. We were on a knoll on the left of the centre of our line (which by this time was about 2½ miles long) overlooking the left flank. Then some Turks got round a ridge about 500 yards away on our left, from which they could get the back of the hill we were on, as well as the front, and we had to dig in as quickly as possible.

Of course, all the units were fearfully mixed up by this time. Major Denton was close to me and about half a dozen of our men; all the other men were a mixture of battalions. I found myself in a trench with some machine gun supports, and borrowed a bit of their trench to haul wounded into and dress there. My sergeant was a little further along the line. When darkness came you could move about a bit as long as you kept off the skyline, and I went and visited Denton and found Barnes, Brockman and Everett along the line with a mixed command. There were not so many casualties now, but every now and then a man would be wounded while digging trenches just over the hill. Altogether it was a very anxious time from the middle of the afternoon until next morning. The firing was continuous, and very heavy. The Turks are wonders at taking cover and would worm their way right up to within 10 yards of the trenches and pot at anything they saw move in the darkness. About midnight, to increase our discomfort, a drizzly rain started, and before long we were wet to the skin. The men in the trench with me had their bayonets fixed all night, and I had my revolver ready. I had already taken off my red cross, as it wasn't much use in such a situation. We all had a few pots at apparently moving shadows during the night. The snipers from the hill opposite came round during the night, and our knoll and the left flank were surrounded, except along the ridge towards the centre. We were all very glad when morning dawned. Time after time during the night the enemy had come right up to the trenches, but they would not face the bayonets, and always retired.

The following five days saw continuous fighting, we holding the position on the top of the ridge, and they trying to break through. Of course, if they had broken through our line anywhere it would have meant that the whole line would have had to retire. An Indian mountain battery got busy on Sunday afternoon, and in spite of severe losses caused by the concentration of the enemy's shrapnel on them, they did wonderful work. Then on Monday, as soon as our line was established, the battleships opened fire over our heads. The 'Lizzie's' shells were a revelation; they would whistle over our heads, and the next, there would be a terrific explosion on the big hill on our left front and when the smoke and dust cleared the whole contour would be changed. Every time that the Turks massed in any spot the observers would pass along the word by field telephone, and the ship's shells would be on them. Of course, they were not quiet either, and there was shrapnel bursting continuously over our trenches.

On Monday and Tuesday our batteries were landing and soon opened fire also. On Monday morning Denton, Everett and Selby formed an observation post on our knoll, a telephone was brought along to my dugout, and they got a dugout just over the hill 10 yards away. They could observe the whole left flank, and shouted messages down all day, which Denton sent on by telephone until he got wounded (not severely) on Tuesday afternoon, and then I sent them on after that. There was a fearful shortage of officers; one after another came over the hill wounded, and some were killed, including Charlie Barnes, while observing for a machine gun. Croly also got a severe wound through the elbow. Later Everett, Selby, and I were the only three left in our section of trenches with a couple of hundred men—all under the few N.C.O.s left. Everett and Selby were kept busy in their posts, and as the wounded were diminishing I took on a bit of army service business, sending down parties for water, food, rum, ammunition, etc., and sent their messages to the head quarters by telephone. Altogether we were going from morning till night, but after dark we could do a bit of a crawl round.

On Monday night I took a stroll down to the beach to get my pack, which I had dropped there as soon as we landed, and luckily found it, and got an overcoat and waterproof sheet out, and took them back. The greatest trouble we had in our part was the removal of the wounded. We could do practically nothing till dark, and even then there were snipers about. Many stretcher-bearers were wounded, and to make matters worse all day and part of the night the valley was swept by shrapnel—in fact, the valley was called 'Shrapnel Valley.' In the dugouts around me were my sergeant and a pioneer sergeant and two assistants looking after the ammunition supply. One of these last was a trick of a kid. He would duck down the hill to the valley to fetch up water and sometimes tea for us, and if a sniper got closer to him than usual he would put down whatever he was carrying, turn in the direction from which the bullet came, and put his fingers to his nose, and then come on again.

There were examples of wonderful bravery all round us. One boy of 19 and a Corporal the only two left out of a machine gun crew [manned] the gun for four days and nights with practically no sleep, and in spite of splinters from bullets which had hit the gun and had embedded in their arms and hands. They only left when the gun was ruined. I could tell you dozens of equally courageous things.

On Thursday we heard a rumour that our Battalion was re-forming on the beach, so I went down to see and found that they had been down resting since the previous afternoon. I went back to tell Everett and Selby to collect my things. They couldn't leave until officers could be spared to relieve them, so I got together the sergeant and the only one I had left of five stretcher-bearers I had managed to collect (all the others were wounded), and I went down to the valley and slept my first decent sleep with Joe Kenny, who had a section of the 4th Field Ambulance there. I arranged with him to see that the section of trenches I had been looking after were evacuated of wounded and went and joined the battalion. Met Dixon Hearder on the beach; he had been doing great work with his machine guns in the centre. When the Battalion reformed there were 11 officers killed, wounded, or missing, and between 500 and 600 men out of the 1,000 odd of the men who had landed.

I am writing this in my dugout and as there is a good deal of shrapnel kicking and whizzing about just outside us we are sitting tight. The food is pretty good; we have tinned meat, bacon, jam, cheese, and biscuits, besides tea and sugar, with rum twice a week; also spuds and onions. The chaps on the *London* have been great. Nearly every day a hamper comes over with the bread, tinned milk, butter, cigarettes, tobacco, matches, chutney, sauce and chocolate, golden syrup, and bootlaces. So we are very happy; even when it rains we rig our waterproof sheets for a roof.

Just a line in conclusion about the effect of being under fire on oneself. You read of men crying and laughing and getting hysterical. I have seen a little of that amongst our reinforcements who were not in the first flutter. But I saw none at all in our lot. Everything was so crisp and sudden, and it seemed just as safe to keep going forward as it did to stay where you were. The different sounds of bullets, shells, etc., we are now experts in. There is the sharp crack of the bullet overhead, with a 'ping' when it hits anything. There is the nasty, unfriendly swish of one that passes close to your ear. Then there is the 'crackle' of a machine gun, changing to a mournful disappointed 'whisp whisp' when the bullets get closer. Lastly, there is the cheerful whistle of the shrapnel shell well overhead, and at which we all used to duck (we don't now, we know they're safe). It's the vicious brute that is just past you as you hear it that makes you take cover in case there's another following it. I heard one fellow in the trenches the other day say to another, 'One of these days we'll be standing at the corner of Hay and Barrack streets and a motor tyre will burst close by, and the people around will be wondering why we're lying on our stomachs.' 'And when a barmaid opens a bottle of soda we'll all be down under the counter', replied his mate.

Private Punch

Private William Joseph Punch was one of the 500 to 800 Aboriginal and Torres Strait Islanders who served in World War I. At least five of these men are buried on Gallipoli, although Punch's war experience was at the western front. Although his death was sadly typical of the Great War, the story of his life is unusual.

Along the Bland Creek (near Frampton, New South Wales) one night in 1880 a group of Aborigines were murdered by settlers as punishment for cattle spearing. A young man named John Siggs from a local settler family came across the site shortly afterwards and found the only survivor, an infant trying to suckle at his dead mother's breast. Filled with disgust at the deed and overcome with pity, Siggs took the baby boy and raised him as a member of the family. The story was put about that the boy was from Queensland, possibly to conceal the fact that he was the sole survivor of the massacre. Under the name William Joseph Punch the boy grew up and went to school along with the other children in the region, and he became a noted sportsman, musician and participant in local social activities.

In December 1915, Punch enlisted. He was in camp with 300 other enlistees at the Goulburn Showground until February 1916 when he was transferred to Sydney. He was reportedly a popular man with the troops and eventually joined the 1st Battalion and fought on the western front. He was wounded in September 1916, though he subsequently returned to duty. He was wounded again the following year in France, shipped back to England and nursed, as many Anzac troops were, in the coastal town of Bournemouth, in Dorset.

We may well never have known about Private Punch's life and death if not for an attempt made by the Returned Services League in 1931 to identify indigenous diggers. That year, the RSL publication *Reveille* issued a request for information that drew a letter from an Australian nurse who had looked after Punch during his last weeks in the hospital at Bournemouth. Sister O'Shea not only wrote to *Reveille* about the black digger but also supplied a photograph of him in his hospital bed.

One of Punch's old mates, W. Scott, also wrote in with his recollections of the man.

I would like to add my quota in remembrance of Bill Punch, of Goulburn, who was admired by all his comrades, and regarded as a 'Dinkum Digger.' Bill was a full blooded aborigine—a Queenslander, I think. He was adopted when a youngster by Mr W Siggs of Woodhouselee, between Goulburn and Crookwell, who educated him and employed him as a stockman and station hand up till the time of his enlistment. Bill, as well as being well educated, was a musician of no mean ability, and very popular with his Digger mates. He went through Goulburn and Liverpool camps, and on to Tel-el-Kebir with our reinforcement, the 17th of the 1st Battalion.

Unfortunately, in Egypt, Bill and several others were quarantined for mumps or something and were left behind. We went on to join the 53rd Battalion at Fleur Baix, and Punch and the others eventually joined the 1st Battalion . . .

On 29 August 1917, Private Punch died of pneumonia in the Mount Dore hospital in Bournemouth. He is buried in the Bournemouth East Cemetery, Boscombe.

A soldier of the cross

He was the Salvation Army minister who allegedly led troops into battle brandishing a shovel. This and other legends formed around the remarkable man known as 'Fighting Mac', properly William McKenzie, Chaplain to the 4th Battalion, AIF.

Born in Scotland, he arrived in Australia at the age of fifteen in 1884 and quickly adapted to outdoor life in Queensland, cane cutting and dairying. He became a Salvation Army minister in 1889—'the true religion for a fighting man', he later said—but retained an intensely practical approach to his duties, which formed the basis of his amazing wartime story on Gallipoli and the western front.

On the transport ship to Egypt he organised sporting events and other recreations for the men, including boxing matches, which he sometimes won against some of the AIF's hardest nuts. These activities gained him the respect of the troops and legends began to attach themselves to his larger-than-life personality. In Egypt he was rumoured to have been incensed at the rather heavily populated venereal disease treatment camp and to have assisted the troops in pulling down the barbed wire around it.

On Gallipoli he worked tirelessly as a water-bearer, stretcher-bearer and chaplain, burying many men and also providing a ready ear for advice and guidance. It was said that in one three-day period alone he conducted 647 burials. One of his earliest burials was that of Lieutenant Colonel Onslow Thompson, the commanding officer of the 4th Battalion, who was killed on 26 April—'It was a relief to find the body of our colonel ... after it had lain out for a full fortnight. We buried it after dark, as it lay in an exposed position. I had to kneel and keep head and body in a crouching posture while reading the service. Hundreds of bullets swept over us while this was going on.'

According to legend, Mac was conducting a service when a Turkish shell exploded nearby, showering him and the congregation with dirt. 'Hallelujah!' he called out, as he picked himself up and continued the service. Although chaplains were officially prohibited from engaging in combat, McKenzie was involved in many battles. At Lone Pine the troops reputedly begged him not to risk his life but he replied, 'Boys, I've preached to you, and I've prayed with you. Do you think I'm afraid now to die with you?'

He continued his hands-on approach on the western front, assisting with the establishment and running of 'comforts' such as coffee stalls. He was present at many of the now iconic battles of the war in including Pozières, Bullecourt and Mouquet Farm in France, and Polygon Wood and Passchendaele in Belgium. In 1917, at the age of forty-eight, he was released from service as a result of the decline in his physical health and the emotional toll of the things he had seen and done. McKenzie was the object of deep respect from his comrades and had also become a national hero—he was sometimes called the most famous man in the AIF. He had been decorated in 1916 and there were rumours that he had several times been nominated for the Victoria Cross.

Despite the poor state of his health, McKenzie continued to actively fill a leading role in the Salvation Army after the war, which included spending some years in China. He was awarded an OBE in 1935 and became a popular presence at Anzac Day observances. McKenzie retired from the Salvation Army in 1939 and died in Sydney in 1947. It is said that weeping diggers marched six abreast at his funeral.

Fromelles

The action officially known as the 'attack' on the French village of Fromelles was the first to involve AIF troops on the western front. It took place around the villages of Fleurbaix and Fromelles on 19 and 20 July 1916 and includes what is generally considered to have been the worst-ever day of fighting for Australian troops. After it was over more than five-and-a-half thousand Australian troops were dead, wounded or imprisoned. The British also suffered heavy casualties and the action was a strategic failure.

This graphic description published four years after the battle mentions Harold 'Pompey' Elliott, a brilliant but independent Australian brigade commander who had already declared Fromelles a hopeless task at the planning stage. His highly trained men were, literally, cut to pieces by the enemy fire and he was seen with tears streaming down his face as he shook hands with the few survivors after the battle.

The morning of the 19th was calm and misty, with the promise of a clear, fine day later. Reports from patrols in No Man's Land during the night indicated that the damage done to the enemy's wire was as yet inconsiderable, but no real importance was attached to that, as the chief part of the artillery preparation had still to come. The patrol reports disclosed also that the enemy was very vigilant, and that close inspection of parts of his wire was impossible owing to the presence of strong enemy posts in No Man's Land. At a quarter past 2 p.m., however, there was a marked increase in enemy counter preparation, and by 3 p.m. a heavy and continuous volume of fire was falling over the front and support line and the saps leading to them, now filled with the assembling infantry. The assembly was reported complete on the 8th Brigade front at 25 minutes past 3 p.m., on the 14th at a quarter to 4 p.m., and on the 15th at 4 p.m. The men had received specially good breakfasts and dinners, and were in high spirits. The enemy fire continued to increase in volume on the front trenches, where already three of the four company commanders of the 53rd Battalion had become casualties.

Punctually at 5.43 p.m. deployment into No Man's Land commenced, and it was hoped that the artillery barrage would be sufficiently intense to keep enemy heads down until the deployment was completed. On the extreme right of the 5th Divisional frontage the 59th Battalion was scarcely over the parapet before a little desultory musketry fire was opened on it, coming chiefly from the Sugar Loaf. Before the men had gone 30 yards this fire had grown in intensity, and a machine gun added its significant voice to the rapidly increasing fusillade. The waves pressed forward steadily, but just as steadily the enemy fire grew hotter, and the enemy front lines were seen to be thickly manned with troops. The losses mounted rapidly as the men pressed gallantly on into the withering fire. Lieut-Colonel Harris was disabled by a shell, and Major Layh took charge of the dwindling line, which, finding a slight depression about 100 yards from the enemy parapet, halted in the scanty cover it provided, and commenced to reorganise their broken and depleted units.

THE THINNING LINES

The deployment of the 60th Battalion was attended by similar circumstances. Heavy fire was encountered almost from the moment of its appearance over the parapet. Into this the troops pressed with the same steadiness as that displayed by the 59th, and with the same result. The ranks, especially on the right, where they were most exposed to the Sugar Loaf, thinned rapidly; but the later waves followed on without hesitation or confusion. On the left flank more headway was made. To halt in No Man's Land in these circumstances was to court certain death, and Major McRae led his troops towards the enemy parapet. It was his last act of gallant leadership. Just at the enemy wire the enfilade fire from the Sugar Loaf became intense, and there, almost at his goal, he fell. His adjutant fell beside him, and there, too, the greater part of the 60th Battalion melted away. Only on the extreme left were the enemy trenches entered by elements of the 60th. They appear to have had some temporary success, for they sent back a few prisoners; but, as the official report significantly states, 'Touch with them was subsequently lost.' Thus on the entire front the 15th Brigade, within half an hour from the time of assault, it was apparent that the 61st Imperial Division had failed to take the Sugar Loaf strong post, which was its allotted task, and that it was beyond human power to cross so wide a No Man's Land in the face of the machine-gun fire that streamed continuously from it. By 6.30 p.m. the remnants of the two battalions were doggedly digging in as near to the enemy parapet as they could. Thirty-five out of 39 of the assaulting officers were already killed or wounded, and with them most of the N.C.O.'s. In these circumstances the survivors could only hold on determinedly to what they had won and await such further action as their trusted brigade commander might devise to meet the situation.

The troops of the centre and left brigades, although they had suffered heavily under the preliminary bombardment, experienced in their assault a vastly different fortune. Immune from the fatal enfilade of the Sugar Loaf, the 53rd and 54th Battalions completed their deployment with comparatively slight additional casualties, and as the barrage lifted the leading wave dashed into the enemy front line. The enemy was caught in the act of manning his parapets, and some bitter hand-to-hand fighting followed. It terminated, as all such hand-to-hand fighting terminated throughout the war, in the absolute triumph of the Australians and the extinction or capitulation of the Germans. The front line thus secured, the later waves streamed over it and made for the enemy support trench, which, according to their information, lay about 150 yards behind his front line. The intervening country torn with shell holes, and intersected by communication trenches, was difficult to cross, and it was swept by a certain amount of machine-gun and musketry fire. A careful search of the terrain failed to disclose anything in the nature of an organised enemy support line at the place indicated on the aeroplane maps, and both 53rd and 54th Battalions spent considerable time in searching for one. Except for certain fragmentary trench sections, all that could be found was an old ditch, containing a couple of feet of water. Whatever the purpose of its original construction, it was now used as a drain to convey away the water pumped by pumping plants from the deep dugouts of the front line. The non-existence of an organised support line at the place indicated in the orders was an immediate and fruitful source of complications, aggravated particularly in the 53rd Battalion by the dearth of senior officers. Instead of stepping into a definite and well constructed line, the men became dispersed in the search for one, and with night closing in and the enemy counter-attacks impending the necessity to consolidate somewhere became pressing. This was done, but the line taken up lacked the continuity and lateral communications that a good trench would have afforded. In the circumstances, the 53rd Battalion's touch with the 54th on its left became intermittent, and finally ceased, while even between the elements of the 53rd itself, communication was irregular. The position of the 54th Battalion was materially better. Although three of its four company commanders and three of its four seconds in command wore casualties prior to the assault, Lieut. Colonel Cass had happily escaped injury, and was thus able to direct the consolidation of his position. By strenuous efforts the line of the drain was improved, and a moderately good fire position along the whole of the 54th Battalion frontage was soon in course of construction.

On the left sector, Major-General Tivey was faced from the outset with the heavy responsibility of securing the extreme left flank of the entire battle frontage. At 6 p.m. the battalions stormed over what was left of the enemy wire, and were soon masters of the enemy front trench. Many Germans were killed, and a good number of prisoners taken. Pressing on to their next objective, they met with an experience precisely similar to that of the battalions of the 14th Brigade. An open ditch, containing about 3ft. of water, 150 yards behind the enemy front line, was the only trace of enemy works in the vicinity, and though Lieut-Colonel Toll personally explored the country for several hundred yards farther, he found no trace of an enemy support line. The search for the expected system took many of the officers and men of both battalions into the area of our own protective barrage, and not a few casualties were suffered thereby. Constrained to make the best of things, Colonel Toll ordered his battalion to consolidate along the ditch.

The general position of the 5th Divisional front at 7.30 p.m. on the 19th was that the attack was definitely held up from the right brigade sector, and successful on the central and left sectors. The 59th and 60th Battalions had suffered terribly, and in the 53rd, 54th, 31st, and 32nd Battalions, the percentage of losses, especially amongst the officers, was very high, and still mounting steadily. The line held was an indifferent one. Consolidation was difficult; the line was not continuous, and later communication along it was irregular and uncertain.

General Elliott received official news of the failure of the 61st Imperial Division (on the right) at about 7.30 p.m., by which time he was also aware that the 59th and 60th Battalions were badly cut up, and quite unable to advance without assistance. On receipt of information at 7.52 that he could use two companies of the 58th to support his attack, in conjunction with the attack of the 184th Imperial Brigade on the Sugar Loaf, he took immediate steps to make the necessary arrangement. Command of the attack was entrusted to Major Hutchinson. Few more gallant episodes than this dashing, hopeless assault exist in the annals of any army in the world. The attack of the 61st Imperial Division had been abandoned (without the battalion knowing it), and the Sugar Loaf defences were thus enabled to concentrate the whole of their organised machine-gun fire on the one thin Australian line which now endeavoured to penetrate it. With wonderful dash the companies pressed on, losing at every step, but undaunted to the end. They reached the remnants of the 59th and 60th Battalions, where they lay grimly waiting in their shallow, improvised positions. They caught them up and carried them on towards the enemy by the impetus of their own heroic charge. Impeded by broken ground and shell holes, the thinning line searched brokenly forward, reeling under the enfilade, enduring everything but the thought of failing. It was in vain. At the enemy wire the fire became hellish, irresistible. Major Hutchinson perished gloriously close to the German parapet. The attack melted into nothingness.

The information that the 8th Brigade could no longer maintain the left flank against the increasing enemy pressure was received at Divisional Headquarters at about 5 a.m. on the 20th. At this moment General Munro, commanding the 1st Army, was, with Major-General McCay and other officers, at Sailly, in conference on the situation, and it was immediately decided that the 14th Brigade should be withdrawn forthwith, from its precarious position. Communication was difficult at this time, and none of the first seven runners despatched succeeded in reaching Lieutenant-Colonel Cass. The eighth runner had better success, and Lieut-Colonel Cass acknowledged the receipt of retiring instructions at 7.50 a.m. He instructed Lieut-Colonel McConaghy who was still in the enemy front line, to provide from his command a rearguard to hold back the enemy during the withdrawal, and Captain Gibbons and several other officers, with about 50 men of the 55th Battalion, were detailed for this desperate duty. Long before the movement was completed Captain Gibbons' small rearguard found itself fighting bitterly against overwhelming numbers of the victorious enemy. No one thought of himself—no one thought of yielding. No one thought of anything save holding on with his last ounce of strength till the brigade could be extricated. So one by one they fell at their posts, and of this gallant band scarce a man was left alive when the last file of their comrades had passed through the trench to safety. Thus it was at about 9 a.m. on July 20, 1916, the survivors of the 14th Brigade regained their old front line and the battle of Fromelles ended.

The total casualties among the Australians from noon on July 19 to noon on July 20 were 178 officers and 5,335 of other ranks.

The Australians are here!

The actions of Anzacs in France and Belgium were deeply appreciated by many of the local villagers, and even today there are many positive memories of the Australian contribution to the ultimate victory on the western front. So well regarded were the Australians that even the simple fact of their return to the fighting could instil great confidence in the battered local populations, as described in this account.

The reception of the Australians by the local population was unmistakable and made their return to the Somme a high romance. In many of the farms and village houses were found still pinned to the walls photographs of individual Australians and flags commemorating Anzac Day 1916. For this country hereabouts had very nearly come to be a little bit of Australia by association during the summer and winter campaigns of that year. Some of the Diggers here found themselves known by name and remembered like intimate friends. They had fought and played, lived and died about the countryside not merely as soldiers but like patriots defending their own homes. And not in vain. To say that the French women and children rejoiced to see them again is to report the fact but mildly. As the Australian advance guards appeared many of these people, packing their old wagons to flee, were suddenly seized with new heart and a great emotion; they tore their household goods from off the carts again, and dragged the old people and the youngest children to the roadside to shout 'Vivent les Australiens'; the word ran from village to village ahead announcing the arrival of the saviours of France. And that they had come to save France the Australians were tempted to believe, not only on the enthusiasm aroused in every man of them by this great reception, but also by their uplifting confidence in themselves and their capacity to thrash the Hun wherever they should meet him. 'Finish retreat', they told the villagers 'beaucoup Australians ici.'

The Roo de Kanga

In September 1917 a correspondent for an unnamed English newspaper visited the western front. The unnamed journalist closely observed the recently victorious diggers and was struck by their casual attitude towards the business of war and their irreverent sense of humour, among other characteristics. Australian forces had just broken the German lines at Mont St Quentin and Peronne in France. Three VCs were won, but the Australians suffered around 3000 casualties.

To test one's psychological impression of the war solely by the Australian front would be rash. For the Australian Corps is very individualistic, and, after its recent victories, very happy, so that it strikes one less as part of a tragic world contest than as a band of Elizabethan adventurers in great fettle, engaged on a high emprise of their own which they pursue with ardour, gaiety, and an immense confidence. The note is well struck in PERONNE. Here and there in the cleared space between shapeless heaps of brick and mortar which is the main street of that town one may pick out the signs of five occupations. Very faint are the traces of its peaceful day . . . The German notice boards of the first occupation are commoner, with traces of the French return superimposed upon them. But in his last tenure, the enemy had plastered it all afresh . . . And suddenly one comes on the largest notice board of all. The effect is like that of a clean and merry wind blowing through a swamp. The board bears the title 'Roo de Kanga,' and it marks the Australian conquest of the ruins of Sept. 1.

And what of the 'Digger', as the Australian private is content to call himself? One could learn much of him quickly, for he has no servility and little shyness. Sometimes one had a quite uncomfortable revelation of him, as when four self-conscious civilians who arrived, not without misgivings, in the forward area met a battalion of him fresh from the trenches and were greeted with the crushing comment: 'Thank God, the Americans at last!' Or one would note him crowding, in the highest spirits, round a cageful of newly captured Germans, comparing notes in a dispassionately professional vein on the recent engagement, or offering, not without success, to exchange a tin of bully beef for an Iron Cross. In the major features of his thirty-mile push the Digger is less interested than in such sporting venture as that of a little party of Australians who pushed across the SOMME into CHIPILLY, whence the enemy was enfilading the line, and bluffed a German force many times their size into surrender. He is delighted, too, with the mule who was set to draw a dummy tank, and did so dejectedly, for a while, but later, satisfying himself with an inquisitive sniff that the thing was vulnerable, kicked it to smithereens. He is, too, most boyishly gleeful about the colossal German gun which he came on in a peaceful glade in the course of his forward rush . . . Its great bulking carriage towers from its concrete base among the trees, a tremendous monument of man's madness. The Digger has written on it 'captured by Waacs,' and Australian names are graven all over it, from that of the Prime Minister downwards.

And everywhere he will have sport. You can see him with his brown chest and arms gleaming in the sun, defending a wicket on a pitch in a bend of the SOMME that he has just captured; or scarcely to be stopped from that super-energetic sort of rugby that is played under his code to watch the 'Archies' peppering a Boche airman; or cheering a famous Australian jockey pelting along in a mule race on a course improvised where the shell holes are fewest. In lazier moments he is regaled by one of the troops of entertainers for which his Corps is famous in a theatre he has knocked together out of nothing; or he is to be found studying with much interest one of the large maps of the front, with which he is kept in touch with the latest news of the whole line, and deciding what he would do at this or the next place if he were Foch [commander of the French forces].

While the Australians took this well-earned rest along the 'Roo de Kanga' they were commended by the commander of the British army to which they were attached. General Rawlinson of the Fourth Army, in the language of the period, paid tribute to the diggers and looked forward to the end of the war.

Since the Australian Corps joined the Fourth Army on April 8th, 1918, they have passed through a period of hard and uniformly successful fighting, of which all ranks have every right to feel proud.

Now that it has been possible to give the Australian Corps a well-earned period of rest, I wish to express to them my gratitude for all they have one. I have watched with the greatest interest and admiration the various stages through which they have passed, from the hard times of FLERS and POZIERES to their culminating victories at MONT ST QUENTIN and the great Hindenburg system at BONY, BELLICOURT TUNNEL AND MONTBREHAIN. During the summer of 1918 the safety of Amiens has been principally due to their determination, tenacity and valour.

The story of what they have accomplished as a fighting Army Corps, of the diligence, gallantry, and skill which they have so thoroughly learned and so successfully applied, has gained for all Australians a place of honour amongst nations and amongst the English-speaking races in particular.

It has been my privilege to lead the Australian Corps in the Fourth Army during the decisive battles since August 8, which bid fair to bring the war to a successful conclusion at no distant date. No one realises more than I do the very prominent part they have played, for I have watched from day to day every detail of their fighting, and learned to value beyond measure the prowess and determination of all ranks.

In once more congratulating the Corps on a series of successes unsurpassed in this great war, I feel that no more words of mine can adequately express the renown that they have won for themselves and the position that they have established for the Australian nation, not only in France, but throughout the world.

I wish every officer, NCO, and man all possible good fortune in the future, and a speedy and safe return to their beloved Australia.

The only gleams of sunshine

Private Vernon Carter left Australia in November 1915, and after training in Egypt went to France in June 1916. He was wounded in the battle of Fromelles where he was taken prisoner and transported at first to Dülmen prison camp in Germany.

For about ten weeks I was in Dulmen camp, and my arm got better. They then sent me through to within eight or ten miles of the Russian border, to what was really an outpost of Schneidemuhl camp. They put me at once to work in a sugar factory, where they work two shifts of twelve hours each, with only a half hour break in the shift. All they gave us was a thing called soup, which you could have put through a colander without a trace of solids being left. It was little better than colored water. Sometimes the diet was varied by a little bit of bread containing strange ingredients, including sawdust. We were entitled to 250 grammes of bread per day, but the stuff was so sodden that the ration would seem no larger than a slice off a toast loaf. I was in that wretched place for five weeks, and during that time they knocked a lot of chaps about. Until that time I had a clean skin, and had not fallen out with any of our oppressors. Some of the men were most cruelly treated, for no reason which we could see, unless it was that none of us understood German.

On the Sunday morning when the five weeks of which I spoke were up a dreadful blizzard commenced to blow—I suppose you can imagine what a blizzard in that place would be like—and we decided to strike work. We had to go to work at 6 o'clock on the night shift. The men, tired of ill-treatment, refused to work. The guards flourished their bayonets over their heads for an hour in the hope of frightening us into working. They got no satisfaction from that, however, so they rang up an officer and told him what had happened. The officer replied that if we refused to work we could stand at attention in the snow until we repented and returned to our toil. But this threat failed to move the men, and they were forced to experience a bitter taste of disciplinary kultur. We had had nothing to eat and nothing to drink since 12 o'clock mid-day; yet from 7 o'clock that night, strangers to food, we stood to attention in that blizzard till 12 o'clock next day. It was a form of punishment so cruel that few would care to undergo it a second time. (I may say here that we have handed to the British authorities the names of the officials responsible for the horror and the British Government is 'pushing it' with the object of having the tyrants punished.)

At 12 o'clock on the Monday, when it was found that this harsh treatment had not broken our spirits, we were sent back to camp, reaching there about 3 o'clock the next morning. And still we had had nothing to eat. We got a little food about 8 o'clock, when some English prisoners gave us some of theirs before we were put into the 'clink.' After five days in confinement we were sent among a party of 500 Russians, French and others to Westphalia, and from December 21, 1916, to August 20, 1918, I worked in a coal mine. For a month I worked on the surface, but was afterwards sent below, where they work shifts of eight hours. It takes an hour going to the face and an hour to return, and the prisoners are the first to go down and the last to return. For a year and eight months I worked in a drive [tunnel] no higher than a table, pushing trucks, and my hips bear the marks today of the knocks I got while slaving in that position. The only thing that saved me from being ill-treated then was that I had the 'boss' bluffed. He was a sergeant who had had twelve months in hospital—no man has a boss-ship in a mine unless he has been a sergeant in the army. Three or four of us had threatened to throw him down a shaft if he did not leave us alone.

About this time I went into hospital with a poisoned foot. At this mine men were beaten every day. If they did not do enough work they were reported to the boss and were kept at attention until they caved in and went back to work. After having spent eleven weeks in hospital with my poisoned foot I was sent to work on a farm and was there until the armistice was signed, and I was soon afterwards given my liberty.

Private Carter was understandably bitter about his harsh treatment as a prisoner of war. His weight had fallen from his normal 14 stone to only 10. But there had been at least one bright spot in the experience:

I cannot conclude without paying the highest possible tribute to the work of the Australian Red Cross. It was wonderful. The packages we got from its workers in Australia, which in my case sometimes included articles from Toolondo and other places near home, were the only gleams of sunshine in the whole dark picture. It is not too much to say that every man's life depended upon them, and that without them not many of us would be alive to-day.

The underground artillery

The 2nd Australian Tunnelling Company (originally No. 2 Company of the Australian Mining Corps) specialised in the highly dangerous job of 'sapping'—burrowing deep beneath enemy lines to place explosives beneath their fortifications. On the western front, the tunnellers became known as 'the underground artillery'. Some of their story was told by one of their number under the pen name 'Willie Wombat'.

It was a certain place in a sector of considerable strategic and tactical importance in which there were at that time keen and active mining operations by the enemy. This part of the line was held by Australians, and with the advent of the miners at this particular period the Huns, for the first time on the Western front, were confronted by Australians in every department of war with the exception of aerial work . . . The enemy knew they were up against Australians, for did they not welcome them by displaying a notice over the parapet with the inscription, 'Advance Australia. If you can!' and the arrival of the miners gave them further opportunity in their publicity department to display in a like manner 'Welcome 500 Australian Miners.'

With these taunts in their minds it was quite natural that our army—I include the New Zealanders—would not take things lying down. Many of the men were hardened veterans of Gallipoli and Egypt, and they very soon put into practice the adage that there should be no peace for the wicked, they organised all sorts of 'stunts,' anything and everything to pester Fritz. 'Keep tickling him up' was their motto; and they did. And, as was only natural to suppose this method of procedure drew retaliation—what was really asked for. Events soon became interesting.

A blow by either party would quickly go the rounds, and, as this branch of warfare increased in activity the front-liners declared that the Miners were pumping more good stuff into the Hun than the artillery, and so it came to pass that as banter continued some wag referred to the diggers as 'the underground artillery.' To be nicknamed by brother-soldiers from the same sunny clime was considered a very great honour and full of good fortune, as well as being accepted in a grand form of brotherly comradeship, for it was on this field that many old mates renewed friendship, and where brothers met, and father and son clasped hands for the first time since the main Expeditionary Force left Australian shores. To the Miners it appeared as a happy omen that they should take up their posts in the front battle line, with their own kith and kin, and as a result a great national pride soon became established throughout the company. It was only natural that they should try to acquit themselves as creditably and as gloriously as their veteran brothers. And I believe this lucky commencement was the real beginning of the fame and honour that have been their reward since coming to France, for today to its credit it must be recorded that it is regarded by General Headquarters as the crack mining company of the Western front.

AUSTRALIANS' FINE RECORD

It is only my intention at present to cover a period of the first 20 weeks of the company in France, in which period the combined effort of the Australians and the enemy resulted in the explosion of 35 mines, 24 of which were blown by the former and 11 by the latter; or, in other words, the Australians blew twice as often as the Huns, plus a shade to spare. And when one comes to realise the explosion on an average of over a mine per week it must be admitted that it was a very creditable performance for human energy can only do its best. In addition, the geological conditions and otherwise were not the best.

For several weeks the enemy had been heard working up in the direction of a certain sap, and it was decided to allow him to come as close up as advisable, and a week after our last blow we fired at half-past 7 in the morning. The listeners had a most anxious and exciting time, for minute after minute and hour after hour they could hear the enemy getting closer and closer. Anyhow, all went well for the miners exploded their mine just as the enemy were about to break through into our subway. This was an exciting piece of work, and proved to be most profitable, by reason of the certainty of the proximity of the enemy's working. After this punishment, and the apparent useless efforts of the enemy miners to get the best of the Australians underground, the Hun subjected this particular part of the workings to a heavy minenwerfer [short-range mortar] fire of the heaviest calibre. These large-sized 'Minnies' are capable of penetrating the ground for some distance, and on explosion blow a crater up to 20ft. deep by 40ft. to 50ft. wide, so that it will be apparent the amount of head-cover necessary for safety in running galleries under no man's land. The attempt was, however, abortive, and no damage was done.

TREMENDOUS EXPLOSIONS

A week after these last desperate attempts of the enemy, as the result of careful preparation and more hard and enduring work, the Australians fired another mine and with a success that was anticipated. Our luck was in, so everyone said, but I firmly believe that, whilst a certain amount of it was in our favour, we had grasped from the very beginning the secret of defensive mining. What evidently perplexed the Huns most was that they were of the opinion that at this particular point our policy was offensive work. Instead it was defensive. The Australian miners' work was to cut Fritz off and let him have it and to wait for him at other places and hand him out the usual medicine.

For a week there was quietude on both sides, the Australians enjoying themselves in addition to exercising great care as to Hun movements in carrying out a tactical move by preparing a mine on the left as the signal for attack on the right of the Australian division in the Battle of Fromelles. It was at 6 p.m. at this strategical point that a large mine was blown, forming an excellent crater in which many Australian infantry took cover, maintaining a withering and punishing fire on the enemy. Six days following this affair the enemy exploded another mine in the vicinity of our workings, doing neither damage nor causing any casualties.

Almost three weeks elapsed before any more activity took place, when early one morning the enemy fired a charge which caused slight damage to our galleries and killed two men. These were the Australians' first casualties underground and were men from an Australian pioneer battalion attached to the company. The same day the Australians replied with a powerful charge and gained their objective. In this part of the sector nothing more was heard from the enemy in the matter of blowing mines for six weeks.

By this time it was generally accepted that in this point of the mining system we had also mastered the Hun. Anyhow, during that period three powerful mines were exploded with great destructive force, having in mind two things, first, to let the enemy know we were still active, and, secondly, to point out to him that he was beaten and that it was useless for him to continue the repairing of the wreckage caused. However, at the end of the time stated, the enemy blew another mine which caused slight damage to our workings but no casualties. It was his last explosion in this part, and as it was the second vital spot of the mining system that had been completely defeated, he had to give the game up.

A week later, after this last effort, we gave him a final charge, which was the end of active mining in a sector which had asked for the best that human energy and endurance could give. After making certain that the Hun had been completely defeated, the company took its departure to a certain place to assist in the good work that was being done in the ground preparations for Messines. And on their departure the officer commanding received a letter from the high command eulogising the patience and perseverance, energy and gallantry of all ranks of the company, and asking that congratulations be conveyed to all for having 'so completely mastered the enemy mining system.'

During the period referred to the company had placed to its credit one mention in despatches, one D.C.M., and five Military Medals.

Matilda goes to war

Although Australia's unofficial national anthem was composed by A. B. 'Banjo' Paterson and Christina Macpherson twenty years before the Gallipoli landings, its journey to the status of national and international musical icon was closely tied to Anzac.

The song began its close association with war when troops from Queensland reportedly sang a version of it during the Boer War (1899–1902). By 1916, C. J. Dennis's *The Moods of Ginger Mick* puts the rabbit-seller mate of 'The Sentimental Bloke' fame on Gallipoli with 'the little AIF', an experience that he says has made us 'all Orstalians now'. As the sequel to the enormously popular *The Sentimental Bloke*, published just before the war began, *The Moods of Ginger Mick* was a great hit with the diggers. One of its poems, 'The Singing Soldiers', has Mick mentioning the song in his letter back home to the Bloke:

'When I'm sittin' in me dug-out wiv the bullets droppin' near,'
Writes ole Ginger; 'an' a chorus smacks me in the flamin' ear:
P'raps a song that Rickards billed, or p'raps a line o' Waltz Matilder',
Then I feel I'm in Australia, took an' shifted over 'ere.
Till the music sort o' gits me, an' I lets me top notes roam
While I treats the gentle foeman to a chunk uv "Ome, Sweet 'Ome".'

The sheet music of the song was also distributed to troops during the war for the community singing that was such a popular pastime of the era. But 'Waltzing Matilda' was not on everyone's lips. It was not until the singer Peter Dawson recorded a hit version of it in the late 1930s that it began to take off, and it took another world war for it to become the national song it is today. By the early 1940s it seems that the song had become widely popular and was recognised as an expression of Australian identity. In 1940, Movietone News covered the arrival at Mascot airport of a Halifax Bomber called 'Waltzing Matilda'. From 1942, British tanks named 'Waltzing Matildas' were used in North Africa, then in Russia and also in New Guinea. The same year, in a guide to Australian manners and customs for American service personnel based in Australia, it was stated that:

A standard favorite all over the country is Australia's own folk song, 'Waltzing Matilda'. In fact, the Aussies have made it a classic all over the world. When the Anzac troops made their first assault on Bardia, they did it to the tune of 'Waltzing Matilda'. They sang it in the heat and fever of Malaya.

The lyrics, with translations, were printed on the following pages.

The song was so well known by this time that it was used as the basis of a new song composed by diggers about their experience of the disastrous campaign in Crete in May 1941. Over 28 000 British, Australian and New Zealand troops were stationed there to repel a determined German air attack for which their commanders had not prepared. A chaotic retreat to the south of the island ensued. At great cost, the Royal Navy managed to save just over half of these troops, leaving the rest as a rear guard to face the advancing Germans. Over 2500 Australian and New Zealand troops were killed and over 5000 captured. This song uses 'Waltzing Matilda' to create a new and different composition with its own significance, deriving from that of the original song and its stature as Australia's unofficial anthem, as well as the dire circumstances in which the Australian troops—including those in the Australian Army Ordnance Corps (AAOC)—found themselves.

Once a private soldier was sitting in his Ordnance store
Down by the shore of the Aegean Sea;
And he said when they asked him what he was a-doing of,
'I'm just a bloke in the AAOC.'

Working in Ordnance, working in Ordnance,
Handling the stores of the infantry;
Truck for your transport, uniforms to clothe you in,
Fixing the guns for the artillery.

Down came the Heinkels and down came the eight-eights,
Came down in thousands—one, two three!
And they blasted the island 'cos they owned the upper air,
So we withdrew to a new country.

Blew up our vehicles, ruined our Ordnance,
Men, we withdrew the majority.
But the Private stood while the transports were pulling out:
'I'll always fight with the rear guard', said he.

So the private soldier burnt down his Ordnance store;
Blew up his workshop with TNT.
And he smiled as he bent to buckle his equipment on:
'I'll always fight with the rear guard' said he.

'Fight with the rear guard, fight with the En Zeds,
Fight with the men of the Sixth Divvy.'
And his ghost may be heard 'round the seas where Ulysses
sailed,
He is the pride of the AAOC.

Tobruk Rats

Together with British and Indian troops, around 14 000 Australians withstood the siege of Tobruk in North Africa from April to August 1941. An army of German and Italian troops commanded by General Erwin Rommel, sometimes known as the 'Desert Fox', aimed to gain access to the Suez Canal to avoid bringing troops and supplies across a large expanse of desert. 'Lord Haw-Haw' (an alias adopted by American-born and Ireland-raised William Joyce), broadcast Nazi propaganda in which he referred to the defenders of the Tobruk garrison as 'rats'. They gladly accepted the insult and turned it back on their enemy, becoming 'the Rats of Tobruk'. Joyce was executed for treason in 1946.

During the siege, Gunner J. M. Stephens wrote home with a graphic account.

Life is just going on the same old way. Any time now we are expecting to get news from home telling us that the war is over and that we have been left here and forgotten. But here we are, all types of guys thrown together and going on as if we could walk out at any time. In a way it's rather a lot of fun being besieged. You never know when there will begin a hell of a rumpus and the boys from the other end will march in to relieve us with all the glamour of historic occasions, bands playing, flags flying and a general welcoming committee to greet them.

On the other hand, we never know when Jerry will start the same sort of rumpus and get tired of being left out in the cold for so long. But if he does, there will be a decent sort of welcoming committee awaiting him.

Of course, we are extremely lucky in a way, because our mail comes in by sea fairly regularly and we hear the news each night on Army wireless which, by the way, are certainly not intended to be put to that use.

It is distinctly not in the rules and regulations of the A.I.F., but each night there is a 'national hook-up' which should make technicians of the A.B.C. turn green with envy. Imagine a regiment scattered over the country-headquarters back a bit, gun positions half-way to the front line and the observation posts right up forward with the infantry. All these parts are connected by army phones.

At night the signaller on duty at headquarters gets an especially hot programme on the Army wireless, mugs it in somehow to his exchange and it is thereby relayed through the phones to all those places I mentioned. The place where I enjoy this relay most of all is at the O'-pip observation post, as only two at a time go there, we have to do rather long watches as one man must be awake at all times. You can imagine the experience of listening to a programme of Harry Roy or someone equally famous—within a thousand yards or so of Jerry's front line. This arrangement and our mail are the only ways we are in touch with the outside world so you can imagine how it is appreciated. Those simple things of life, which we all took for granted at one time, we are learning to appreciate pretty fast.

In my opinion, there is nothing better these days than a cup of tea boiled on a primus stove round about midnight and a good yarn about old times. War has really taught me two things, appreciation and patience, two valuable assets in the periods to come after it is all over. That is about the main thing in our lives these days—just thinking of what we will do when the war is over. I look forward to that time more than I looked forward to Christmas or birthdays when I was a kid.

About four days ago I saw the best air show I have ever seen. As Jerry doesn't seem to be able to shell us out with his artillery, he sent over what I thought must have been his whole Air Force to try and bomb us out. The only thing he accomplished was to provide an exciting half hour's entertainment for the troops. When Goering taught his Huns to fly he did a good job, but he didn't concentrate enough on teaching them to drop bombs accurately.

There were all types of planes everywhere you looked, diving and mucking around like two-year-olds at the barrier. They must have dropped tons of bombs, but I don't think they did anything but stir up a few desert fleas. When they see that the bombs have no effect they get very liverish and dive at us in an endeavour to machine-gun civility into us. But we were well in the comparative safety of our slit trenches and he drew a blank. When they come over in droves like that everyone gets into a slit trench and blazes away with any weapon he can lay hands on.

There are some duds among the stuff Jerry drops and I can't think of a more uncomfortable experience than to be lying in bed, hear a plane go over, hear that very unwelcome whistle of a falling bomb (the blasted things seem to take an hour to land), increasing in sound as it comes nearer, and then, when you are all keyed up for the bang, all you hear is a dull plop. You get the same sort of feeling during the shelling.

There is a popular saying of the last war that you never hear the shell that gets you. I used to wonder how that could be, but I know it is true now because it is the same with a near miss. The other night we heard the guns and in an instant everything went black. I expected to find myself flitting around the clouds with a brand new pair of wings, but the blackness was due to the blast, dust and, I suppose, momentary concussion. But we didn't hear the whistle at all because the shell travels faster than the noise.

I have just had my nightly cup of tea and listened to the B.B.C. news which never seems to be any different. It is just about midnight and I am writing in the light of a well shaded hurricane lamp, the reason being that that man is around again. It is bright moonlight outside and Jerry thrives on that, so I don't want to have a beacon to light him on his way.

It is funny in a way the manner in which we disregard his nightly visits. Every night without fail we have a raid, and at any time of the night you like to go outside you can bet on one of these crates being overhead. If ever we got to London I am afraid that we would be the worry of the air warden's life as we have got so used to visits. Of course, being in open country makes us feel safe, and it would doubtless be vastly different in a thickly populated town.

One thing in particular I will appreciate when I get back is unrestricted lighting without some raucous voice bellowing through the night, 'Put that ——— light out. Where do you think you are; Luna Park?' Except on one or two occasions I don't think I've seen a car with head lights on since I left Australia. Those occasions were in Palestine a long way from here.

By the way, in the letter I just received you mentioned that you had sent over some more parcels. Parcel delivery is rather awkward here, but we get them all in time, though they take a while longer than other places. It's great to know we are not forgotten and your thoughts are appreciated more than you can think.

For the first time in weeks, the horrible 'un has begun booping off his big guns at night. He must be getting a little excited over something, or is trying to frighten us. At this moment he is landing them about a thousand yards away and until he begins to land them within yards of us we can afford to be blase.

Well, I seem to have run out of any more to say, so, in the words of Fitzpatrick, the travel expert, we say goodbye to this glamorous city of the Western Desert and, to the music of our jovial friend Herman's bung bungs [artillery], we come to the close of another perfect day and hope to shake the dust of this gigantic, enormous and magnificent b—— place off our army boots very shortly. V for Victory, or something.

P.S.—He seems to be getting closer. Always like a tense and dramatic finish to my letters.

'Bluey' Truscott

Keith 'Bluey' Truscott was one of Melbourne Football Club's finest players and a scoring member of the club's 1939 premiership team. When he joined the RAAF in July 1940, his enlistment was widely publicised in the press, with even more coverage when he returned to play in his club's next grand final win in September 1940. He joined the Empire Air Training Scheme and then flew Spitfires in Britain, where he was promoted and awarded the Distinguished Flying Cross (DFC) after shooting down six enemy planes. He continued to destroy German aircraft, was promoted to squadron leader and gained a bar to his DFC. Truscott's winning personality, auburn hair and flying skills made him a celebrity in Britain, where a fund was organised to raise money to buy a Spitfire for 'Bluey'.

Truscott returned to Australia on leave in May 1942, playing once again with his club. He was reportedly out of condition, but the crowd loved him anyway and cheered him enthusiastically.

It is said that after the game he bumped into one of his old teachers who asked him what he thought of returning to football. Truscott reportedly answered that it was 'too dangerous'.

Truscott's fame increased when he was posted to New Guinea just before the Japanese attacked Milne Bay in mid-1941. He took over the command of No. 76 Squadron and led the Kittyhawk fighter-bombers through several dangerous days of fighting. He was mentioned in dispatches for this work.

Another RAAF squadron involved in the battle for New Guinea was 75 Squadron. Their deeds, real and not so, live on in a rollicking ballad about their exploits that reflect the devil-may-care attitudes of the young Australians who risked their lives in the primitive airplanes of the time. P40s were fighter-bombers, also known as 'Kittyhawks', while the Zero was the Allied name for the Japanese Mitsubishi A6M fighter plane.

. . . So we grabbed some P40s and went to the fight,
And we soon found the Nips had a nice little kite.
It was bright shining silver and Zero by name
And a bloody fine show as it goes down in flames.
Down in flames, down in flames,
And a bloody fine show as it goes down in flames.

Now the papers they tell of this squadron's success
And Nippon has many an aeroplane less.
But the pages don't say how the hell it was done—
Without our replacements and at seven to one.
Yes to one, yes to one,
Without our replacements and at seven to one . . .

Back in Australia to help defend Darwin and the north against the possibility of invasion, Truscott destroyed another enemy plane. But on 28 March 1943 he misjudged a training manoeuvre and was killed when his Kittyhawk dived into the sea in Exmouth Gulf in Western Australia. His tally of enemy aircraft was sixteen destroyed, three probably destroyed and three damaged. Despite this record, Truscott was notorious for his bad landings.

Angels of the Owen Stanley Range

'Fuzzy-Wuzzy Angels', as they were dubbed, are a permanent part of the Anzac legend. While there has been some controversy about over-romanticising the motives of the 'Angels' and about the paternalism towards them inherent in the attitudes of the day, there is no doubt that the diggers were deeply grateful for their sacrifice. Letters home praised the Angels unreservedly. Captain Trevor King wrote from New Guinea to Miss Clare Theobold of Newtown in Sydney, NSW:

The Papuan natives have done a wonderful job up here. I personally owe my life to one of these chaps. During one part of the show I was trapped crossing a mountain stream. The river was about 40 yards across and running very fast, and with a Jap machine-gun blazing away I decided to cross in an endeavour to sneak up and put Tojo's gun out of action. I became stranded on a wet, slippery log midstream, and with lead flying in all directions it is not the most comfortable feeling. After a period of shouting for assistance, using as much native language as I knew, one of these chaps spotted my predicament and, in a flash, despite machine-gun bullets, cut a rope of lantana vine and threw it out from a ledge of rocks, soon to haul me to safety.

Private A. Johnson wrote in similar manner to Miss B. O'Brien in Melbourne:

I am in hospital in a back area. Had to be carried by the native bearers for over a day. They are worth their weight in gold, and are doing great work in getting the wounded back. Then I was lucky, and came the rest of the way by plane, and it was only a matter of minutes getting over the country that took weeks to cover on foot.

Probably the most famous Australian poem of World War II celebrated the Angels of the Owen Stanley Range. It was written by Bert Beros, a Canadian veteran of World War I who served with the second AIF in the Middle East and New Guinea. Beros said he wrote the poem hurriedly on '14th October, 1942, at Dump 66, the first Range of the Owen Stanley'. It began:

Many a mother in Australia,
When the busy day is done,
Sends a prayer to the Almighty
For the keeping of her son,
Asking that an angel guide him
And bring him safely back.

And went on to describe the actions of the Angels:

Bringing back the badly wounded
Just as steady as a hearse,

Using leaves to keep the rain off
And as gentle as a nurse.
Slow and careful in bad places
On the awful mountain track,
The look upon their faces
Would make you think that Christ was black . . .

Australia's secret submariners

Australian submariners played central roles in some pivotal incidents of World War II, including the raid on the German battleship *Tirpitz*, the D-Day invasion and the dropping of atomic bombs on Japan.

In 1942–43, the Royal Navy developed a secret class of miniature submarines known as *X*-craft. With a four-man crew, they were designed to attack enemy shipping in port. At around 50 feet (15 metres) in length and weighing 30 tons (27 tonnes), they were towed—on the surface or submerged—to their targets. Lacking torpedoes, they were instead armed with clockwork detachable mines that could be placed beneath enemy ships by a diver, allowing plenty of opportunity for the submarines to escape before the blast. But this all proved to be difficult in practice, a situation worsened by the sometimes fatal buoyancy problems of the *X*-craft. Many submariners were lost in these extremely hazardous vessels, quite a few of them in non-combat accidents.

The *X*-craft first went to war in an attempt to sink the German battleship *Tirpitz* at her Norwegian base at Kåfjord in September 1943. Submarines *X5* through to *X10* were deployed, towed submerged and surfacing every six hours to change crews. The tow of *X9* parted on the way to the target and two men were lost with the vessel. *X8* was also lost on the way to the attack. On 22 September, the three remaining miniature submarines, *X5*, *X6* and *X7*, did attack *Tirpitz*, causing substantial damage that delayed her deployment for some vital months. All three submarines were lost during the action or afterwards.

Over the next two years, *X*-craft carried out other operations in Bergen harbour in Norway, off the French coast, and in the Pacific. Australians were prominent in *X*-craft, including NSW-born Lieutenant Brian 'Digger' McFarlane, West Australian Lieutenant Jack Marsden and Victorian Lieutenant Ian McIntosh. McIntosh was destined to become Vice Admiral of the Royal Navy and was knighted in 1973. McFarlane and Marsden were both lost with *X22* in a collision with another ship in February 1944.

In January 1944, Tasmanian Lieutenant Kenneth Robert Hudspeth, Royal Australian Naval Volunteer Reserve, a school-teacher before the war, was in command of *X20* conducting reconnaissance off the French coast in preparation for the D-Day landings. He had already won a Distinguished Service Cross for his part in the *Tirpitz* raid and now won a second. The citation read, in part:

For outstanding courage and devotion to duty whilst commanding HM submarine *X-20* in a hazardous operation. He showed great coolness, grasp and ability in manoeuvring his *X* craft submerged in shallow water close under enemy defences during the first experimental beach reconnaissance from *X* craft in January 1944 . . .

At a similar location later the same year, Hudspeth received a third DSC 'for gallantry, skill, determination and undaunted devotion to duty...'. Hudspeth and crew spent two cramped and humid nights beneath the waters of the English Channel reconnoitring what was to become known as Juno Beach. As the bombardment that launched the invasion began, *X20* surfaced and used her lights to illuminate the safest passage for the landing craft.

In 1945, six *XE*-craft, refinements of the earlier versions, were sent to Pearl Harbor to take part in the Pacific war. Admiral Nimitz of the United States Navy, himself a submariner, observed that they were 'suicide craft'. The Americans were reluctant to put them into operational roles—until they discovered that the *X*-craft had a longer operational range than they had assumed. The *XE* submarines then went into training off the Queensland coast to prepare attacks on Japanese warships and on underwater telegraph cables. This would eventually be known as Operation Sabre, designed to cut the cables linking Tokyo with Singapore, Saigon and Hong Kong, an important communication channel for the Japanese high command. Special tools and techniques had to be developed for this unprecedented operation.

After training in Hervey Bay in Queensland, during which two divers were lost in accidents, a group of *XE*-craft were deployed in missions against the Japanese. On 31 July 1945, Perth engineer Lieutenant Max Shean was in command of *XE4*. Also aboard were Sub-Lieutenant Ken Briggs from Glenn Innes in New South Wales, Engine Room Artificer Level 5 'Ginger' Coles, Sub-Lieutenant Ben Kelly and Sub-Lieutenant Adam 'Jock' Bergius. On that day, *XE4* and her crew were submerged off the Mekong River in what was then French Indo-China, now

Vietnam. They were dragging a grapnel hook across the seabed in an attempt to locate underwater telegraph cables. After several futile runs, they finally located the southbound cable beneath sand and silt at a depth of fifty feet (15 metres). At 1229 hours Ken Briggs left *XE4* through the exit hatch, found the cable and cut it with the hydraulic cutters specially developed for the task. He was back aboard in thirteen minutes, carrying a length of cable as evidence of his success. Adam Bergius RNVR then left the submarine at 1402 and, after several attempts, managed to sever the northbound cable and return by 1452.

The cutting of the undersea cable forced the Japanese to use radio for their communications. The Americans had already cracked the Japanese radio codes and so were now able to gain access to vital information that had been unavailable when transmitted beneath the sea. *XE4*'s action that day provided intelligence that was reportedly a factor in the decision to use nuclear bombs on Nagasaki and Hiroshima. Max Shean added a bar to the Distinguished Service Order he had won for his previous *X*-craft service and the United States awarded him a Bronze Star. The other members of the crew were also decorated, with Ken Briggs and Adam Bergius both receiving the Distinguished Service Cross for their bravery.

During their brief but decisive careers, *X*-craft submariners, British and Australian, were highly awarded with four Victoria Crosses, four Distinguished Service Orders, seven Distinguished Service Crosses, one Conspicuous Gallantry Medal, two Distinguished Service Medals, one Bronze Star (USA) and eleven mentions in dispatches.

Today, *X24* can be seen at the Royal Navy Submarine Museum in Gosport, Hampshire, in the UK. The remains of two others, thought to be the remains of the *XT*, or training versions of the *X*-craft, lie at Aberlady Bay in Scotland's East Lothian region. The Imperial War Museum at Duxford, UK, has an exhibition of *X*-craft, including the remains of *X7* and an intact *X51*. There is a memorial to the 12th Submarine Flotilla, of which the *X*-craft were a part, in Sutherland in Scotland and two other memorials near the *X*-craft training base at Bute, also in Scotland.

The home front

Even though there were no hostilities within Australia during World War I, and limited enemy action during World War II, home fronts in Australia and Britain have played a vital role in mass conflicts. As well as being the place to which all soldiers wish to return as quickly as possible, home is the location of essential industrial, medical, political and social support. Home fronts are as much a part of Anzac as battlefronts—not only during a war but also for many years afterwards. It is on home soil that the national community will attend to the inevitable aftermath of broken minds and bodies, as well as to the expression of grief and commemoration.

Scots of the Riverina

In 1915, the alcoholic, depressed and impoverished writer Henry Lawson became the subject of a rescue mission by his friends and journalistic colleagues. A number of them approached then-NSW premier Holman who suggested that the writer be given a literary commission in the recently established (1912) Murrumbidgee Irrigation Areas. The job had a number of advantages. It provided Lawson with somewhere to live rent-free; it got him away from his unhealthy Sydney lifestyle; and, most of all, it provided him with a degree of self-respect. All Lawson had to do was write verse and stories that related in some way to the great experiment in large-scale agricultural irrigation, a subject in which he had a strong interest.

Lawson took up the position, on and off, between January 1916 and the end of 1917. He produced a considerable number of poems and sketches during this period, some published in *The Bulletin* magazine and in a few other newspapers, by then mostly filled with often grim war news. Now ageing, the once-radical firebrand had become a staunch supporter of the British Empire and of Australia's role in the war then raging at the other end of the world. Lawson was unfit for service himself, but his experiences and observations of life in the Riverina allowed him to compose his last great poem. It tells a story of the wrenching effects of war, of one among many similar tragedies suffered by families throughout the country.

The boy cleared out to the city from his home at harvest time—
They were Scots of the Riverina, and to run from home was a
   crime.
The old man burned his letters, the first and last he burned,
And he scratched his name from the Bible when the old wife's
   back was turned.

A year went past and another. There were calls from the
firing-line;

They heard the boy had enlisted, but the old man made no
    sign.
His name must never be mentioned on the farm by
    Gundagai—
They were Scots of the Riverina with ever the kirk hard by.

The boy came home on his 'final', and the township's bonfire
burned.
His mother's arms were about him; but the old man's back
    was turned.
The daughters begged for pardon till the old man raised his
    hand—
A Scot of the Riverina who was hard to understand.

The boy was killed in Flanders, where the best and bravest die.
There were tears at the Grahame homestead and grief in
    Gundagai;
    But the old man ploughed at daybreak and the old man
    ploughed till the mirk—
There were furrows of pain in the orchard while his housefolk
    went to the kirk.

The hurricane lamp in the rafters dimly and dimly burned;
And the old man died at the table when the old wife's back
    was turned.
Face down on his bare arms folded he sank with his wild grey
    hair
Outspread o'er the open Bible and a name re-written there.

The Durban Signaller

Ethel M. Campbell was a well-born Durban socialite whose fiancé was killed early in World War I. She became a patriotic icon to the diggers sailing to and from the battlefields of France and the Middle East. Born in Glasgow in 1886, Ethel (sometimes known as Edith) Campbell became known as 'the Durban Signaller' because of her practice of semaphoring messages of support to the troopships passing through Durban harbour. Also known as 'the Diggers' Idol' and 'the Durban Angel' she sometimes threw fruit and other gifts aboard the ships, all much appreciated by those aboard. She renamed her house 'Little Australia' and entertained thousands of soldiers there, assisted by her dog 'Digger' and the provision of facilities for playing 'two-up'.

As well as these practical contributions to the war effort, Ethel Campbell composed a large number of patriotic and inspiring verses, publishing them herself and distributing them to the troops at every opportunity with unflagging enthusiasm. The poems' combination of patriotism, wry observations and humour made them appealing to the soldiers, who often preserved them in their diaries.

Gunner Millard passed through Durban on his way to England during World War I and kept some of Ethel Campbell's verses for over sixty years, including this one.

We stand on the shores of Durban
And watch the transports go
To England from Australia,
Hurrying to and fro.

And what can we do to show them
Our love, our pride, our thanks?
We can't do much (I own it),
But give them a passing cheer
While the real elite beat a shocked retreat,
Why, they saw one drinking beer!

If they were lucky enough to survive the war, homeward-bound diggers might be greeted yet again by Edith Campbell as their ships passed back through South Africa.

So highly thought of was Ethel Campbell's war work that she was made a Member of the British Empire (MBE) in 1919, and in 1923 was invited to Australia to officially open a war memorial. Despite advancing age, the Durban Signaller answered the bugle call again in World War II with a repeat performance of her pastoral work, and more verse.

Ethel Campbell never married. She died in 1954 and was fondly remembered by diggers, including Mr Uhr-Henry of Tasmania.

As one of the thousands of Australian servicemen privileged to meet Miss Ethel Campbell and accept her hospitality and motherly interest, it is with a saddened heart and a feeling of personal loss that news of her death is received. Following her kindness in the First World War, when as the 'Durban Signaller' she waited on the wharf to greet and farewell every Australian troopship at Durban, she began the same practice early in 1940, but soon found it necessary to move to Hilton, about 70 miles from Durban, for health reasons. Her love for the Digger was such that she would journey to Durban when she knew a troopship or the Navy was in. Her name became a legend, and when, one day, she was not at the wharf, a crowd of fellows 'thumbed' their way to her home, where they received a royal welcome. From then on thousands of troops were entertained by her at Hilton, and the boys seemed to think it was their duty to visit her.

I have been inside 'Little Australia,' have played two-up on the two-up tower, patted her dog, whom she called 'Digger,' sang the songs she wrote about us, and listened to the glowing tales she recited about the old Diggers. But most of all I was privileged to know and learn to love this grand lady, who thought so much of Australians, and who worked so hard, at her own expense, to make their passing through South Africa a happy one. Indeed did she earn the title of 'The Angel of Durban.'

Should there be any ex-serviceman who would care to contribute to the cost of a small memorial plaque, to be placed on her grave. I would be only too willing to arrange details and to have the work completed.

The chalk Rising Sun

England's Salisbury Plain was the location of extensive military camps, depots, hospitals and related facilities throughout World War I. Many Australians and New Zealanders spent time there, either in training or in hospital, often both. On a hillside near one of the local villages, Codford, in Wiltshire, can still be seen a memento of the Great War Anzacs. A large Rising Sun badge, 53 by 45 metres, was carved into the chalk in 1917 by diggers stationed near the village. According to the story, a local commander decided that something striking on the hillside would improve his view. He assigned the 13th Training Battalion to the task as a form of punishment for their malingering. The hill, properly known as 'Lamb Down', became 'Misery Hill' to the soldiers who had to spend long, cold days building and then maintaining the carving. They did have one consolation, though. According to local historians, the soldiers used beer bottles to dig up the grass to form the design and also to embed in the carving, giving it the appearance of the actual bronze of the Rising Sun badge. Presumably they had to empty the bottles first.

A Tasmanian visitor to the area in 1918 provided some colour to the story and also indicated that the Anzacs had carved other symbols into the hillside, not entirely to the satisfaction of all the locals.

The country all around is very pretty, and both Hurdcott and Fovant camps are well situated on a hill and very healthy. Opposite, with a narrow valley between, there is another low hill; this is of chalk, with a thin coating of grass. The Australian badge, 'The Rising Sun', has been formed by cutting away the grass, it is beautifully done; also Y.M.C.A. badge, map of Australia and Tasmania, a kangaroo, and various crosses, etc. I was told that the owner had sued the Commonwealth for damages. He was offered £1500, but refused it, went to law, lost the case, and had to pay his own costs. Truly a just punishment. He should have been well pleased to have his entirely useless hill turned into a work of art for all time.

By 1938 the Codford badge had become so badly eroded that it had to be restored, and its subsequent upkeep was accepted by the Commonwealth government as part of its war memorial program. But it was not long before the carving had to be covered up to avoid its bright outline being used by German bombers as a navigation aid. It has since been uncovered and restored.

Codford was also the location of a New Zealand military hospital during World War I, the inmates producing a lively newspaper called *The Codford Wheeze* (incorporating *The Wiltshire Wangler*, *The Wyle Wail* and *The Salisbury Swinger*). The paper contained many examples of soldier humour, related especially to injury and, hopefully, convalescence. A patient under the pen name 'Zeaffirm' contributed some verses under the title 'Codford' that give a good idea of life in the hospital.

A place of wood and rusty tin,
Long corridors that leak like sin,
A dismal place, without, within,
Just Codford Hospital.

In Summer time it's hot as well
The place of which the Padres tell,
And don't the paint and Ronuk [wood polish] smell?
In Codford Hospital.

In winter time it gets the worst
Of mud! It takes an easy first
For frozen taps and pipes that burst,
This Codford Hospital.

Still, Diggers, if from fell disease,
From leadswinging or feet that freeze,
You suffer—come, we cure all these
In Codford Hospital.

For, if discomforts we have got,
Are we downhearted? Rather not;

We are a very happy lot
At Codford Hospital.

'Zeaffirm' was perhaps feeling happier than usual as he knocked out his rough and ready poem during Christmas, 1918, and having survived the war he probably also survived Codford. At least ninety-seven patients did not. Sixty-six New Zealanders and thirty-one Australians are lying still in Codford cemetery, the largest of its kind in Britain. The cemetery is the site of Anzac Day observances each year.

A similar design, 51 by 32 metres, together with a number of regimental badges of Australian and British army units and the YMCA logo, was also cut into a hillside at nearby Fovant, also in Wiltshire. These striking examples of folk art date mostly from 1919 when Anzacs were encamped in the area awaiting return home. Together with some post–World War II carvings of British regimental badges, they are looked after by the volunteers of the Fovant Badges Society, which traced its lineage to the local Home Guard—or 'Dad's Army'—of World War II, with assistance from the Australian War Memorial. Thanks largely to the society and its fundraising efforts, the carvings can still be seen today.

Another British Anzac memento of the Great War was created not too far from Codford. At Hurdcott, in Wiltshire, an outline of Australia was cast in cement across a hillside that was re-christened 'Australia Hill'. It took volunteer diggers seventeen weeks to finish in 1918. Apparently the structure was still visible in 1999, at least from the air, though unlike the chalk carvings this English home-front monument does not seem to have been maintained.

Blighty

In World War I, Britain was known to all British, Canadian and Anzac troops as 'Blighty', derived from a Hindustani term for 'foreign' or 'away'. For the British it was home and for the Anzacs and other Empire troops it was an opportunity to get away from the fighting, on leave—or for recuperation if they had been wounded. The time taken to sail to and fro between the Pacific and Europe meant that it was difficult for Australians or New Zealanders to return home for even fairly lengthy periods of leave. When asked by an English woman how often he had leave, an Australian soldier was rumoured to have replied 'Once every war'.

As well as getting 'Blighty leave', many soldiers hoped to receive 'a Blighty one', meaning a wound serious enough for them to need treatment in Britain, while not serious enough to be life threatening. As the Adelaide journalist and soldier Hugh Garland (DCM) wrote in his *Vignettes of War*, this ditty was popular with the Australian troops at the front:

Dear Lord our ways we're wending
To toil and strife again.
Where Fritz is always sending
His shrapnel down like rain.
O, teach us, Lord, to dodge 'em
And, if you don't do that,
Please tell old Fritz to lodge 'em
For blighties neat and pat.

Sadly, Garland was not lucky enough to receive a Blighty one. He was killed in action in May 1917.

If a digger did win some time in a British hospital, there was an opportunity to spin a few yarns to the locals. Diggers were notorious in Britain during the Great War for the whopping lies they frequently told gullible 'pommies' about their goanna farms and the like back home.

I've heard Aussies tell stories to the unsophisticated of many different kinds of farms we have 'out there'—there's the jackeroo [sic] farm, the nulla-nulla farm, the wombat farm, etc., etc. But the boy with the flea farm is the best novelty I've struck. He was a badly wounded inmate of an English hospital. At every opportunity he would tell the nurse about his wonderful flea farm. Finally, the nurse concluded that he had gone off his block and reported the matter to the doctor.

'What do you do with this flea farm of yours?' the doctor asked him.

'Oh', replied the Aussie 'we make beer out of the hops.'

While recuperating from his 'Blighty one', a digger would often be visited by well-meaning citizens doing their bit for the war effort by cheering up recovering soldiers. While this was appreciated, it could often be a little wearing as the citizens, ignorant of the reality of the front line, invariably asked lots of silly questions. Anecdotes on this theme were many.

In a British hospital a lady had put more questions to a wounded Australian than an insurance agent could. 'Do you get much windy weather in Australia?' she at length asked. Then the soldier departed from the strict truth. 'Windy weather!' he exclaimed. 'Why, I should reckon. For instance, sometimes a cold south gale will come on, and blow so darned hard, that it blows the sun out. Then you've got to sit round in the dark sometimes for a week, 'till a hot northerly sets in and lights it up again.'

And while being away from the front—even with over-inquisitive locals—was pretty good, it was 'not all beer and skittles'. A battle-scarred Gunner Millard was welcomed to England as he left his hospital ship by scores of girls carrying fresh fruit for the wounded. But things went downhill from there, not only for himself but also for the British people, as he wrote home from No. 4 Convalescent Camp on Salisbury Plain, Wiltshire.

In camp we never taste sugar or butter and get very little meat. The main ration is mostly fat at that. Things are getting fairly serious with the civilian population. The people have to wait in queues for hours to get a few ounces of margarine, butter being a thing of the past. The same applies to meat, tea, etc. Hundreds have to go away empty-handed as there is seldom enough to go around. A lot of the London butchers are now selling horse-flesh, having given up the unequal contest for other meat . . .

London was also the location of the Australian Army Headquarters in Horseferry Road. Most Australians would turn up here sooner or later if they were in London, either for some official reason or for the social facilities. It seems the encounters they had at headquarters were not always pleasant. A story about a digger just off the boat from the trenches being upbraided for the state of his uniform by a staff member at Horseferry Road became a poem and a famous soldier song.

He landed in London and straightaway strode
Direct to Headquarters in Horseferry Road.
A Buckshee Corporal said 'pardon me, please,
But there's dust on your tunic and dirt on your knees.
You look so disgraceful that people will laugh,'
Said the cold-footed coward that works on the staff.

The Aussie just gave him a murderous glance,
And said 'I've just come from the trenches in France,
Where shrapnel is falling and comforts are few,
And Aussies are fighting for cowards like you.
I wonder, old shirker, if your mother e'er knew
That her son is a waster and afraid of the strafe,
But holds a soft snap on the Horseferry staff?'

By the time the Anzacs went home after the war, the song had
changed a bit, but the sentiments remained the same in this
version from a homeward-bound troopship in 1919.

Your hat should be turned up at the side like mine,
Your boots, I might state, are in want of a shine,
Your puttees are falling away from your calf;
Said the cold footed b—— of Horseferry staff.
The soldier gave him a murderous glance,
Remember I'm just home from the trenches in France.
Where shrapnel is flying and comforts are few,
Where the soldiers are fighting for b——s like you!

So well did 'Horseferry Road' capture the attitude of diggers
towards authority that it was also sung in various versions in

Australia's next few wars. By 1941 'Horseferry Road' had grown a chorus and become the famous 'Dinky-di' with the chorus 'Dinky-di, dinky-di, "I am a digger and I won't tell a lie . . .'.

Other versions were still being sung in the Vietnam War.

Homecoming

Around 10 am on 3 August 1915, the troopship *Ballarat* entered Outer Harbour at Semaphore in Adelaide. She carried a cargo of wounded men from Gallipoli. A local journalist reported the scene.

Many persons went to the Outer Harbour to meet the soldiers but in view of the fact made public that the South Australian warriors would be conveyed without delay to Keswick, and would there be permitted to be welcomed, the crowd was not so large as would otherwise have been the case. As the *Ballarat* was nearing the Outer Harbour wharf the signal 'Welcome home,' displayed from the local flagstaff, caught the eyes of the troops, many of whom lined the rail and gave rousing cheers. No attempt was made by the returned heroes to hide the nature of the wounds they received. Some were minus a leg, others without an arm, several with an eye gone, and a large number with an arm still resting in a sling, crowded to the vessel's rail. All were in a merry mood, and frequently the spectators ashore would hear a shout, 'Are we downhearted?' and the ready response from others—a long-drawn-out 'No.' Immediately the stretcher-bearers on the wharf received an order to march, the troops on board called 'Left, right, left, right' as the men marched, and other-wise good-humoredly chaffed them.

A squad of the A.M.C. lent assistance to those who were unable
to walk down the gangway, but although many of the returned
warriors needed no help, there were a few who could not have
reached the wharf without it. If anything was required to bring
forcibly home to Australians the awful effects of war, the sight of
maimed and shell-torn men carried down the gangway on the
backs of comrades must have done so. Three South Australians
among those who landed were minus portions of their legs, but
all bore their bufferings cheerfully, and one could not but admire
their spirit. At the foot of the gangway Captain Butler checked the
names of the sick and wounded as they crossed to the wharf, and
the soldiers were at once escorted to the waiting ambulance train. In
a little more than half an hour the disembarkation was completed,
and at 10.45 the train moved off for Keswick amidst the cheers of
the spectators and farewells from those still on the troopship . . .

The premier and other dignitaries welcomed the soldiers home
with patriotic words and expressions of gratitude for their bravery
and sacrifice. The reporters interviewed some of the men, mostly
wanting to know the more grisly details of the hand-to-hand
fighting. Some yarns were spun.

There is a more kindly feeling than ever between themselves,
and though they make light of their own wounds there is
obvious sympathy in their demeanour to the other wounded. But
when it comes to killing an enemy it is only a matter of business,
and if they felt a pity for their antagonists they would not be so
well fitted to do their work. It is not surprising, therefore, that
they chat about the number of Turks they have bayoneted without
the slightest shudder. 'War is murder,' said one, but 'War is good'

said most of them. 'It is tip-top,' said Private Sheppard. 'I advise all the lads to go and have a cut at it. There is plenty of fun and plenty of good shooting to be had. The Turks are not such bad fellows. During the 24 hours armistice some Turkish soldiers exchanged money and cigarettes with our own boys who were burying the dead. Some of the Turks can talk a little English, and the German officers seem to understand English well.'

On the same page of the newspaper that carried this account was a report of 1000 men out of work at Broken Hill in New South Wales.

Very irritated

Civilian questions to soldiers returned home from the front often betrayed such ignorance of what the soldiers were experiencing that they were parodied in digger humour. On this occasion, the question seemed to be a sensible one, though the answer could perhaps be taken with a grain or two of salt.

'Do the Australians still keep up their cheerfulness at the front?' I asked a soldier at the Cheer-Up Hut [a solider's comfort facility—see 'The Lady of Violets' in the chapter entitled 'Memories'], Adelaide, recently. He had just returned from France.

'Yes, easy,' he replied. 'I only struck one feller who didn't. He was as cheery a chap you ever seen too. 'E was all grins and jokes. 'Is smile was like a sunrise on a patch o' golden wattles. One day 'e went with 'is battalion bayonetin' Germans. It was a 'ell of a scrap. 'E was singin' "Australia will be there" all through it, and every time 'e notched a German, 'e'd yell somethin' funny.

'E got six wounds in different parts of 'is frame. When 'e was bein' carried on a stretcher to the dressin' station 'e laughed over the fight as it is 'ad been a little game o' ticky touchwood. 'E was fixed up with bandages until 'e looked like a bloomin' mummy, and every time 'e moved 'is wounds stung 'im like scorpions. But 'e just laughed as merry as a baby in a bath tub. Suddent 'e lost all 'is joy, and began to swear like—like—lemme see—well, like an A.S.C. man 'e was wild!'

'And what made him so cross?' I asked.

'Why, 'e found 'e'd lost 'is pipe in the fight.'

Death's soldier

Just sixteen when he enlisted in the AIF, 'Ted' Lording's story is one of horror and fortitude that highlights the usually forgotten aftermath of war. Born in Balmain, Sydney, Lording served in Egypt and on the western front as a signaller in the 30th Battalion. In July 1916 he was savagely wounded by a burst of enemy machine-gun fire at the battle of Fromelles. This shattered his chest and right arm, and a few minutes later several scraps of shrapnel embedded themselves in his spine. Miraculously still alive, Lording spent the rest of the war undergoing medical treatment after medical treatment in Britain and in Australia, where he returned in 1917. These treatments continued after the war and by 1928 he had undergone fifty-two mostly serious surgical operations. Lording should have died many times but refused to surrender to what must have seemed the sweet release of death.

In 1935 he published his memoir under the title *There and Back*. It is an unvarnished account of his suffering and survival, which is described by the journalist, soldier and historian F. M. Cutlack in his original review of the book.

When the doctors opened up his chest in the field hospital, the full extent of Lording's dreadful wounds was revealed. His left lung was shattered and the remnants collapsed. His heart had moved and was visible through the gunshot wound in his left chest. His right elbow was smashed and the four shrapnel wounds in his back had partially paralysed the spine.

He was operated on incessantly, sometimes daily, and sometimes without anaesthetic because his condition was too precarious for the doctors to render him unconscious. During one of these operations a four inches (ten centimetres) section of his ribs was removed. The pus in the chest cavity, 'which sometimes amounted to as much as a kidney-dish full' had to be drained twice daily, involving an incredibly painful procedure of rolling him on his side. During the course of his treatment, Lording developed tetanus; needed to be force fed; and had the blood of others injected into his veins.

The medical authorities got him back alive to Blighty, where he had to be cut up again to remove pieces of six of his ribs from his opened chest. Recovery from this procedure required rubber tubes to be inserted into his chest and left there for many weeks to drain the area. They were also used to pump in glycerine—'like a blanky Murrumbidgee irrigation farm'. Lording kept his extracted ribs in a bottle by his bed and insisted that the nurses dusted it every day.

He was shipped home to Sydney, Australia where he endured more operations at the soldiers' hospital in Randwick and was discharged with a morphine habit. He later entered Prince Alfred Hospital for yet more operations, survived them and managed to overcome his addiction. He studied to become an accountant but had to return to hospital in 1932 for another series of operations. For weeks he resisted death and finally won the battle, recovering sufficiently to return to everyday life and gain his professional qualification.

Despite his health, or lack of it, Lording married in 1922 and fathered three children. This relationship eventually ended in divorce and Lording married again in 1943. But the following year, at last overcome by the enormity of his suffering, Lording was admitted to Sydney's Callan Park Mental Hospital where he died on 1 October. His experience has been accurately described as 'an epic of human suffering' and the medical historian of the Australian forces, A. G. Butler, wrote that Lording deserved 'a special place (if anyone does) among the immortals of the A.I.F'.

For his gallant service and decades of suffering Lording was given no special military awards, simply a minimal invalid pension and the campaign medals that all soldiers were entitled to receive.

A stitch in time

As well as physically supporting soldiers at the front through their involvement in making munitions, providing transport and, of course, making uniforms, women working on the home front found ways to provide a little unofficial moral support. This story dates from World War II and suggests that army equipment and clothing were in short supply. It might even be true.

Many of the old Diggers will recollect the discovery in their greatcoat pockets of nice little notes from work-girls, whose nimble fingers had stitched the cloth of the garment. Some of these notes were answered, meetings were arranged and romance brightened the lives of soldier lad and lassie.

Which leads up to the fact that a member of the AIF at Redbank (Q) [Queensland] was issued with a greatcoat which contained such a slip of paper in one of the pockets. But the new digger didn't write to the girl. The coat was a hangover from the last war, the note bearing the date, 1917.

The Nackeroos

In response to Japanese air strikes on Darwin and other northern Australian towns from early 1942, a unique force was raised to protect Australia's northern boundaries. The North Australia Observer Unit (sometimes titled 'Observation Unit', but in either case NAOU) was a 550-strong group of mounted observers who patrolled Australia's immense northern border in search of enemy activity. Known sometimes as 'Curtin's Cowboys' after John Curtin, the then-prime minister, they referred to themselves as 'the Nackeroos', a title that well described their rough and ready nature.

Operating in small groups, mostly on horseback, they lived off the land. The Aboriginal members, whose knowledge of the harsh country was unequalled, played a vital role. The Nackeroos established food and ammunition dumps across their patrol territory in preparation for the eventuality of a Japanese invasion, in which case they were expected to operate behind enemy lines as a guerilla resistance unit. The unit's commanding officer was the noted anthropologist W. E. H. Bill Stanner, whose knowledge of the region made him the inevitable choice for the position.

The intelligence gathered by the NAOU went by radio to the larger Northern Territory Force, known as 'Norforce'.

One of their members, Des Harrison, recollected that the unit had over one thousand horses, donkeys and mules. Sometimes these had to be overlanded across the Top End. During one wet season, five Nackeroos drove eighty horses 700 kilometres across the Northern Territory and Western Australia. They lost four horses to crocodiles but arrived at their destination with the other seventy-six in reasonable condition. Some of the unit's patrols extended for 800 kilometres and lasted for two months, seeking evidence of enemy infiltration, finding downed airmen and also conducting bush rescues when required. Harrison made a point of recognising the astonishing bush skills of the Aboriginal members of the unit. Their ability to track and to find food and water saved patrols from perishing on more than one occasion.

The Nackeroos were quietly disbanded at the war's end and their story is relatively little known. One of the few tangible remnants of their existence is a memorial dedicated to Norforce in Timber Creek, in the Northern Territory. Unveiled in 1999, the memorial is in the form of a boulder on which is mounted a brass plaque reading: 'Australia Remembers. Norforce Ever Vigilant 1945–1995. They guarded Timber Creek, and the NW coast, from 1942 onwards in the War against Japan. Lest We Forget'.

There were a total of ninety-seven confirmed Japanese air raids on Australian targets between February 1942 and September 1943, including Broome (three times) Derby, Exmouth Gulf, Wyndham, Port Hedland and Onslow in Western Australia; Darwin, Drysdale, Katherine, Milingimbi and Port Patterson in the Northern Territory; and Townsville, Mossman and Horn

Island in Queensland. The Nackeroos may not have been the only response to the bombing of the north. There have long been rumours that another, similar force known colloquially as 'the black guard' was established specifically to mount subversive resistance operations in the event of a Japanese invasion. These rumours probably relate to other home-front units formed with largely indigenous members.

The Torres Strait Light Infantry Battalion was tasked with the defence of the Torres Strait region. In 1941 the Northern Territory Special Reconnaissance Unit was established under the command of yet another anthropologist, Donald Thomson. The unit consisted of Torres Strait Islanders, Aborigines, South Sea Islanders and a few white members. Like the Nackeroos, they used bush skills to move around and live off the land, ready to conduct a guerilla resistance against any Japanese incursion. The unit patrolled the coastline and engaged in missions into Japanese-occupied Dutch New Guinea. Other indigenous units were formed and it is thought that eventually almost every able-bodied male Torres Strait Islander was in uniform. According to the Australian War Memorial's account of these activities: 'In proportion to population, no community in Australia contributed more to the war effort in World War II than the Islanders of the Torres Strait'.

Yanks Down Under

After the fall of Singapore in February 1942, Australia turned towards America for strategic support in the Pacific war. Australia rapidly became an extended American base, with hundreds of thousands of US servicemen and women 'invading' Australia until the end of the war in 1945. To prepare the American visitors for their Australian sojourn, the Americans issued a booklet titled *Instructions for American Servicemen in Australia 1942*. It contained information about the customs, attitudes, manners, likes and dislikes of Australians, as seen from an American perspective.

The book acknowledged that Australians had 'through courage and ingenuity made a living and built a great nation out of a harsh, empty land. They built great cities, organized a progressive democracy and established a sound economic system, for all of which they're justly proud'. The booklet went on to profile 'The People "Down Under"'.

And they're proud too of their British heritage and to be a member of the British Commonwealth—but they still like to run their own business and they take great pride in their independence. They resent being called a colony and think of themselves as a great nation on their own hook, which they are. And it's natural that they should find themselves drawn closer and closer to Americans because of the many things we have in common. They look at the swift development that has made the United States a great power in a few generations, and compare our growth with theirs. Nearly 40 years ago, an Australian states-man said of the United States: 'What we are, you were. What you are we will some day be.' And just a short time ago Australian War Minister Francis Forde said: 'We feel that our fate and that of America are indissolubly linked. We know that our destinies go hand in hand and that we rise and fall together. And we are proud and confident in that association.'

You'll find the Australians an outdoors kind of people, breezy and very democratic. They haven't much respect for stuffed shirts, their own or anyone else's. They're a generation closer to their pioneer ancestors than we are to ours, so it's natural that they should have a lively sense of independence and 'rugged individualism'. But they have, too, a strong sense of cooperation. The worst thing an Australian can say about anyone is: 'He let his cobbers (pals) down.' A man can be a 'dag' (a cutup) or 'rough as bags' (a tough guy), but if he sticks with the mob, he's all right.

If an Australian ever says to you that you are 'game as Ned Kelly', you should feel honored. It's one of the best things he can say about you. It means that you have the sort of guts he admires, and that there's something about you that reminds him of Ned Kelly. Kelly was a bushranger (a backwoods highwayman) and not a very good citizen, but he had a lot of courage that makes Australians talk about him as we used to talk about Jesse James or Billy the Kid.

Of course, the best thing any Australian can say about you is that you're a 'bloody fine barstud'.

You'll find that the Digger is a rapid, sharp and unsparing kidder, able to hold his own with Americans or anyone else. He doesn't miss a chance to spar back and forth and he enjoys it all the more if the competition is tough.

Another thing, the Digger is instantaneously sociable. Riding on the same train with American troops, a mob of Aussies are likely to descend on the Yanks, investigate their equipment, ask every kind of personal question, find out if there's any liquor to be had, and within 5 minutes be showing pictures of their girls and families.

One Aussie, a successful kid cartoonist, who got himself trans-ferred to an American unit for a week, could have run for mayor and been elected after 2 days in camp. He knew the first name and history of every man and officer and had drawn portraits of some of the officers.

Being simple, direct and tough, especially if he comes from 'Outback', the Digger is often confused and non-plussed by the 'manners' of Americans in mixed company or even in camp. To him those many 'bloody thank you's and pleases' Americans use are a bit sissified. But, on the other side of the fence, if you ask an Australian for an address in a city you happen to be, he won't just tell you. He'll walk eight blocks or more to show you.

There's one thing about Americans that delights him. That is our mixed ancestry. A taxi driver told an American correspondent about three soldiers he hauled about one night: 'One was Italian, one was Jewish, and the other told me he was half Scottish and half soda,' said the hacker, roaring with laughter.

There's one thing you'll run into—Australians know as little about our country as we do theirs. To them all Americans soldiers are 'Yanks'—and always will be.

Australians, like Americans again, live pretty much in the present and the future, and pay little mind to the past.

If they are still in effect, you might get annoyed at the 'blue laws' which make Australian cities pretty dull places on Sundays. For all their breeziness, the Australians don't go in for a lot of drinking or woo-pitching in public, especially on Sundays. So maybe the bars, the movies, and the dance halls won't be open on Sundays, but there are a lot of places in America where that's true too.

There's no use beefing about it—it's their country.

IT'S THE SAME LANGUAGE TOO. We all speak the same language—the British, the Australians, and us—our versions of it. Probably the only difficulty you'll run into here is the habit Australians have of pronouncing 'a' as 'i'—for instance, 'the trine is lite today'. Some people say it sounds like the way London Cockneys talk, but good Australians resent that—and it isn't true anyway.

Thanks to our movies, the average Australian has some knowledge of our slang, but it'll take you a while to get on to theirs. To them a 'right guy' is a 'fair dinkum'; a hard worker is a 'grafter' and 'to feel crook' means to feel lousy; while 'beaut', means swell. Australian slang is so colorful, and confusing, that a whole chapter is devoted to it at the end of this book.

Also, the Australian has few equals in the world at swearing except maybe the famous American mule skinner in World War 1. The commonest swear words are bastard (pronounced 'barstud'), 'bugger', and 'bloody', and the Australians have a genius for using the latter nearly every other word. The story is told of an old-timer who was asked when he had come to the continent. He replied 'I came in nineteen-bloody-eight.'

The book observed that Australians were keen on community singing and provided the lyrics of 'Waltzing Matilda', 'A standard favorite all over the country'. It went on to describe what Australians liked to eat and drink.

THE AUSTRALIANS EAT AND DRINK TOO. Australians are great meat eaters—they eat many times as much beef, mutton and lamb as we do—a lot more flour, butter, and tea. But they don't go in for green vegetables and salads and fruit as much as Americans. Some of the best fruits in the world are grown along the tropical coast of Queensland, but the Australian, nevertheless, is strictly a 'meat and potatoes guy.'

There are a couple of libelous stories going around about Australian food. Housewives 'down under' are supposed to make coffee with a pinch of salt and a dash of mustard, but that's probably just another Axis propaganda story. The other one is that 'outback', as the Australian call the dry country, when you order your dinner of beef or lamb and two vegetables, the vegetables you get are fried potatoes and roasted potatoes. That probably isn't true either. You may think it's a gag, but you will get kangaroo steak or kangaroo tail soup in the 'outback', especially if you go hunting yourself. They're supposed to be tasty.

Meat pies are the Australian version of the hot dog, and in Melbourne, the substitute for a hamburger is a 'dim sim', chopped meat rolled in cabbage leaves which you order 'to take out' in Chinese restaurants. But because of the demand, hot dog and hamburger stands are springing up in large numbers. So you'll probably see signs like this when you get around the country a bit: '500 yards ahead. Digger Danny's Toasted Dachshunds.' But you won't find drug stores selling sodas or banana splits.

Drinking in Australia is usually confined to hotel bars during the few hours they're allowed to open—they close at 6 pm in most places. The main drink is beer, stronger than ours and not as cold. Hard liquor is fairly expensive and much less commonly drunk than in America. They also make some good light wines.

But the national drink is still tea, which you will find is a good drink when you get used to it. Along the roads you'll see 'hot water' signs displayed—Australian motorists take along their own tea and for a few pence, from the roadside stands, they can get hot water and a small tin can (billy can) in which they brew their tea. But since the war began, there isn't any motoring.

The guidebook also accurately identified the Australian love of sport and a flutter.

As an outdoor people, the Australians go in for a wide variety of active sports—surf, bathing, cricket, rugby, football, golf and tennis. The national game is cricket and the periodic 'test matches' with England are like our World Series. Cricket isn't a very lively game to watch, but it's difficult to play well. Not much cricket is being played nowadays.

The Australians have another national game called Australian Rules Football, which is rough, tough, and exciting. There are a lot of rules—the referee carries a rule book the size of an ordinary Webster's Dictionary. Unlike cricket, which is a polite game, Australian Rules Football creates a desire on the part of the crowd to tear someone apart, usually the referee—some parks have runways covered over, so the referee can escape more or less intact, after the game is over. The crowd is apt to yell 'Wake up melon head' or some such pleasantry at the umpire, but they don't think it good sportsmanship to heckle the teams. Australian soldiers play it at every chance. In one camp the boys used Bren gun carriers to clear a field to play on and that afternoon 500 out of an outfit of 700 got into the game.

Yes, and the Australians play baseball too. We think we have a monopoly on the game, but the first American units found out differently after being walloped by Australian teams. Before the Americans arrived not many Australians turned out to watch a baseball game—it was primarily a way for cricketers to keep in shape during the off-season. Now crowds of 10,000 turn out to see Australian and American service teams play—and they're getting into the sport of our national game by yelling 'Slay the bloke' when the umpire pulls a boner.

If you're good at sports you'll probably be more popular in Australia than by being good at anything else. One of the National heroes is Don Bradman, a stockbroker from Adelaide, who was the nation's greatest cricket player—he rates more lines in the Australian Who's Who than the Prime Minister.

A good many Australian sports champions are familiar names on American sports pages. Bob Fitzimmons, who won the heavyweight title from Jim Corbett, was Australian-born. And American tennis fans have seen the great Australian teams in action—with men like Jack Crawford, Vivian McGrath, Adrian Quist and John Bromwich, who took the Davis Cup from us in 1939, just before the outbreak of the war. The Aussies also won the cup from us just before the last war, in 1914.

And in golf, there is the famous trick shot expert, Joe Kirkwood, who is a familiar figure in American professional tournaments.

Probably more people in Australia play some sport or other than do in America. There are a lot of good tennis courts and golf courses, in some cases provided by the municipal authorities, which are inexpensive to play on.

But above all the Australians are the No. 1 racing fans in the world. Most cities and towns of any size have race tracks and some like Perth have trotting tracks which used to be lighted up for night racing before the 'brown out' (the Australian version of the black out). The big event of the year is the running of the Melbourne Cup, established in 1861, 14 years before our Kentucky Derby. It's a legal holiday in Melbourne the day the race is run. There's one main difference between Australian racing and ours. Their horses run clockwise.

THE GAMBLING FEVER. As one newspaper correspondent says, the Americans and Australians are 'two of the gamblingest people on the face of the earth'. It's been said of the Australians that if a couple of them in a bar haven't anything else to bet on, they'll lay odds on which two flies will rise first from the bar, or which raindrop will get to the bottom of the window first. If an American happened to be there, he'd probably be making book.

The favorite, but illegal, game among the Diggers is 'Two-Up' which is a very simple version of an old American pastime, matching coins—that is, it's the favorite game after the one of putting a buck or two on a horse's nose. The Australians wouldn't approve of the Chinese who said he didn't want to bet on a horse race, because he already knew one horse could run faster than another.

Finally, the digger was described:

YOUR OPPOSITE NUMBER, THE AUSSIE. You'll have a good deal to do with the Australian people, probably, but you'll sleep, eat, and fight alongside of your opposite number, the Aussie.

American newspapers and magazines have been full of stories about the Aussies—in Greece, in Crete, in Libya, at Singapore, and in the Burma jungles. All Americans who've had anything to do with them say they're among the friendliest guys in the world—and fine physical specimens of fighting men.

So far in this war the Australians have been in all the hot spots—wherever the going has been tough. And they have the reputation for staying in there and pitching with anything they can get their hands on—and if there isn't anything else they use their hands. During the early days of the threatened Jap invasion of their continent, Australian pilots fought off armored Jap bombers with the only planes they had—often just trainers.

The Aussies don't fight out of a textbook. They're resourceful, inventive soldiers, with plenty of initiative. Americans and British have the idea that they are an undisciplined bunch—they aren't much on saluting or parading and they often do call their C.O. by his first name—but when the fighting begins, there isn't any lack of discipline or leadership, either.

Officers most often come up from the ranks, and they are a young group. The average age of Australian generals today is less than 50 years—about the same as our own. The greatest Australian general in the last war was a civil engineer by trade, and one of Wavell's best desert generals was Sir Iven Mackay who was a school teacher and who put soldiering under 'recreation' in his biography in the Australian Who's Who.

The story is typical of the attitude the Anzac has toward the business of fighting. During some tough going on the El Alamein sector in Egypt, recently, a group of Australians volunteered to knock out a dangerous machine gun nest, manned by members of Rommel's Afrika Korps. As they were dashing in, one Aussie yelled to another: 'Cripes, Bill, I tell you if the (censored) food in this outfit doesn't get any better, I'm bloody well going to quit.'

Australians are immensely proud of the record their men made in the last war—any country would be proud of it. You'll see memorials to the dead of World War 1 all through Australia and they're honored greatly by all the people.

The Brisbane Line

Was there a 'Brisbane Line' or not? Controversy about the existence of a line that would be defended to the death in the event of a Japanese invasion has persisted since World War II.

Even the reality of the Japanese threat to Australia has been questioned by some historians. But whether the Japanese really did intend to conquer and occupy the Australian mainland or not, there was a strong belief in 1942 that this was likely. 'He's coming south' screamed official posters and advertisements of the period, and Prime Minister John Curtin's government (which had been elected in 1941) was so alarmed by the fall of Singapore and its implications that Curtin made his famous speech in which Australia turned away from Britain as its primary ally and looked towards the United States.

What was the 'Brisbane Line'—if there was one at all? It was an imaginary line drawn from Brisbane to Perth that represented the final line of defence against any Japanese invasion. Everything north of this line would be sacrificed to the invaders. These were dramatic days for Australia. In February 1942 Singapore had fallen to the Japanese who were rapidly advancing southwards. Darwin and many other northern cities were bombed, including Broome, Wyndham and Townsville. The Americans were forced to flee the Philippines and establish a Pacific base in Australia.

After an Australian press briefing from the American General Douglas MacArthur in mid-March, 1943, the Brisbane Line was reported in Brisbane's *Courier-Mail* newspaper, causing considerable public consternation. The issue was, of course, highly political and Curtin was forced to establish a Royal Commission to determine the truth or otherwise of claims that the conservative Menzies government had concocted the Brisbane Line policy when it was in power from 1939 to 1941. This accusation was strongly denied and the Royal Commission could find no evidence of it existing.

Having coined the term 'Brisbane Line' and set the controversy in motion, MacArthur subsequently distanced himself from the idea. But in his reminiscences he claimed that, at one point, the Australian military authorities did have a plan to defend the country along a line stretching southwards from Brisbane to Adelaide, consigning the country's western third to the possibility of foreign occupation along with the entire Top End. Whatever the truth of the Brisbane Line policy, it was eventually determined that the best way to defend Australia from the Japanese was to oppose them before they arrived, a decision that led to the fighting in New Guinea and the creation of a new Anzac icon, the Kokoda Track.

Controversy about the Brisbane Line is still never far away in contemporary Australia. There are strong opinions held by proponents and opponents of its existence. Some point to the remains of tank traps and other defences in the Tenterfield area of New South Wales and elsewhere as tangible evidence of the plan. Others point out that such fortifications are, of themselves, insufficient evidence. The Brisbane Line has become entwined with the larger issue of a potential Japanese invasion with stories about special 'invasion currency' being printed by the Japanese and maps in Japanese featuring southward-pointing arrows. These are in fact spoofs, and while the 'invasion money' existed, it was for use in Britain's Pacific territories, not in Australia.

One way to understand the Brisbane Line controversy is to see it as a projection of justifiable wartime anxieties reflecting some traditional regional rivalries and cleavages. The north of Australia, or the 'Top End', has always had a strong sense of its own identity and an occasionally well-founded distrust of politicians and almost everything else in the 'soft south'.

Similarly, the possibility of the Brisbane Line extending only to Adelaide reflects the traditional psychological and cultural distance between the east and west of the country, only magnified by the dividing immensity of the Nullarbor Plain. Like modern 'urban myths', such beliefs trade on often unspoken social fears and hidden conflicts and, true or not, are often found believable by large numbers of people.

Miss Luckman's journal

Just before and during World War II, Miss Grace Luckman kept a journal. It was only a cheap notebook that opened out to a bit less than an A4 page, its pages ruled for keeping basic accounts. In the notebook, Grace, a country girl, jotted down her thoughts and feelings and pasted in many clippings taken from the newspapers of the time. Most of these clippings are poems, some of her own homilies, 'Thoughts for the Week', and other uplifting creations, together with items on romantic love, including 'My heart pants for you' in pictogram form.

The family was fully involved in the war. Private E. Luckman was in camp with the 11th Battalion, and Signaller H. Luckman was in the Signal School Base with the New Zealand Expeditionary Force in the Middle East. Grace also recorded the birthdays of friends and family, including 'Ernie' who had turned eighteen the year before the war began. His address at

C Coy, 2/2 Infantry Battalion, is carefully pencilled into the last page. Many other entries relate directly to the war and how it appeared to those at home.

Scribbled on one page of the notebook are two homespun verses concerning the devastating loss of HMAS *Sydney* in November 1941 and the fundraising undertaken by the community for the families of the lost sailors.

Here's to the *Sydney* brave and true,
Here's to the men who manned her too.
Ever in our thoughts they'll be,
This gallant ship and her company.
Day by day they sailed the sea
To keep beloved Australia free.
So listen to the Lord Mayor's pleas,
Enclose a stamp for the new *Sydney*.

'In Praise of Tanks' celebrated the victories of tanks in New Guinea and the Middle East.

Cast not in beauty's mould your feature,
Born of man's inhuman brain;
Yet we have learned your worth—you monstrous
Product of a world insane . . .

The poem went on to praise the tanks for the defeats of Rommel and the Japanese.

Some items manage to combine both Miss Luckman's romantic interests and the war, as in this poem about the 'lovelorn blokes at Darwin' who are 'a sitting shot for me'.

Put me somewhere near to Darwin
Where there's romance in the air,
Where a score of eager suitors
Answer every maiden's prayer.
For the wedding bells are calling,
And there's still a chance for me,
On a balmy night in Darwin
Where the moon is on the sea . . .

One of the many newspaper clippings carefully pasted into the notebook also concerned Darwin and the visiting Americans.

L ife in the lonely desert country around Darwin was summed up by an American soldier on leave at Melbourne.

'It's this way, buddy. When you're there a few weeks you find yourself talking to yourself. After that you find yourself talking to the lizards. After another couple of weeks you find the lizards talking to you. Then you find yourself listening.'

Other entries reflect nostalgia for 'old England' and the need for Australia to answer the call and act in her protection, sentiments that also featured in World War I. Like many Australians, Miss Luckman had family in Britain. She kept her journal after the war and in a brief note about it written forty years later, she still signed herself 'Miss Grace Luckman'.

Laughter

THE OLD SAYING that 'an army marches on its stomach' is a truism that could easily be matched by 'an army survives on its laughter'. Military life is often difficult and dangerous and one way of coping with it is to laugh, especially about things that are not very funny at all. Anzac humour reflects the famous larrikinism and anti-authoritarianism of the digger, whether at Gallipoli, the western front, Tobruk, Kokoda or Vietnam.

Lovingly told and retold, the peppery yarns of the digger never failed to raise a laugh at the front, in the pub or at reunions after the war. While some may have lost a little of their original bite as the years have passed, these brief snippets of humour are powerful expressions of Anzac attitudes, then and now.

A million cat-calls

In the 1914–18 war, the Anzacs were notorious among British troops for indiscipline and a casual attitude towards the military in general. They tended to address officers by their first names and, of course, rarely saluted. This was beyond the understanding of the disciplinarian British army and led to many confrontations, sometimes serious, sometimes amusing. One such incident occurred in northern France at a place called Strazeele. The Australians were camped across the road from the 10th Battalion Royal Fusiliers, as recounted by Fusilier Private C. Miles.

The Colonel decided that he would have a full dress parade of the guard mounting. Well, the Aussies looked over at us amazed. The band was playing, we were all smartened up, spit and polish, on parade, and that happened every morning. We marched up and down, up and down.

The Aussies couldn't get over it, and when we were off duty we naturally used to talk to them, go over and have a smoke with them, or meet them when we were hanging about the road or having a stroll. They kept asking us: 'Do you like this sort of thing? All these parades, do you want to do it?' Of course we said, 'No, of course we don't. We're supposed to be on rest, and all the time we've got goes to posh up and turn out on parade.' So they looked at us a bit strangely and said, 'OK, cobbers, we'll soon alter that for you.'

The Australians didn't approve of it because they never polished or did anything. They had a band, but their brass instruments were all filthy. Still, they knew how to play them.

The next evening, our Sergeant-Major was taking the parade. Sergeant-Major Rowbotham, a nice man, but a stickler for discipline. He was just getting ready to bawl us all out when the Australians started with their band. They marched up and down the road outside the field, playing any old thing. There was no tune you could recognise, they were just blowing as loud as they could on their instruments. It sounded like a million cat-calls.

And poor old Sergeant Rowbotham, he couldn't make his voice heard. It was an absolute fiasco. They never tried to mount another parade, because they could see the Aussies watching us from across the road, just ready to step in and sabotage the whole thing. So they decided that parades for mounting the guards should be washed out, and after that they just posted the guards in the ordinary way as if we were in the line.

The Pommies and the Yanks

Rivalry between Australians and the British and Americans was often played for laughs.

Two Aussies on leave from France were occupying a first-class non-smoking compartment of an English train, when an irascible old bloke blew in. The old killjoy got nasty because one of the Aussies was smoking, and without any preliminary diplomatic negotiations handed the cigar-puffer an ultimatum that he would have him removed from the compartment if he didn't stop smoking. This annoyed the Aussie, and he counter-attacked behind a strong smoke barrage. At the next station Mr. Killjoy called a porter and read out the Aussie's crime sheet:

'This man is smoking in a non-smoking compartment.' He demanded that the Aussie should be removed. The porter told the Aussie that he would either have to stop smoking or stop travelling in a non-smoker.

'Well, I plead guilty to smoking in a non-smoker,' said the Aussie 'but this old nark has no kick coming against me. He's travelling first on a second-class ticket!'

The porter demanded old Killjoy's ticket and found that the Aussie's statement was correct. Exit old Killjoy.

'How did you know he was travelling wrong class?' asked the second Aussie, later.

'Oh, I saw the ticket sticking out of his vest pocket,' replied the other, between puffs, 'and it was the same colour as my own.'

Sometimes these yarns involved the ability to understand, or not, the 'great Australian slanguage'.

THE YANK: 'Say, Guy, how far to battle?'
AUSSIE: 'Well sonny, I guess it's about five kilos. Just "pencil and chalk" straight along this "frog and toad" till you come to the "romp and ramp" on the "Johnny Horner". Then dive across that "bog orange" field till you run into a barrage. That lobs you right there. D'ye compree?'

Being able to speak the right lingo could mean the difference between life and death, as highlighted in an Australian yarn.

The weary pongo [soldier of low rank] was wending his way frigidly along the duckboards when he encountered a sentry.

'Halt!—password?' The weary one carefully searched his thought-box, but couldn't recall the required word. He remembered, however, that it was the name of a place in Australia, so he began to run through all the places he knew, in the hope of striking it: 'Bondi, Woolloomooloo, Budgaree, Wangaratta, Cootamundra, Murrumbidgee, Wagga Wagga, We—.'

'Pass on, Digger,' interrupted the sentry, 'you've got the dinkum talk!'

The dialogue between the American and the Australian was a popular form of digger humour. Possibly because the Australian always tops the exaggerations of the American. This one was already old when it was first published in 1917.

A yankee and an Aussie were having a quiet drink in the canteen. After a while the conversation came around to the subject of wildlife. 'Your dingo is nowhere near as savage as our coyote', the American claimed. 'And our cougars can outdo any of your wild beasts.'

'Is that right?', said the Aussie.

'Yeah. Take our rattlesnake. It bites you and you die in under two minutes.'

'Oh, that's nothing', replied the Aussie. 'Our taipans come at you so fast you're dead two minutes before they bite you.'

It was not only the wildlife that featured in tall tales of this type.

It was at a military hospital in England, and the convalescents were sitting in the garden chatting. The topic was cold weather. The American had the floor.

'Wal, I reckon it was a bit cold in those French trenches this winter. But shucks! It was a heat wave compared with some of the cold snaps we get in America. Why, look here, children; I remember one day over'n New York it got so darned cold, kinder suddent like, that everybody's whiskers froze, and the people had ter shave themselves with dynamite. Of course the explosions shook up ther old city a trifle, but, by George Washington, some whickers got shifted! Another day a cold jerk put in without notice and froze up all the whisky. The bartenders had to go about with axes chipping' nobblers off the whiskey blocks. Some cold, I reckon!'

An Australian scratched his right ear with a crutch, and put in:

'Dunno much about cold in Australia, but I ken talk heat a bit. It does warm up over there. Now, once I was humpin' me bluey in ther bush. A heat wave came up. You could see it comin' in the distance by ther kangaroos 'oppin' about with their tails on fire. I picked up a bit of old fencin' wire and lit me pipe with it. That was a sure sign too. In a few minutes that wave struck me, dealt with me, and then passed on, leavin' me with only me pocket knife and a quart pot to go on with. Of course I was new to the bush, or I couldn't have felt it so much. I met another bloke soon after. He was eatin' a baked goanna he'd picked up. I sez 'Warm, mate, eh?' He sez, 'Oh, it's been just nice to-day. Reckon it'll be fairly 'ot to-morrow.'

It was on again in the next war as well.

Overheard on Townsville beach one night in 1944—a Yank calls to an Aussie: 'Hey, Buddy, break down the language! I'd like you to know I have a lady with me here!'

The Aussie calls back to the Yank: 'And what the hell d'ya think I have here—a ruddy seagull?'

Religion

Religion was another point of difference and potential sectarian dissension within the ranks. Personal experience stories featured frequently in trench tales. These were sometimes simple accounts of unusual and/or humorous experiences; at other times they were retellings of traditional yarns and tall stories. Often they were in all likelihood apocryphal, though nonetheless revealing for that, as in this slice of sectarian rivalry under the title 'We'll Have That Moment Again'.

An R.C. Padre was tripping gaily along somewhere near supports, when he noticed a burying party just putting the finishing touches to the graves of four of their comrades. He pulled up, and finding that three of them were of his creed, asked who had read the service. 'Some Tommy C of E Padre, sir' was the reply. The R. C. Chaplain asked nothing more but walked straight to the graves, and, in a voice like a sergeant-major, gave the order 'Numbers 2, 3 and 4—As you were!'—Then proceeded to re-read the burial service.

Many years after World War II ended in 1945, Mr R. F. Young of Tasmania remembered an incident that typified the predominant digger attitude to formal religious affiliations.

When I was joining the A.I.F. back in 1940, a big bushman ahead of me in the line was being asked by the Recruiting Depot Lieutenant about his name, age, and so on. When it came to his religious denomination he drawled, 'Aw, I'm not fussy. What are you short of?'

Monocles

This anecdote is from the Boer War (1899–1902) and so cannot be considered a strictly Anzac yarn. But it suggests that the attitudes of the diggers were already in formation a long time before 1915.

It was during the Boer War. He was walking down the street in a city in South Africa when he noticed a very polished and obviously very new British Army lieutenant complete with monocle and swagger stick, walking across the road.

About to cross the road from the other side was a very dirty and obviously very experienced Australian Light Horseman, complete with slouch hat, the inevitable 'makings' hanging from his lower lip, and a saddle over one arm.

The young lieutenant halted the Aussie, apparently with the intention of asking him what he meant by appearing in the streets in such an untidy getup.

The Aussie spat his cigarette on to the road and eyed the young officer up and down. 'The Queensland Bushrangers,' he answered casually. Then he lifted a saddle stirrup to one eye in imitation of the monocle, and said with a forced accent. 'And you, my good man—what bloody regiment, may I ask, do you belong to?'

The diggers of the Great War didn't have it all their own way when it came to British officers and monocles. One Australian unit had a posh-talking officer who wore a monocle. One morning when the men came out to parade before the officer, they all lined up with a coin in one eye. The British officer looked at them, then tossed his head upwards, sending his monocle spinning into the air, catching it in his other eye.

'Now, which one of you bastards can do that?', he asked in an impeccable English accent.

It is said that the diggers were so impressed they all wanted to buy the officer a drink.

Food and drink

If troops are not properly fed they cannot fight well, due both to physical and psychological decline. Sometimes it becomes necessary to resort to deception to improve the menu, as recounted in this tale from Gallipoli.

The ration problem on Gallipoli was at times a very real one, but probably the most trying part of it, to the troops at any rate, was that the only commodity in the 'sweets' line of business was apricot jam. Australians often wondered why that particular form of preserve seemed to be unlimited. The explanation was that in 1914 the English crop of 'cots was one of the heaviest on record. Thousands of tons of the fruit were jammed and canned, and some makers (can any of us ever forget Tickler, with his picture on the label?) made fortunes, though all of them didn't deserve to. Naturally the troops, and especially the Australians, got sick of the sight of the stuff.

One dark night in November, '15, it fell to my lot to take a fatigue party of 20 men down from 'Q Pip' (Quinn's Post) to the beach. None of us knew the route we had been ordered to follow, and we got helplessly bushed until I espied a light in what turned out to be an ASC sub-depot. 'I've been lookin' for you,' said a voice. 'You'll be the party for the stuff for the Jocks' (Scottish Horse). Scenting something good, I took the risk and said that we were. Darkness aided in hiding the Aussie uniform and silence did the rest. We afterwards discovered that we had got away with over 200 jars of Keiller's Dundee marmalade, among the best of Scotia's products. I have often wondered what happened to the wight who issued the stuff without a murmur. But in those days one could do a lot and get away with it.

Alcohol has always featured heavily in the life and lore of soldiers. During the Great War, rum and other forms of alcohol were often issued to troops when at the front line—and greatly appreciated it was, as reflected in this World War I ditty.

The Frenchman likes his sparkling wine,
The German likes his beer,
The Tommie likes his half and half
Because it brings good cheer.
The Scotsman likes his whisky,
And Paddy likes his pot,
But the Digger has no national drink,
So he drinks the blanky lot.

Many yarns were spun around the subject of grog. This one allegedly took place in the French town of Le Havre immediately after the war's end on 11 November 1918. The reference to the '8 chevaux ou 40 hommes' (8 horses or 40 men) was a favourite World War I digger term for the very basic French rail carriages in which they were often transported. As this story tells it, four days of this form of travel put the diggers in the mood for a drink.

After the Armistice the troops were sent to Le Havre in a car de-luxe of the '8 chevaux ou 40 hommes' brand. The weather being cold, the food crook, and the journey taking anything up to four days, the troops arrived at their destination in a somewhat peevish mood.

Our crowd was reported to have busted open some railway trucks at Abbeville and helped themselves to cognac, and the O.C. No. 5 Company at the Australian delousing camp was deputed to intercept the train . . . and search it. He carried out his duties faithfully telling the O.C. train his orders and saying 'I shall be back in twenty minutes with my staff and I will search thoroughly. If I find any cognac, heaven help anyone found with it.'

When the search was made the honour of the AIF was vindicated. Next morning the O.C. No. 5 found a bottle of cognac on his bunk.

Babbling brooks

The tradition of the dreadful cook is a long one, stretching back to Australia's pioneering days. It often features in the lore of shearing; for example, in the tale of 'Who called the cook a bastard?'. In this story, the shearers are so fed up with the appalling food their cook serves up that there is an argument in which one of them calls the cook a 'bastard'. The cook complains to the boss, who comes into the men's shed to find the culprit. 'Who called the cook a bastard?' he demands to know. 'Who called the bastard a cook?', comes the rapid-fire reply.

The tradition continued into the First AIF where, in a variation on the theme, a digger is being questioned by the officer in charge of his court-martial. "'Did you call the cook a ———?" "No", the digger answers, "but I could kiss the ——— who did!'"

And in another incident involving bad food and bad language:

I came out of my dugout one morning attracted by a terrible outburst of Aussie slanguage in the trench. The company dag [character] was standing in about three feet of mud, holding his mess tin in front of him and gazing contemptuously at a piece of badly cooked bacon, while he made a few heated remarks concerning one known as Bolo, the babbling brook. He concluded an earnest and powerful address thus:

'An' if the ——— that cooked this bacon ever gets hung for bein' a cook, the poor ——— will be innocent'.

Cooks were usually known by their rhyming slang name as 'Babbling Brooks', or simply 'Babblers'.

'What's this the Babbling Brook has given me—tea or stew?' asked the new hand perplexedly, as he contemplated the concoction in his Dixie.

'It's tea', announced his cobber.

'How can you tell?' said the new hand.

'You can always tell when you've got tea or stew by where he puts it. If he puts it in the Dixie lid it's stew, but if he puts it in the Dixie itself it's tea.'

Repetition of the same offering could also cause concern.

During the advance towards the outer defences of the Hindenburg Line early in September, 1918, the supply of rations got a bit disorganized, and for three solid days the cookhouse menu was stew, made of biscuits and bully-beef, with sundry dehydrated vegetables put through the mince, and boiled with a little water. Every man who came to the cookhouse made practically the same remark: 'Struth! Stoo again!' Then followed a wider range of language.

It nearly drove the cook mad. On the evening of the third day a notice was chalked up outside the cookhouse: 'It's Stew Again! But the first insulting cow who says so will be made Fresh Meat!'

Cooks were usually considered to be less than hygienic in both their trade and their personal characteristics.

Back in the First World War days there was a company cook— we'll call him Bill—who was probably the finest spoiler of Army rations in the whole A.I.F. He was also the greasiest trooper ever to don uniform.

'I learnt to cook from me old mother,' he would reminisce. 'Every Saturday she useter boil a sheep's head for Dad and us 14 kids; and she always cooked the head with the eyes in, as she reckoned it'd 'ave to see us through the week.'

Old Bill returned home after the armistice, sound in wind and limb, his nearest approach to a 'Blighty' being up at Messines in '17, when a whizzbang shell struck him fair and square in the chest. But he was so greasy the shell merely glanced off him and killed two mules attached to the cooker.

The tradition, and the problem, continued into the next war.

The boys hated the new cook, and one of them filled his boots with pig-wash in the dead of night. The cook said nothing next day when the lads visited the cookhouse after dinner, and the jester said:

'Well, cookie, who filled your boots with pig-wash?'

'Dunno', cookie said, 'but I know who ate it.'

In another place during the same war:

'How you liking it?' the cook said to the new recruit eating his first camp dinner.

'What is it?' the new recruit said.

'Horseflesh', the cook said. 'How'd you feel about that, eh?'

'I don't mind horseflesh', the new recruit said, 'but you might have taken the harness off.'

And, according to Tobruk legend:

An officer was inspecting the cooking arrangements in a darkened dugout. 'You've got too many flies in here, Cookie', he told the individual entrusted with feeding the troops.

'Ave I sir?' came the puzzled reply—'Ow many should I 'ave?'

Army biscuits

Perhaps the single most detested item of army food was the biscuit, also known as a 'tile' or 'hard tack', all names suggesting the unnatural solidity of the food. There was much to be lampooned about the biscuit, as O. E. Burton of the New Zealand Medical Corps wrote on Gallipoli, the extravagance of his prose suggesting the depth of feeling towards the offending item.

BISCUITS! Army biscuits! What a volume of blessings and cursing have been uttered on the subject of biscuits—army biscuits!

What a part they take in our daily routine: the carrying of them, the eating of them, the cursing at them!

Could we find any substitute for biscuits? Surely not! It is easy to think of biscuits without any army, but of an army without biscuits—never.

Biscuits, like the poor, are always with us. Crawling from our earthly dens at the dim dawning of the day, we receive no portion of the dainties which once were ours in the long ago times of effete civilization: but, instead, we devour with eagerness—biscuits porridge. We eat our meat, not with thankfulness but with biscuits. We lengthen out the taste of jam—with biscuits. We pound them to powder. We boil them with bully. We fry them as fritters. We curse them with many and bitter cursings, and we bless them with few blessings.

Biscuits! Army biscuits! Consider the hardness of them. Remember the cracking of your plate, the breaking of this tooth, the splintering of that. Call to mind how your finest gold crown weakened, wobbled, and finally shrivelled under the terrific strain of masticating Puntley and Chalmer's No.5's.

Think of the aching void where once grew a goodly tooth. Think of the struggle and strain, the crushing and crunching as two molars wrestled with some rocky fragment. Think of the momentary elation during the fleeting seconds when it seemed that the molars would triumphantly blast and scrunch through every stratum of the thrice-hardened rock. Call to mind the disappointment, the agony of mind and body, as the almost victorious grinder missed its footing, slipped, and snapped hard upon its mate, while the elusive biscuit rasped and scraped upon bruised and tender gums.

Biscuits! Army biscuits! Have you, reader, ever analysed with due carefulness the taste of army biscuits? Is it the delicious succulency of ground granite or the savoury toothsomeness of powdered marble? Do we perceive a delicate flavouring of ferro-concrete with just a dash of scraped iron railings? Certainly, army biscuits, if they have a taste, have one which is peculiarly their own. The choicest dishes of civilized life, stewed or steamed, fried, frizzled, roasted or toasted, whether they be composed of meat or fish, fruit or vegetable, have not (thank Heaven!) any like taste to that of army biscuits. Army biscuits taste like nothing else on the Gallipoli Peninsula. It is a debatable question indeed whether or not they have the quality of taste. If it be granted that they possess this faculty of stimulating the peripheral extremities of a soldier's taste-buds, then it must also be conceded that the stimulation is on the whole of an unpleasant sort. In short, that the soldier's feeling apart from the joy, the pride, and the satisfaction at his completed achievement in transferring a whole biscuit from his outer to his inner man without undue accident or loss of teeth, is one of pain, unease and dissatisfaction.

It may seem almost incredible, wholly unbelievable indeed, but armies have marched and fought, made sieges, retired according to plan, stormed impregnable cities, toiled in weariness and painfulness, kept lonely vigils, suffered the extremes of burning heat and of freezing cold, and have, in the last extremity, bled and died, laurel-crowned and greatly triumphant, the heroes of legend and of song, all without the moral or physical, or even spiritual aid of army biscuits.

Agamemnon and the Greeks camped for ten years on the windy plains of Troy without one box of army biscuits. When Xerxes threw his pontoon bridge across the Narrows and marched 1,000,000 men into Greece, his transport included none of Teak Green and Co.'s paving-stones for the hardening of his soldiers' hearts and the stiffening of their backs. Caesar subdued Britons, Gauls, and

Germans. Before the lines of Dyrrhachium his legions lived many days on boiled grass and such-like delicacies, but they never exercised their jaws upon a rough, tough bit of—army biscuit.

Biscuits! Army biscuits! They are old friends, now, and, like all old friends, they will stand much hard wear and tear. Well glazed, they would make excellent tiles or fine flagstones. After the war they will have great scarcity value as curios, as souvenirs which one can pass on from generation to generation, souvenirs which will endure while the Empire stands. If we cannot get physical strength from army biscuits, let us at least catch the great spiritual ideal of enduring hardness, which they are so magnificently fitted to proclaim.

The seasons change. Antwerp falls, Louvain is burned, the tide of battle surges back and forth: new reputations are made, the old ones pass away; Warsaw, Lemberg, Serbia, the stern battles of Gallipoli, Hindenburg, Mackensen, each name catches our ear for a brief moment of time, and then gives way to another crowding it out; but army biscuits are abiding facts, always with us, patient, appealing, enduring. We can move to other theatres, we can change our clothes, our arms and our generals, but we must have our biscuits, army biscuits, else we are no longer an army.

The casual digger

A good many Anzac yarns play with the diggers' casual attitude to war:

There was once an Australian V.C. winner who was exceptionally modest. It was only with great reluctance that he agreed to attend a ceremony at which he was to be presented with his decoration.

When it was all over, a friend asked him how he felt after such a tumultuous reception.

'They got on my nerves,' said the V.C. winner. 'They made that much fuss, you'd have thought I'd won a medal in the Olympic Games.'

Queenslander, Jim Matheson had a yarn about his war:

In France during 1917, the Eighth Brigade was moving up in open formation under intense rifle fire. My Queensland mate and I were under fire for the first time. As the bullets whizzed and spatted around us, my mate said to me, 'Didya hear that one, Jim?'

'Yes,' I replied, 'twice. Once when it passed us, and once when we passed it.'

The diggers' favourite gambling game of two-up needed to be played, regardless of the circumstances:

Recently, one of our patrols was overdue, and I was detailed as one of a search party . . . Suddenly we saw the shadows of a number of men standing silently in the darkness. 'Fritzes!' said someone, and we all ducked into shell-holes. Fritz's next flare revealed a small party, all stooping and gazing intently on the ground. Then one of them cried softly and exultantly, 'Two heads are right!' picked up the pennies and pocketed the winnings. It was the lost patrol. They were making their bets and tossing the coins in the darkness, and then waiting for the light from a Fritz flare to see the result.

This one was reported in the British *Evening News* and reprinted in the *Australian Corps News Sheet* in 1918 under the title 'Taking the war calmly'.

An Australian told me this:—We were advancing, and had been going about an hour, and my platoon numbered about fifteen men. Going over a ridge we saw a pill-box. We poured machine-gun fire at it, and threw grenades too. No reply came, and we congratulated ourselves that we had no casualties.

All the time we could see smoke coming from the aperture; this worried us so we decided to charge it. We had our charge, with whoops and yells. I got to the door-way, and was met with, 'Say, Digger, what the ——— is all the noise about?'

There stood an Australian, with a frying-pan in his hand, cooking bully beef over a fire which the Huns had left.

And, in digger lore at least, even the British Tommies recognised the bravery of their Anzac allies.

Tommy (to Australian): 'That was a rare plucky thing you did this morning, to bring your mate in under that heavy fire.'

Australian: 'Yairs, the blasted cow, he had all me b—— tobacco with him.'

Officers

In a much-told tale a very proper British officer addresses a group of Australians in what was the normal British army style. The Anzacs found this unacceptable and proceeded to count him out, a practice relatively common in the AIF though unthinkable in the British army. The 300 soldiers each sang out their number, ending at 300. The conclusion was the chorus 'Out you Tommy Woodbine bastard'. The men then dispersed, some reportedly playing two-up, and leaving the outraged British officer to complain that this was an act of mutiny. But a staff sergeant, more experienced with the ways of the AIF, told him that such things were nothing remarkable and that no-one in authority in the Australian hierarchy would take such an accusation seriously.

True or not, the many yarns about officers, usually highlighting the anti-authoritarian aspect of the digger's worldview, were legion in both world wars, as in this anecdote from the first war.

A digger is travelling on a train with two English officers. The officers are discussing their family backgrounds, relationships and pedigrees. After listening to this conversation for a while, the digger introduces himself to the officers as 'Bluey' Johnson . . . not married, two sons—both Majors in the British army.

Identity is the theme of another yarn from the 1914–18 war.

Two diggers on leave in London fail to salute a passing British officer. The outraged officer demands of the diggers: 'Do you know who I am?' One digger turns to the other and says, casually: 'Did you hear that, Dig? He doesn't even know who he is'.

The theme persisted into the next war:

During World War 2 a couple of diggers were on leave in Damascus. They visited a number of drinking establishments, sampling the local spirit known as 'arrack', a strong and fiery brew. Not surprisingly, they became lost. Unable to speak Arabic they could not get any help from the locals. Fortunately, a British general suddenly appeared in full dress uniform. 'Hey mate', one of the tipsy Australians called out 'can you tell us where we are?'

The general stiffened with indignation at being addressed in such an insubordinate manner and replied frostily 'Do you men know who I am?'

'Cripes Bill', said the digger turning to his mate, 'this bloke's worse off than us. We mightn't know where we are but the poor bugger doesn't know who he is!'

This one allegedly took place on a footpath in Tel Aviv during October 1942:

An older English colonel and a younger American major were deep in discussion about the war. Four young Australian soldiers, fairly intoxicated, came along towards them, divided into pairs, passed the officers and went unsteadily on their way.

'Who in the blazes are that golddarned rabble?' asked the American major.

'They're Orstralians', replied the English colonel.

'And whose side are they on?'

'Ours Major, they are our allies', said the Colonel.

'But dammit, they didn't salute us', bleated the Major.

The Colonel admitted that this was so. 'But at least they had the decency to walk around us. If it had been their fathers from the last war, they would have walked right over us.'

The same egalitarian tone is heard in many other digger yarns. The two diggers who fool the sentry into believing that they are leaving camp rather than returning to it late by facing the other way is just one of many. Often these are tinged with anti-British sentiment.

Saw a digger on leave in London walk past a young officer without slinging a salute. On being pulled up and asked didn't he know whom he had passed, Dig said that the face was familiar but that he could not place him.

'I'm an officer in His Majesty's Imperial Army' exploded the 'Sir', 'and entitled to a salute!'

'Oh, garn, you little b——!' says the Dig, and walked on.

Coming across an Aussie sergeant shortly afterwards, the officer unfolded his tale, repeating the Digger's last blessing.

'But you're not one, are you?' mildly asked the sergeant.

'Certainly not!' exploded the officer.

'Well, go back and tell him that he is a blinking liar,' drawled the sergeant.

It was not only British or American officers who were the butt of digger yarns, as in this one from the western front.

Digger Jones (of the 1st Div. ASC) was washing down his two donks, in a shell hole at Fleureaux, about fifty yards from the old duckboard track, where the mud and slush was about two feet deep, in 1916. Having cleaned and groomed one down, he led him back and stood him on the duckboard track. A Staff Officer dressed in white corduroys, glittering spurs and polished leggings wending his way to battalion headquarters, was annoyed to find a mule blocking his pathway. Approaching the mule he gave it a heavy shove, forcing it back into the slush, much to the annoyance of Digger Jones. 'Here, what the h—— do you think you're doing?' he yelled indignantly.

'What do you mean by blocking the track with your confounded mule?' said the officer. 'I'll have you arrested for this. What is your name and number?'

Digger Jones surveyed the ground between them, and then replied: 'You come over and get it.'

On another occasion:

General Braithwaite, known more or less affectionately to New Zealanders as 'Bill the Bight', was taking his Brigade up into the line when one of those inevitable hold-ups occurred at a crossroad. This caused a halt of the Brigade alongside an Aussie battery wagon lines. Bill rode up on his charger as natural as ever (that is, he was fuming!), and roared out, 'De-lay, de-lay! What is the meaning of this de-lay?' To which the Aussie's greasy cook took it upon himself to answer, 'It's French for milk, you silly old basket.'

And the soldier who took the sergeant major's suggestion too seriously:

Sergeant Major to a Private who has missed eleven shots out of twelve: 'What, eleven misses; good heavens, man, go around the corner and shoot yourself.'

Hearing a shot around the corner, the Sergeant Major rushes around, to be confronted by the bad shot—

'Sorry, sir, another miss,' the Private murmurs.

This problem also continued into World War II:

In Whitehall recently an English Major-General stopped a non-saluting Aussie, and demanded to know who he was.

'I'm a kind of Aussie soldier', was the reply.

Said the officer: 'Well, I'm a kind of major-general and you owe me a salute.'

Said the Aussie: 'Okay, brother, I'll give you a kind of salute.' And he did.

A sergeant major is calling the role at parade:

'Johnson!'

'Yair,' drawled Johnson

'Simpson!'

''Ere.'

'Jackson!'

'She's sweet.'

'Smith!'

'Here, sir.'

'Crawler!' shouted the platoon.

An opposite form of this situation is the well-travelled tale about the officer who is expecting an inspection from the top brass. He assembles his men to brief them and when he has finished tells them, 'And whatever you do, for Christ's sake don't call me Alf'.

A certain Australian sergeant major during World War I gave his commands in a most unorthodox manner:

'**S**lope arms—you, too!'

    'Present arms—you, too!'

'Forward march—you, too!'

After the parade one day, a young lieutenant approached the sar'major and asked him the reason for his unusual commands.

'Well, sir,' he replied, 'it's like this. Those men are a tough mob. Every time I give an order I know they're going to abuse me, so I get in first.'

Birdie

On Gallipoli and at the western front, the Anzacs created a whole cycle of yarns about a character known as 'Birdie'. In reality, this was General Birdwood, commanding officer on Gallipoli, who earned the deep respect of ordinary Australian and New Zealand soldiers. This was something particularly difficult to achieve given their problems with military authority, and was based on Birdwood's concern for the wellbeing of his men and his willingness to appear at the front line when necessary. General Sir Ian Hamilton, overall commander of the campaign and effectively Birdwood's boss, generously summed up the man's impressive reputation, calling him 'the soul of Anzac', and stated 'Not for one single day has he ever quitted his post. Cheery and full of human sympathy, he has spent many hours of each twenty-four inspiring the defenders of the front trenches, and if he does not know every soldier in his force, at least every soldier in the force believes he is known to his chief'.

In the many stories about him, Birdie is portrayed as a good bloke who understands the attitudes of his men and is prepared to bend the rules to accommodate them, especially those related to military rank, as in this favourite Birdie story.

Geneneral Birdwood is talking to an English staff officer outside the Australian Imperial Force headquarters in Horseferry Road, London. The staff officer is amazed and annoyed Australian soldiers passing by do not bother to salute the general. 'I say, why don't you make your men salute you?'

'What!' exclaims Birdwood. 'Do you think I want to start a brawl in the heart of London!'

And at Gallipoli:

Birdwood was nearing a dangerous gap in a sap on Gallipoli when the sentry called out: 'Duck, Birdie; you'd better ——— well duck!' 'What did you do?' asked the outraged generals to whom Birdwood told the story. 'Do? Why, I ——— well ducked!'

As well, there is the Gallipoli reinforcement who mistakes the general for a cook, again because he is not wearing his badges of rank.

A new reinforcement was going to Rest Gully when he got away from his track and, seeing a soldier studying a paper, went up to him and said: 'Can you tell me the way to my crowd?' The reinforcement has failed to recognise General Birdwood who replies 'You'd better go and ask the cook just there.'

'Oh, I beg your pardon,' answered the reinstoushment. 'I thought you were the cook.'

Birdwood maintained his good image with the diggers on the western front:

We were holding a nice, quiet sector of the line at le Touquet, when General Birdwood decided to pay our Brigade a visit. To me fell the job of conducting his party. On arrival at the reserve lines, Birdy decided to pay the 'Gas Alarm post' a visit. The sentry was a reinforcement, and failed to either salute Birdie or notice the party, so the General decided to have a little yarn, and the following dialogue took place:

Birdie: 'Do you know me, son?'

Dig: 'No. Don't want to!'

Birdie: 'Been in France long?'

Dig: 'Too blanky long.'

Birdie: 'Do you know that I am General Birdwood?'

Dig (very surprised): 'Go on! I 'ave heard of you. Shake hands!'

The brass hats nearly fainted, but to Birdie's everlasting credit let it be recorded that he shook hands heartily.

The piece of paper

A favourite Anzac yarn of both world wars is usually known as 'The Scrap' or 'The Piece of Paper'. In its World War I version it appeared in *The Anzac Records Gazette* of November 1915 in this form and under the title 'Anzacalities'.

The Australian soldier in a well-known hospital in Egypt developed a habit of picking up every bit of paper he could find. A Medical Board decided he was harmless and might be better for a trip to Australia. On the trip to Australia he still continued the practice and on arrival there he was again boarded and the Board decided he was too eccentric for active service. On receiving his discharge he looked at it closely and remarked with a dry smile. 'Thanks! That is the piece of paper I have been looking for.'

By 1942, the story had been updated and was much more elaborate, as in a version by Sergeant F. Oliver-Seakins that was published in a number of places, an indication of its popularity.

Sandy was a popular figure in his unit, always cheerful and high-spirited. But once, when he got back from leave, he told his mates he'd met a 'beaut Sheila' and was anxious to get out of the Army to marry her. As many others were similarly placed little notice was taken of Sandy when he 'got down in the dumps' occasionally.

One evening he was out with two friends taking a stroll when he saw a piece of paper on the ground ahead of him. He ran forward, picked it up, scrutinized it carefully, and threw it away again, sadly shaking his head. His mates asked him whether he'd expected to find a fiver, but he only said, 'It isn't what I'm looking for.'

As time went on Sandy became the talk of the section. Every time he saw a piece of paper he picked it up and looked at it carefully; but he always shook his head and threw it away, saying sadly, 'That's not what I'm looking for.'

It began to be rumoured that Sandy was 'troppo'. The orderly sergeant thought he might need a break from his usual routine, so he placed him on pioneer fatigue. But one of Sandy's new jobs was to empty the orderly room wastepaper basket.

His 'disease' now really manifested itself. He closely studied each piece of paper in every basket he emptied. And, as usual, the paper wasn't what he was looking for.

Everyone was now thoroughly worried about Sandy.

The climax came when the section was on parade for an inspection by some visiting brass. The Colonel was highly pleased with his tour and was just about to compliment the Major when Sandy stepped forward three paces, picked up a piece of paper that had floated down to the ground in front of him, looked at it sadly and then returned smartly to his place in the ranks.

Later, Sandy was paraded before the Major, who nonplussed at his behaviour, told the orderly sergeant to take him to the Medical Officer.

In the M.O.'s tent Sandy's first action was to pick up a couple of sheets of paper from the table and examine them, putting them back down with a shake of his head. The M.O. couldn't get much out of Sandy. All he would say was that he hadn't found what he was looking for.

'Acute neurosis.' Was the M.O.'s verdict. He recommended that Sandy be sent down to have his case examined by a medical board. This was arranged and Sandy went south.

In due course the board considered his case. Obviously acute neurosis. It was agreed that Sandy should be discharged medically unfit.

As the Officer at the G.D.D. [Genearl Details Depot] handed Sandy his discharge certificate, he remarked with a grin, for he'd heard all about Sandy's case. 'Hang on to THAT bit of paper, won't you!'

'By cripes I will!' said Sandy, laughing as he folded up the form and put it in his pocket. 'That's the bit of paper I've been looking for!'

Baldy becomes mobile

Those things that amused the diggers do not necessarily amuse everyone, though this story shows how the Anzacs dealt with the impositions of officialdom in a characteristically straightforward manner.

About the end of March, 1918, when the wilting flower of England's Fifth Army was doing a marathon for home and mother, pursued by the beastly Bosche, the heads broadcasted one hateful word throughout the A.I.F.

'Be Mobile!' was the official edict. Every five minutes, it seemed, some bird of brass-hat plumage would flutter in gasping as if he'd brought the news from Ghent. Then, he'd cast an eagle eye over the collective water-bottle and the blancoed bandolier, and swoop off to some other harassed unit twittering, 'Be Mobile!'

After the first few days the whole place came a hot-bed of mobility. Everyone from the boss to the last bandsman wore a mobile look. 'Are you mobile?' became a form of greeting. The very stew we ate seemed to have a mobile flavour. Such a positive nightmare did the word become that many a brave soldier shuddered at its sound.

After the first few days the only living soul in our unit that couldn't be quite called mobile was Baldy, the mule, whose fairy footsteps were usually guided by Blackie Crayton. Blackie himself was sufficiently mobile to pass muster. As a combination, however, he and Baldy delayed every 'mobile' exercise, and held up every 'mobile' route march.

'Can't you make the mule more mobile, Crayton?' the Sergeant-Major used to roar.

Late one night on the way up to Ypres Sector, Baldy who had been respectably mobile for the greater part of the day, suddenly became immobile. Baldy just stubbed his toes, so to speak, in the pave and stopped dead. Blackie was at his wit's end. A desperately cold night, another three or four kilometres to get to the prepared billets and a hot meal, and Baldy reneging!

For nearly two hours Blackie, wet through and finished, struggled—coaxing, bullying, blaspheming and getting madder every minute. His frantic efforts proving futile—the jibbing animal never budged an inch—Blackie went absolutely berserk.

'You bald faced atrocity!' he howled. 'I'll lay a shade of odds THIS'LL shift you, you ——— that's what you are!' With which solemn incantation he placed a couple of Mills' [small bombs] beneath the noble beast, and fled. By the time he reached safety, the bombs had made their presence felt, and Baldy shifted according to forecast.

The first person the fed-up Blackie met as he trudged along wearily into the village was our dear old friend and soul-mate, the Sergeant-Major.

'Where's that cranky mule?' he questioned. The almost hysterical Blackie stood silent for fully thirty seconds before he responded.

'Baldy?' queried Blackie in tense tones. 'Baldy? Baldy is mobile. Mobile at last. In fact, he's so blanky mobile that he'll be on the move from now till the Resurrection, pulling himself together and collecting his scattered remains. Baldy's gone to his long home. An' it's so darned long he'll never reach it. Yes! Take it from me, Baldy's more blinkin' mobile than any of us! Now, tell me where's the mobile cook-house?'

Characters

They come in all shapes and sizes, with many different names, from 'Happy Henry' to 'The Section Dope'. What they all have in common is the ability to raise a laugh, whether through their wit or their stupidity. Here are just a few of the many 'character' yarns that diggers have enjoyed telling one another.

Our prize Section Dope was trying to put the hard word on the Quarter Bloke for a tin of butter.

'But I gave you a large tin of butter the day before yesterday,' said the QM testily. 'You don't want to make it too hot!'

'You didn't give me a large tin of butter, it was a small tin.'

'You dopey cow, I gave you a large tin of butter and a small tin of axle grease.'

'Cripes! Then I've eaten the ruddy axle grease and put the butter on the axles!'

*

'Dopey' in our unit didn't seem to have any liking for soldiering, so one day I asked him why he had joined up.

'Well, you see, a cobber stole five pounds from me and ran away with my wife. There was nothing else to do but enlist.'

'That was certainly tough luck,' I sympathised.

'Yair, it was every penny I had.'

*

As soon as it became known in the battalion that Andy had been a kangaroo shooter before the commencement of war in 1914, a sergeant put it to him that he was the right man to do a bit of sniping. Andy declined without thanks.

'Why?' snarled the sergeant.

'I just don't like it, that's why. I've shot kangaroos, wallabies, dingoes and brumbies, an' I ain't goin' to finish up with men—at least, not sniped men, anyhow.'

The sergeant seethed, but Andy was adamant. Sniping a kangaroo, he maintained, was a different thing from sniping a man.

'Well,' blew up the sergeant, 'if you're THAT finicky, I'll go over and ask Fritz to hop!'

*

They called him Happy Henry. He was one of those grim humorous Australians who could no more resist joking about anything than he could resist accepting a cigarette. A friend remarked that his dial was hard enough to dent a railway pie at half a mile.

Happy Henry was well into the Somme scrap, and got out of it with a lump on each side of his head like young coconuts. He could hang his tin hat on either. He told the boys about it in the camp afterwards. He said:—'I'd just sent a Hun over the Never Never with the sunning end of me bayonet, when another Fritz weighin' about 'alf a ton swung the butt of his rifle against me block. Me head gave out a musical G. sharp, and as I made a smack at 'im I sez, 'If yer do that agen, cobber, I'll be rude.' I missed him, and he swung agen and got me a clout on the other side of the block. His rifle smashed to pieces and of course I fixed 'im then. Y'see that was where 'e made the mistake.'

'How mistake?' asked somebody.

'Well, he should 'ave lobbed me on the same place twice!'

*

Sandy was attached to our unit, 1 Div., 1st A.I.F. Like most diggers from the outback he had unorthodox ways of doing things. One day we were on parade for inspection by the Colonel. Sandy was in the front rank and was highly conspicuous by having several buttons of his tunic undone. When the Colonel reached him he stopped, bug-eyed, his pink face rapidly taking on a purplish hue. His hand shot out to point to the buttons left undone, Sandy seized the Colonel by the hand and nearly shook it off. The old boy glared at him. 'I don't know you, my man,' he roared.

'Sorry, mate,' said Sandy, 'I thought you was an old shearer bloke I knew out the back of bloody Bourke.'

*

The Australian platoon was under heavy Japanese frontal attack. The commander yelled out, 'Fire at will!'

'Cripes,' growled Chiller, 'if you can pick Will outa that mob, you're a better man than I am!'

*

'Yes, Nugget, I tell you it was cold,' said one of the 'Diamond Dinks,' [old hands] trying to impress an open-eyed 'reinstoushment' with his experiences of the winter on the Somme, 'as cold as the gaze of the Quarter Bloke when yer put the hard word on him for a new Aussie tunic! Struth! I tell you at Bazentin it freezed so hard that you couldn't blow a candle out! Y'ad ter knock the flame off with a stick!'

'The Unofficial History of the AIF'

Smith's Weekly began publication on 1 March 1919. It was a weekly Sydney broadsheet, the creation of its long-time editor Claude McKay and cabin boy turned millionaire Sir James Joynton Smith. From the beginning, the paper was aggressively nationalistic and very much on the side of the returned soldiers. It was quickly dubbed 'the diggers' Bible'. At first, the paper did very well. But by 1939 circulation had fallen to 80 000, though World War II led to a revival in which sales reached 300 000.

The paper's historian and one-time staffer, George Blaikie, wrote that '*Smith's*' created 'what was generally called "The *Smith's Weekly* Soldier". And there was a very curious phenomenon associated with this figure. It looked completely different when viewed from different angles'. One of these angles provided the classic view of the digger as: '. . . an undisciplined larrikin who would not button his tunic, delighted in insulting his officers and dodging his proper duties, and made a virtue out of going AWL [absent without leave] and resisting Military Police'.

Smith's encouraged the submission of 'pars' or paragraphs and 'gags' from its predominantly digger readers. These became a regular feature of the paper under the title 'The Unofficial History of the AIF'. The column ran most weeks throughout the 1920s, carrying a mix of personal experience stories, reminiscence and yarns. On 14 February 1925, for instance, the column carried the story of twin brothers who received exactly the same wound on the same day. The 28 March edition printed the yarn about the digger who was not worried about the dangers of trench warfare unless a shell had his regimental number on its base. A few days later the soldier was lucky to escape extinction as a 'dud' dropped near him. Upon examining the base of the defective shell the soldier discovered that it indeed bore his regimental number.

But the most popular story that *Smith's* ever published appeared under the heading 'The Most Amazing Story of the War'. For the readers of the newspaper, this yarn about the toughness of the digger was hilarious.

Here is told the amazing fact of a Digger who, to all intents and purposes, had passed into eternity; who returned from the brink of the grave into which he was being rolled. It is the closest thing to a resurrection from the dead in the 1942 years that have passed since the first Christmas.

It is related by a member of Smith's editorial staff who is an officer of the A.I.F. Names quoted are those who played parts in this real life drama, and are not fictitious.

THE MOST AMAZING STORY OF THE WAR!

Just before Christmas 1942, there wasn't any peace and goodwill round Sanananda [PNG, then New Guinea] way. There was mud, heat, mosquitoes, hate, and the strong sweet, smell of death.

'A' Company, Thirty-six Bn. Attached to the Seventh Division, A.I.F., had attacked an unsuspectedly strong Nip position just forward of Kessel's. A well-placed Woodpecker and two LMGs [machine guns] had driven our boys back with heavy casualties. Seven men were posted missing, and as the withdrawal had been for only a couple of hundred yards there was little hope for them.

Three days later a corporal of 'A' Company volunteered to make a lone patrol into the Nip lines to locate the Woodpecker and LMGs. He couldn't find them, but he returned with information that an Australian body was lying in a Jap slit trench under the corpses of two very High Nips. Accompanied by a stretcher bearer he went out and carried the body back to his own perimeter.

Padre N. G. Anderson, chaplain of the Thirty-Sixth Bn., formerly Presbyterian minister at Moruya, New South Wales, was asked to perform burial rites. He ordered his batman to prepare a grave inside the wire. The grave was almost ready when the Padre arrived. The body lay beside it. No dead man is a pleasant sight after the jungle heat and the flies has worked on him. The one beside the grave was unusually horrible. The head was swollen to almost twice normal size. The eyes, wide open, stared fixedly. The body, clad only in tattered green shirt, was thin as a wafer and grey as dawn light.

Padre Anderson felt under the shirt for the identity discs that should have been on the chest. There was none. Placing a hand under the hip, the Padre rolled the body on to its stomach. As he did so he had a queer sensation that all life had not gone out of it.

'Do you think this man is really dead?' he asked his batman who was busy digging.

'Looks as if you're going troppo, too, Padre,' the sweating batman commented.

Still the Padre was not satisfied. He sent for the battalion M.O., Captain W. J. Pullen. The doctor took one look at the grey still form and shook his head. However, he placed his stethoscope against his shirt.

'Good God,' he shouted, 'the heart's still beating.' Hurriedly the body was carried from the graveside to the company first aid post. After half an hour the soldier had been cleaned up and his main wound located—a bullet had entered his right ear and stopped at the base of his skull. He was given a few hours at most to live.

Nothing more could be done for him. A small group stood beside the stretcher discussing his identity. He certainly wasn't a member of 'A' Company. General opinion was that he was from Seventh Division Cavalry.

In the middle of the discussion a tiny voice squeaked, 'I'm one of you!'

Everyone spun around. The body still lay stiff and grey. The glazed eyes still stared into space, but the lips were moving very, very, slightly.

'What's your name?' asked the Padre.

'Gordon!'

That was the name of one of the 'A' Company men posted missing after the attack three days earlier.

'What's your number?'

The squeaky voice whispered an NX [AIF identification number] number. It was Gordon's number.

But Gordon had weighed more than thirteen stone, and this man wasn't more than eight. Several men from Gordon's Company were called in and also his company commander. All agreed the man was not Gordon. The voice squeaked out the nicknames of numerous members of 'A' company while the eyes still focused on the canvas roof of the tent.

'What happened to you?' the man was asked.

'I went in with the attack. Then I remember coming to consciousness with Nips tearing off my boots and pants. They ripped off my steel hat and hurt my head. I groaned and they bashed me with the helmet until I passed out again. The second time I came to I was alone and very thirsty. There was a Nip slit trench near by. I crawled to it hoping there was water in the bottom and fell in. I was so weak I couldn't get out. A 25-pounder barrage from our guns came over and shells fell around me. Then came a mortar barrage. Two Nips jumped into the trench on top of me. A mortar bomb hit the lip of the slit and killed them both. Their bodies saved me.'

'So you know where the machine guns are?'

'They were moved this morning.'

'In which direction were they taken?'

'How was my body lying when I was discovered?'

'Head north, feet south.'

'The guns were taken west. The Nips stepped across my slit trench from right to left.'

The voice stopped. For the first time the eyes closed. Obviously death was near. Next morning the Digger's heart was stronger then ever. He was moved back to an advanced dressing station where he was again placed to one side to die quietly. His heart beat even more strongly.

From the ADS he was sent back to a main dressing station where the bullet was removed from the base of his skull. Within a few days he was recovering rapidly, and soon after he was evacuated to the mainland.

Eighteen months later, in Martin Place, Sydney, Padre Anderson met the man he set out to bury on the Sanananda Trail. 'The body' was thirteen stone again and perfect in all respects except for a deafness in the right ear.

'Did you know I almost buried you?' asked the Padre.

'Know it! I heard every word you said to the gravedigger. I couldn't speak then but I wasn't worried. I only hoped you'd get it over quick. Then the things the flies put on me wouldn't worry me any more. Guess it was the merriest Christmas I ever had!'

Please Let Us Take Tobruk

During the siege of Tobruk in 1941, the 'Rats' were assailed with propaganda leaflets dropped from enemy planes. Addressed to 'Aussies', the sheets pointed out that Germany and her allies were closing in and that the 'offensive from Egypt to relieve you

[is] totally smashed'. The sheet went on to claim 'You cannot escape. Our dive bombers are waiting to sink your transports' and, finally 'SURRENDER!'.

The diggers thought the Germans had it all wrong. After finding a hygienic use for the propaganda sheets they wrote their own version of what the enemy should have said if they really wanted the Rats to surrender.

AUSSIES

We have been trying to get you out of your 'rat holes' for the past three months, and we're getting a bit fed up with it. Every one of your chaps we get costs us about ten, and it's getting a bit thick.

Do you think that's fair? Play the game, you cads! Come out and give yourselves up. The German beer is the best in the world, and we have millions of gallons of it here. And if you can't stand our Sauerkraut, we'll give you steak and eggs any time you want them.

We look after our prisoners very well, and every Aussie is supplied with a Batwoman; this is on the instructions of the great and farsighted Fuhrer, who hopes in time to improve the fighting quality of the German race.

Our prison camp is the most luxurious in the world—two-up schools every night, coursing every Wednesday, trots on Monday afternoons, and the gee-gees every Tuesday, Thursday and Saturday.

It's all yours, if you ....
PLEASE, PLEASE LET US TAKE TOBRUK

So famous were the Rats after the siege that they became the subjects of impersonation. This ditty displays the same resilient sense of humour.

In all the Aussie papers
That have chanced to pass my way,
It seems that every Digger
Returning home must say,
That he's a gun-scarred warrior
Who went through Greece and Crete
Who saw the show in Syria,
And braved the desert's heat.
They never missed a battle,
They were always in the ruck.
And there's not a man among them
Who wasn't in Tobruk.

Well, they can have the limelight,
Though some have got it free.
But if they're the veterans of Tobruk
THEN WHO THE HELL ARE WE?

Parable of the kit inspection

The Vietnam War generated its fair share of digger humour, including this exaggerated parody of a biblical parable.

And it came to pass, that there cometh one which bore on his shoulder, three stars, who spaketh; saying; 'Bring unto me the Sergeant Major.'

And there cometh one who bore on his arm a golden crown. Then he of the three stars saith unto him of the golden crown; 'Tomorrow at the ninth hour, parade before me one hundred men and all that is theirs.'

195

And the one of the golden crown answered, saying, 'Lord it is done.'

And behold! On the morrow, at the ninth hour, there did parade before him of the three stars, one hundred men, with all that they did have, as had been promised him. Then cometh others which bore on their shoulders two stars and yet others who bore one star. These were called 'Subbies', which being translated from the Latin meaneth 'Small Fry' or 'Little Potatoes'. Then he of the golden crown, standing before the one hundred men, cried out with a loud voice, and did cause them to become pillars of stone.

And behold! There cometh one which was called 'Quartermaster.' This man held great power, for he belonged to that tribe which said; 'These men must purchase from us.' Thus did they wax fat in the land! And, passing amongst one hundred men, he did say unto this man and unto that man; 'Where is this thing,' and 'Where is that thing.'

And they all had save one which was called. 'Spudus Murphy', and he lacked. Then he, the one which was called Quartermaster, saith unto him; 'Friend, where are thy drawers woollen long and thy boots ankle, pair of one?' And Spudus Murphy answered saying; 'Lord, on the third day of the week, I did thirst and had not the wherewithal to satisfy my thirst, for I had not received my reward. And I did take my drawers woollen long and my boots ankle pair of one, unto mine uncle of the tribe of "Love", and did say unto him "How many pieces of silver for these things?" And he saith unto me, "Seven" And I saith unto him; "Give to me that I may thirst not." And he did trade with me. Then I took the pieces of silver unto the abode of him that sold wine and did say unto him; "Give me to drink that I may thirst not."

And he gave me, and I knew no more until the fourth day of the week.'

Then he of the three stars waxed exceeding wrath, and calling two men. He placed one to the East, and one to the West of Spudus Murphy and, turning sharply on his left heel and right toe, he was led away and cast unto the prison.

And on the morrow, he was brought before one which bore on his shoulder a crown and a star, showing him to be above all men! This one was called CO, which, being translated, meaneth; 'Putter up of the wind.' And he saith unto Spudus Murphy; 'What are these things that I hear concerning thee? Sayest thou aught?'

Then Spudus Murphy related to him how that he had exchanged his drawers woollen long and his boots ankle pair of one, for silver for wine. Then he that was called CO, waxed exceeding wrath, and his anger was kindled against Spudus Murphy, and he saith unto him. 'Why has thou broken the laws which I have made? Knowest not that thou has sinned? Now because thou has done this thing, thou shalt be punished. Twenty and eight days shall thou labour.'

Then was Spudus Murphy led away to a place where he would hear the tick of the clock, but could not tell the passage of time. And the name of that place was 'The House of Glass.' And he was in that place twenty and eight days.

So my friends, be not as the one, but rather as the ninety and nine. Where thou thirsteth and has not the wherewithal to satisfy thy thirst, wait until the day of reward; then shall the joy be increased a thousand fold.

And now may the blessing of that great Saint, The Regimental Paymaster, be amongst you, now and always.

The Air Force wife

The trials and tribulations of the long-suffering air force wife were graphically described in this bittersweet account from the Vietnam War years.

An Air Force wife is mainly a girl. But there are times, such as when her husband is away and she is mowing the lawn or fixing a flat tyre on a youngster's bike, that she begins to suspect she is also a boy.

She usually comes in three sizes: petite, plump or pregnant. During the early years of her marriage it is often hard to determine which size is her normal one.

She has babies all over the world and measures time in terms of places as other women do in years. 'It was at Amberley that we all had the mumps . . . in Butterworth Dan was promoted.'

At least one of her babies was born or a posting was accomplished while she was alone. This causes her to suspect a secret pact between her husband and the Air Force providing for a man to be overseas or on temporary duty at such times as these.

An Air Force wife is international. She may be a Wagga farm girl, a South Australian nurse, a Victorian typist or Queensland meter maid. When discussing service problems they all speak the same language.

She can be a great actress. To heart broken children at parting time, she gives an Academy Award performance: 'Melbourne is going to be such fun! I hear they have Australian Rules Football and briquettes and trams!' But her heart is breaking with theirs. She wonders if this is worth the sacrifice.

An ideal Air Force wife has the patience of an angel, the flexibility of putty, the wisdom of a scholar and the stamina of a horse. If she dislikes money, it helps. She is sentimental, carrying her memories with her in an old footlocker.

One might say she is married to a bigamist, because she shares her husband with a demanding entity called 'duty'. When duty calls, she becomes no. 2 wife. Until she accepts this fact her life can be miserable.

She is above all a woman who married an airman who offered her the permanency of a gypsy, the miseries of loneliness, the frustration of conformity, and the security of love. Sitting on her packing boxes with squabbling children nearby, she is sometimes willing to chuck it all in until she hears that firm step and cheerful voice of the lug who gave her all this. Then she is happy to be . . . his Air Force wife.

Legends of Anzac

WAR IS A fertile field for the making of legends. In the case of Anzac, the potential for powerful stories is enhanced by the imprinting of Gallipoli, the western front, Tobruk, Kokoda and other events on the development of national identity. The character of legends is that they are told as true stories about events that could well have happened at a particular time and place. But usually they turn out to be, at the least, elaborate versions of more mundane events. The stories of these events, and sometimes of the characters taking part in them, are burnished through repetition in the succeeding years. But whether they contain a greater or lesser amount of historical truth, legends are powerful stories to which many people relate, emotionally as well as intellectually. They are told and retold, often gaining even greater appeal as they progress down the generations and their meanings become ever more valued. There are many legends of glory and gallantry, as well as mystery and mayhem, in the rich traditions of Anzac.

The Eureka sword

In 1854 the Irish-born Peter Lalor (pronounced 'Lawler') was elected leader of the disaffected miners on the Ballarat goldfields. The 'diggers' were protesting primarily against the amount of tax levied on them by the Victorian government and the often-brutal manner in which the police administered and collected the money. They also demanded political representation. After a series of violent incidents and mishandling of the situation by the authorities, the miners armed themselves, erected the famous wooden stockade at Ballarat and raised the Southern Cross flag. This armed act of treason was violently suppressed by police and military forces on the morning of 3 December 1854. Lalor barely escaped, in the process severly injuring his arm, which was amputated as a consequence. Thirteen rebels were tried for treason. All were acquitted. The Eureka Stockade was already a much-mythologised event by the time World War I began, and the story of Lalor's sword was well suited to the Gallipoli legend.

There are a number of conflicting accounts of the origins and ultimate fate of the sword. The most persistent version is that Peter Lalor carried the sword and even used it during the bloody defence of the Eureka Stockade. Greatly treasured by the Lalor family, the weapon was eventually passed to Captain Peter Joseph Lalor, grandson of the leader of the Eureka rebels and a professional soldier who led a group of 12th Division men at Gallipoli on the first day of the landings.

Lalor was a colourful and apparently impetuous character who had enlisted in the Royal Navy at an early age but subsequently deserted to join the French Foreign Legion. He had been involved in a South American revolution and eventually became a member of the Australian forces. Known in the AIF as 'Little Jimmy', Lalor carried his grandfather's sword with him as he and his men scrambled up the hills from the beach towards the areas known as Baby 700 and the Nek. Lalor was supposed to remain at the Nek, but when he did not hear from another party that had advanced further, he became impatient and decided to push on. He stood up to survey the scene, began to rouse his men to advance and was immediately killed by a Turkish bullet. A comrade picked up the sword but lost it later in the fighting. Another Australian soldier retrieved the sword and returned with it to the beach, where he handed it to a naval officer. It has never been seen since.

Considerable legendry has built up around these incidents and the whereabouts of the sword. The image that is most persistent, supported to some extent by a Turkish account of an Australian officer bearing a sword, is that Lalor died gallantly brandishing the sword as he called on his men to advance. This has certainly featured in media coverage of the story over the years. Where the sword ended up remains a mystery. There was a renewal of interest during and after World War II and at one point the official historian of the war, Charles Bean, published a claim that it might be in a Turkish museum.

To add to the confusion, there is also a story that another soldier carried Lalor's Eureka sword into an earlier battle far from Turkey. In the obituary of Captain Osborne O'Hara, an officer in the 2nd Royal Irish Fusiliers, published in the *Truth* newspaper in February 1915, is the tale of how the sword came into his family.

Captain O'Hara fell fighting with the self same sword with which the celebrated Peter Lalor fought and defended the famous Eureka Stockade during the great Miner's Rights' Riots at Ballarat in the early fifties. This sword was a beautiful Damascene blade as light as a feather, as keen as a razor, whose swish was like a soldier's song when swung by a strong arm. How Peter Lalor's sword came into the possession of the O'Hara family and in the death grip of the young captain as he fell fighting at the front, is no mystery, but a story reading like a romance.

Either before or soon after young Osborne O'Hara was born, his father, the Doctor, had a pressing professional call to operate for cancer on a poor woman, who, so it subsequently turned out, was unable to pay the fee. The operation was so far successful as to relieve her from pain and prolong the patient's life. She was grateful but could not pay the fee, and consequently was not asked to do so. But in her gratitude she asked Dr O'Hara to accept an old sword, hanging on the wall, which he had been admiring. The woman told the doctor that the sword was the identical sword with which Peter Lalor had fought at the Eureka Stockade fifty years before. She explained how the sword had come into her possession, traced its ownership to Peter Lalor and absolutely established its identity as his own once beloved blade.

Recent historical research has also thrown up further possible trails through which the Eureka sword—or swords—might have travelled from the Ballarat battlefield to the battlefields of World War I. The same research has also confirmed that, despite the robust life of the legend of Peter Lalor's Eureka sword, there is no evidence that he actually carried it, or any other sword, at the Eureka Stockade. But even if 'Little Jimmy' Lalor's sword was not wielded by his grandfather at that momentous event, the persistent belief that it was highlights the need for folklore to link two important events in Australian history.

The lost submarine

When war between Britain and Germany was declared in August 1914, Australian ships were tasked with attacking Germany's East Asiatic Cruiser Squadron under the command of Vice-Admiral Count von Spee. The submarines *AE1* and *AE2*, with their parent ship *Upolo*, joined an Australian flotilla near Rabaul, New Britain (then the main island of what was German New Guinea) as part of the hunt for the enemy ships and the capture of Rabaul and the Bita Paka radio station. On 14 September, *AE1* and *Parramatta* were patrolling together near Cape Gazelle in case von Spee's cruisers appeared. The ship and the submarine—called a 'devil fish' by the local indigenous people—were exchanging visual signals until shortly before *AE1* was last seen, just before 3.30 pm. *Parramatta* returned to *AE1*'s last known position but did not sight the submarine. Assuming that *AE1* was returning to harbour as planned, *Parramatta* made for Herbertshöhe, anchoring at 7 pm. An hour later *AE1* had still not returned and Australian Fleet Commander Rear Admiral Patey ordered a search for the missing submarine. *Encounter*, *Parramatta*, *Warego* and *Yarra* spent the next two days combing the area. But *AE1* was not found, nor was any wreckage. What had happened?

Lieutenant Stoker, commander of *AE2*, the lost submarine's sister boat, was asked for his expert opinion. His speculations were contained in a report he made from Suva, Fiji, a month later. The possibility of enemy attack was dismissed, as was a mechanical breakdown that may have led to her being swept away. Stoker considered that the most likely causes of her disappearance were that *AE1* had either suffered a catastrophic mechanical failure while submerged or been wrecked on one of the many treacherous reefs in the area.

In his diary, A. B. Wheat, a sailor aboard *AE2*, recorded that 'The cause of her disappearance is still a mystery' and also speculated along the same lines as Stoker's official report. Wheat, and probably his fellow crewmen, thought that *AE1* might have been sunk by an old tug armed with a five-barrelled Nordenfelt gun. When the burnt-out and beached wreckage of this German vessel was discovered it was thought that she might have surprised *AE1*, which had no deck gun. The possibility of a mine was discounted after diligent sweeping of the area. Wheat included the suggestion that *AE1* may have overtrimmed [unbalanced buoyancy] after having one of her motors disabled—'that is had not buoyancy enough with her one remaining motor to give complete control and finally she had become unmanageable and sank'. Given the troubled trimming procedures of *AE1* in England and *AE2*'s later stability problems in the Dardanelles, this is perhaps the most likely explanation for the loss of Australia's first submarine. The failure of the search to reveal anything of *AE1*'s fate hit the officers and men of *AE2* especially hard. Wheat wrote that it 'cast a great gloom over us as we all had friends who had gone and we were the only two submarines in Southern Waters'. The dedication that prefaces his diary reads, in part:

To the memory of our sister ship *AE1*, and her crew, Lost September 14th, 1914 in St. Georges Channel, between German New Guinea and New Ireland.

We took the first patrol on the 13th, they took the second next day. We came back, they didn't. The path of our duty became the high-way of mystery for they never came back. They lie coffined in the deep, keeping their silent watch at Australia's North Passage, heroes all.

Similar speculations appeared in the Australian press. Revealing the impact that the loss of *AE1* produced, the *Sydney Morning Herald* of 21 September 1914 contained a lengthy account, together with the official statement on the incident. The prime minister's sympathies were extended and there were sections on the crew and officers. Newspapers carried photographs of *AE1* titled 'The Lost Australian Submarine' and reprinted the expressions of sympathy and condolence from near and far, including those from New Zealand and from the commanders in chief of the East Indies and China. Also included was the official statement from the Navy Board, noting that '... although our men did not fall by the hand of the enemy, they fell on active service, and in defence of their Empire, and their names will be enshrined with those of heroes'. There were messages of sympathy from the king and queen and from Winston Churchill in his role of first lord of the admiralty. The Royal Australian Navy produced a black-edged memorial booklet and special payments and arrangements were made for the wives and families of the officers and crew. A number of poems were composed in commemoration of the tragedy.

These expressions of grief and remembrance echoed the public shock at the loss of *AE1*, along with the concern in official circles. But the fate of the submarine and her crew would soon be forgotten by most as the war unfolded, bringing news of even greater tragedies. The lost submarine soon faded from the pages of the newspapers, and *AE1*'s sister submarine sailed to the Mediterranean. *AE2* became the first to 'force the Dardanelles', penetrating the Narrows section of the Dardanelles and entering the Sea of Marmara. In the mounting body count of World War I, the relatively minor disaster of *AE1* in a colonial sideshow to the main theatres of war was soon forgotten by the public and by the government. It was not until the 1970s that John Foster of the Royal Australian Navy initiated an investigation into the fate of *AE1*. The search continues today.

The vanished battalion

In December 1915, the Gallipoli commander General Sir Ian Hamilton penned a dispatch on a mysterious battlefront incident that had taken place a few months earlier.

The 1/5th. Norfolk were on the right of the line and found themselves for a moment less strongly opposed than the rest of the brigade. Against the yielding forces of the enemy Colonel Sir H. Beauchamp, a bold, self-confident officer, eagerly pressed forward, followed by the best part of the battalion. The fighting grew hotter, and the ground became more wooded and broken. At this stage many men were wounded, or grew exhausted with thirst. These found their way back to camp during the night. But the Colonel, with sixteen officers and 250 men, still kept pushing on, driving the enemy before them . . . Nothing more was ever seen or heard of any of them. They charged into the forest and were lost to sight or sound. Not one of them ever came back.

Hamilton's sober and professional account of this incident was only in stark contrast to a much more sensational version of the mystery in which the missing Norfolks disappeared into an ominous cloud rather than a 'forest'.

The 1/5th Norfolks were a British regiment, in part composed of raw recruits from the Sandringham Royal Estate, who were known colloquially as 'the Sandringham Pals'. Their unaccountable disappearance was the subject of more than usual concern. In the absence of hard information about their fate, a legend developed that had a good deal in common with other stories of vanished battalions on the western front. These stories usually involved the appearance of a mysterious cloud or mist over the battlefield, into which marched the doomed regiment or other unit, never to be heard of again. In the Gallipoli incident a group of New Zealand sappers claimed to have seen on 21 August (not 12 August):

Six or eight 'loaf of bread' shaped clouds—all shaped exactly alike, which were hovering over Hill 60. It was noticed that in spite of a four or five mile an hour breeze from the south, these clouds did not alter their position . . . Also stationary and resting on the ground right underneath this group of clouds was a similar cloud in shape, measuring about 800 feet in length, 220 feet in height, and 200 feet in width. This cloud was absolutely dense, solid-looking in structure, and positioned about 14 to 18 chains from the fighting in the British-held territory . . .

According to this account, a British unit said to have been the 1/4th (not the 1/5th) Norfolks, 'had marched straight into it, with no hesitation, but no-one ever came back out'. After an hour or so the unit had disappeared into the large ground-level cloud, and three-quarters of an hour later the cloud rose to the level of the others and they drifted northwards until 'they had all disappeared from view'.

The signatories to this account were New Zealander Frederick Reichardt and two other Anzacs. The discrepancies between the dates and correct designation of the Norfolks unit, together with the impossibility of the New Zealanders seeing what was happening four miles (6.5 kilometres) from their position at the time, strongly suggests that the event described was a battlefield delusion. Similar circumstances gave rise to such beliefs as the Angels of Mons, the Comrade in White and other apparitions supposedly experienced by battle-stressed men on the western front. However, it was close enough to what had actually happened to the Norfolks to generate the legend of the vanished battalion.

What did happen to the 1/5th Norfolks? In September 1919 a mass grave was discovered on the Anafarta Plain, as reported by the commander of the Gallipoli Graves Registration Unit.

We have found the 5th Norfolks—there were 180 in all; 122 Norfolk and a few Hants and Suffolks with 2/4th Cheshires. We could only identify two—Privates Barnaby and Cotter. They were scattered over an area of about one square mile, at a distance of at least 800 yards behind the Turkish front line. Many of them had evidently been killed in a farm, as a local Turk, who owns the place, told us that when he came back he found the farm covered with the decomposing bodies of British soldiers which he threw into a small ravine. The whole thing quite bears out the original theory that they did not go very far on, but got mopped up one by one, all except the ones who got into the farm.

The bodies included their colonel. There remains a lingering suspicion that the men were executed. Whether that is true or not, the nearly 300 officers and men of the 1/5th Norfolks had advanced well past their own front lines and deep into enemy territory. They were tired, in unfamiliar terrain and, it seems, not well led. A bayonet charge failed, they were surrounded and then felled by machine gun and sniper fire. Those who apparently made it to the farmhouse also died. Fourteen survivors were taken captive by the Turks, though the legend takes no account of this.

The two men with donkeys

The story of Simpson and his donkey has become part of the legend of Anzac. Once taught to every child at school, it is the subject of frequent recollection in print and in the media, and is commemorated in many other ways, including in the well-known statue at the Australian War Memorial in Canberra. According to most accounts, John Simpson Kirkpatrick, an Englishman serving with the AIF, continually took one or more donkeys up to the firing lines at Gallipoli and brought back wounded soldiers for medical treatment, at great personal risk. One morning, 'Simpson' as he was known, was winding his way towards the firing line when a cook called out to him to come and get some breakfast. 'I'll be back soon; keep it hot for me', he is said to have replied. That morning he was killed by enemy fire and the enduring legend of selfless courage and sacrifice was born, as outlined in one of the early accounts of the story.

We have had numerous inquiries for information with regard to Private John Simpson, 'The Man with the Donkey' as he is perhaps better known, and mainly owing to the courtesy of a soldier who was a member of his section at Gallipoli, we are able to throw a little additional light on the career of that hero.

In the first place, it has since been gleaned his full name was Private John Simpson Kirkpatrick, though he dropped the latter name on enlisting. He was born in South Shields, England 22 or 23 years ago and of latter years was the sole support of a widowed mother. A tall, well-set, finely figured, clean-cut young Englishman, he took to the sea as a career, and about five or six years ago came out here and joined one of the interstate vessels as a fireman, and in that capacity he travelled from port to port on the Australian coast, often touching Fremantle. In fact, of later years he is said to have been keeping company with a Fremantle girl, who saw him off when he left these shores on the Empire's errand, the goal of which was death. But we are beginning to anticipate.

On the outbreak of war, Simpson, to give him his better-known name, was still a fireman (we understand on the *Kooringa*) and he quickly heard the call and enlisted at Blackboy. Needless almost to say, this cheery, brawny, presentable young fellow was cordially welcomed, and on accepting him for the À.M.C. Captain M'Whae made an unconscious prophecy in remarking. 'You're just the man we want.' He was.

Simpson duly went through his training and participated in that march through Perth of the original first contingent, and may have been noticed by onlookers as carrying a possum, the mascot of his corps. With the men he was always popular, he sang a good song, possessed a cheery disposition and the ideal soldier spirit.

He was with the A.M.C. in the landing that electrified the world, and was busy during the first day assisting in the tending of the wounded. Then he was missed, and for a couple of days could not be found. About the Wednesday they came across him. He had been about his country's business. Then for the first time they beheld him in his role of 'The Man with the Donkey.'

It was soon found that he was accomplishing splendid work with the little animal he had picked up in conveying the wounded men to the base from difficult places where stretcher bearers could not go. His new military position was unorthodox, 'not on the strength' to use a military term. But the authorities were wise enough to see that he was achieving great things, and they let him be. 'The Man with the Donkey' he thereafter became, and 'Simmo,' as he was affectionately nick-named, and 'Murphy' the wiry little donkey with its eternal burden of wounded men, became familiar figures on the peninsula. Those who knew not his name, or whence he came, knew 'The Man with the Donkey,' and many a stricken soldier blessed the pair with his fevered lips.

One day the donkey walked down to the familiar goal, the dressing-station, with a wounded man as burden but otherwise alone. Its master was not in sight. A search was made, and the hero was found dead—shot through the heart by a stray bullet. As he would have wished to die he passed away, discharging the self-appointed duty he had for weeks carried out so faithfully. This was on May 19 but for many a long day afterwards in the dug-out and in the trench was the name of 'The Man with the Donkey' on Australian lips.

The donkey was taken and cared for by an Indian officer, and up to when our informant left Gallipoli it was still alive, its new master declaring that he would not part with it on any account. Whether the animal (there is talk of a movement to bring it back to Australia) was unavoidably slaughtered with the other dumb servants in the evacuation, or taken off as a special mark of affection, it is hard to say.

And Simpson? He was buried on the evening of May 19, and a roughly carven cross erected over his grave with the simple but sufficient inscription: 'Private John Simpson—The Man with the Donkey.' And so he sleeps, in desolate Gallipoli.

There was considerable agitation for a decoration for poor Simpson, but for some reason still unexplained it never materialised. 'If ever one deserved recognition, he did,' is the general verdict of those who knew the man and could judge of what he had done.

The story of Simpson and his noble sacrifice was immediately popular in Australia. A Mr Frank F. Keon of Melbourne sent a newspaper clipping about Simpson to Simpson's mother in England. Mrs Kirkpatrick wrote back in due course.

Dear Sir—Thank you very much for the cutting that you sent me about the grand work my dear beloved son has done in Gallipoli. I should have written before now, but I have been so poorly and broken-hearted about him that I have not been able to answer to all the kind friends that sent me their sympathy, so that I hope you will excuse me for not answering your kind letter sooner. I am sending you the cutting of our Shields daily, and you will see what a tribute his officer, Captain Fry, gives him. Now, sir, hoping that you will let all my son's friends in Melbourne know that John Simpson Kirkpatrick, that sailed in the s.s. *Kooringa* for two and a half years, is the donkey-man of Anzac, and tell the Australians from me, his mother, that my heart is bursting with sorrow and with pride to know that my beloved son, and the light of my life, died with the brave Australians. Now, sir, I can say no more at present, only that I have lost one of the best and most faithful sons that a mother ever had. Thanking you again for your kindness, I remain, your [sic] truly.

Sarah Simpson Kirkpatrick.

But Simpson was not the only man using donkeys to rescue the wounded at Gallipoli. After he was killed, the donkeys and their dangerous task were taken over by a New Zealander named Dick Henderson. And it was Henderson who actually appeared in the most famous photograph of 'Simpson' and his donkey, due to a mistake in the editing of the original editions of the official history of the war. This was not corrected until many years later in subsequent editions of the history. Henderson was luckier than Simpson and survived the war. He had apparently been well aware of the mistaken identities in the photograph but had chosen not to reveal the truth until the 1950s when, by then blind and ageing, he felt the need to 'clear the story up' so the mistake could be righted.

There have been many calls over the years for Simpson to receive a posthumous Victoria Cross, beginning with recommendations from serving officers who witnessed the man and his donkeys at work. There was even an attempt to have him sainted. To date, though, these efforts have not met with official approval, perhaps because of the difficulty in deciding which of the two 'Simpsons'—and probably others—was the bravest.

Also full of controversy and rumour is the story of where Simpson's donkey came from, and whether or not the animal was killed or managed to escape Gallipoli with the evacuating troops. As usual, there are various versions. A popular one is that the beast was the property of a Colonel Pope, commander of the 16th Battalion, AIF. Another is that it was a member of Pope's battalion, one T. Gorman, who should have the credit. Most stories agree that the donkey was obtained at Lemnos.

Did the donkey die when Simpson was killed? Possibly, though some said that the donkey led rescuers to Simpson's body, surviving to the end of the campaign to be taken off Gallipoli with the troops. In some strands of this tale, the donkey died aboard ship and was buried at sea. There was another claim that 'Murphy' was rescued by an Indian soldier. There was also a story that, like many supposedly deceased folk heroes, Murphy was alive and well in another place, in this case somewhere behind the lines at Abbeville, France. As a newspaper article recollecting the events and rumours put it in 1936, the donkey was 'one of the many dumb heroes of the Great War'.

Murphy's daughter

A further element of the story of Simpson and the donkey involves 'Jenny', the offspring of Murphy and another Gallipoli donkey also known as 'Jenny'. F. C. Dunstan of B Depot, 6th AASC wrote about young Jenny in *The Anzac Book*.

For the delightful diversion which little Jenny, with her frolics and gambols, provided for the A.S.C.'s when they really had a moment to spare another medium will have to be sought. Though of short duration, her life appeared a charmed one whilst it lasted. Her freedom of action was the envy of every soldier along the beach. Her disregard for the enemy's bullets and shells commanded our unbounded admiration. But whether her immunity for six months was due to the kindness of the Turks or their bad shooting, or her own good judgment, who can say?

Jenny's origin is enveloped in some obscurity; but it is said that with her parents, Murphy of Red Cross fame and Jenny Senior, she toddled into our lines when quite a mite; and, once having crossed over the border into civilization, the three emphatically refused to return whilst the objectionable Hun element obtained in their native country.

Jenny the younger was no mere mystic mascot for the humouring of an especially created superstition. Her congenial company and high spirits, her affectionate ways and equable temperament, were the factors which gained for her the obvious rank of 'Camp Pet.' Her friendly regular visits will be missed, and the picture of her patrician head and dark-brown shaggy winter's coat. Her refined voice was music compared with the common 'hee-haw' which characterizes her kind, or the peremptory foghorn of the sergeant-major.

But now she is no more. Our sorrow is immeasurable. The mother never left the babe whilst it suffered excruciating agony through a deadly shrapnel pellet. Skilful, indefatigable attention, invincible iodine, proved futile. Jenny Senior is grief-stricken, and now lies upon the neat little grave in which her infant was placed by the big Australian playmates who now mourn their irreparable loss.

The souvenir king

Souveniring—also known as 'ratting'—was a popular pastime of Australian troops. It involved obtaining items of enemy equipment—clothing, weaponry, medals or anything else that might be worth a few bob. Whether these items were obtained from Germans after they no longer had a need for them or were 'liberated' from prisoners was of no consequence. Possession, as they say, was nine points of the law.

The Anzacs were not the only troops to souvenir all manner of items from the field of battle, but they were noted exponents of the art, as suggested in a couple of digger yarns.

On the Western Front, a sergeant halted the enormous Private Smith, who was wearing a spiked German helmet.

'Who gave you permission to wear German issue?' he asked.

'Please, sergeant', said Private Smith, 'don't make me give this lid up; I had to kill seven Germans to get my size.'

The sergeant looked at Private Smith's feet. 'If you ever lose your boots,' he said, 'the flamin' war's over.'

And one about the enthusiastic war photographer:

It is well known to most front line Diggers that the Aussie official photographer was one of the gamest men in the war. One day he was taking the usual risks, oblivious of all considerations but that of getting a good picture. A purposeful Digger was seen stalking him from shell-hole to shell-hole.

'What in the cell yer doing, Ginger?' yelled a cobber.

'Oh, it's all right. I'm just waiting for this photo bloke to get knocked. I want to souvenir his camera!'

The story of the colourful character who became known as 'the souvenir king' is full of folklore as much as fact. John Hines, known as 'Barney', was born in Liverpool in 1873. After many years of roughing it around the world he ended up in Australia, enlisting in the AIF in 1915 and becoming a member of the 45th Battalion. On the western front he proved to be, like so many other 'bad characters', as good at soldiering as he was bad at staying sober, obeying orders and otherwise knuckling down to military discipline. In addition to his apparent fearlessness and talent for taking large numbers of prisoners, Barney had a very special ability with souvenirs.

So efficient was Barney at obtaining his trophies that he was dubbed 'the souvenir king'. It was not only the number and range of items that Barney managed to filch from enemy sources, or elsewhere, that was impressive, but also their occasional oddity or extravagance. On one occasion he souvenired a grandfather clock; on another he added a full barrel of English beer to his stocks.

To be fair, he was far from being the only collector of questionable mementos in the AIF or any other army. It was the publication of an evocative photograph, taken by Frank Hurley, of Barney sitting with a pile of his keepsakes that provided him with a raffish celebrity around which grew quite a few legends. The most widespread of these is the most unlikely tale that when the German head of state, Kaiser Wilhelm, heard of Barney's looting, he placed a price on his head, encouraging German troops to hunt down the souvenir king. His notorious reputation for unhappy dealings with authority also generated the story that he was once arrested by British Military Police but caused them so much trouble that he was soon handed back to his unit. His battlefield bravery led to the folk belief that he had killed more German soldiers than any other member of the AIF.

Barney was wounded on several occasions and was given a medical discharge in 1916. But he re-enlisted and went back to fight and souvenir for another year or so until he was again discharged for health reasons in 1918. He returned to Australia where he set up house in a humpy on the fringes of Sydney, eking out a living through various forms of manual and itinerant labour and, of course, selling souvenirs. It is said that he took the train into the suburbs each week to deliver a sack of vegetables to ex-soldiers in the repatriation hospital. Occasional republication of the famous photograph briefly revived his notoriety from time to time. When war again broke out in 1939, Barney tried to enlist but was rejected due to his age. He died in 1958.

The crucified soldier

One especially potent legend of the Great War is best known in its Canadian version. But the story also circulated among British and Allied forces, with the alleged victim being a British officer or an Anzac.

Canadian troops had been training in England from October 1914, arriving in France the following February. By May a disturbing new rumour was spreading through the trenches. The *Times* of 10 May 1915 ran the first press report of the story, which claimed that a group of Canadians wounded in the fighting near Ypres had come across one of their officers who had been literally crucified.

'He had been pinned to a wall by bayonets thrust through his hands and feet, another bayonet had been driven through his throat and, finally, he had been riddled with bullets.'

A similar horrific tale was picked up by the Canadian press and retailed in a number of versions, and stories of crucified Canadians, as well as British and Australian troops, continued throughout the war. There were questions in the British Parliament, some street riots and numerous official and unofficial attempts to verify the stories. But they never were proven, although the belief that the event—or something like it—had occurred was certainly strong among Canadian troops at the front and also among many on the home front. It has been suggested that the story was a propaganda piece developed by the Allies in response to the German sinking of the liner *Lusitania* on 7 May 1915. Regardless of its origins—and there were similar stories in circulation before April 1915, including allegedly on Gallipoli—the story has never gone away, with a recent television documentary attempting to verify it.

As with all such rumours and legends, details will vary. There is also a tendency for various stories to become mixed up in their telling and retelling. In this case, it may be that the actual crucifixion myth became tangled up with another tale in which a soldier is discovered bound across a wagon wheel or stakes in a crucifixion-like position. Known as 'Field Punishment No. 1', this unpleasant form of discipline was practised in the British and some other armies and was known to troops colloquially as 'crucifixion'. It could be incurred even for minor offences. Field punishment involved the unlucky soldier attending parades in a full pack, after which the pack was taken off and the luckless victim was trussed up across a wagon-wheel with fetters or handcuffs for an hour in the morning and an hour in the afternoon. This treatment went on for as many days as the inflicting officer determined, up to twenty-eight days in the field. If sentenced by a court martial it was possible for 'No. 1' to be carried out for up to ninety days. The soldier who suffered 'crucifixion' was also given hard labour and lost pay.

New Zealand conscientious objector Archibald Baxter experienced 'No. 1' in Belgium at the hands of a New Zealand sergeant at a prison compound called 'Mud Farm'. Baxter was bound to stakes rather than a wheel and, according to his account, for a good deal longer than the regulation two hours.

He took me over to the poles, which were willow stumps, six to eight inches in diameter and twice the height of a man, and placed me against one of them. It was inclined forward out of perpendicular. Almost always afterwards he picked the same one for me. I stood with my back to it and he tied me to it by the ankles, knees and wrists. He was an expert at the job, and he knew how to pull and strain at the ropes till they cut into the flesh and completely stopped the circulation. When I was taken off my hands were always black with congested blood. My hands were taken round behind the pole, tied together and pulled well up it, straining and cramping the muscles and forcing them into an unnatural position. Most knots will slacken a little after a time. His never did. The slope of the post brought me into a hanging position, causing a large part of my weight to come on my arms, and I could get no proper grip with my feet on the ground, as it was worn away round the pole and my toes were consequently much lower than my heels. I was strained so tightly up against the post that I was unable to move body or limbs a fraction of an inch. Earlier in the war, men undergoing this form of punishment were tied with their arms outstretched. Hence the name of crucifixion. Later, they were more often tied to a single upright, probably to avoid the likeness to a cross. But the name stuck.

A few minutes after the sergeant had left me, I began to think of the length of my sentence and it rose up before me like a mountain. The pain grew steadily worse until by the end of half-an-hour it seemed absolutely unendurable. Between my set teeth I said: 'Oh God, this is too much. I can't bear it.' But I could not allow myself the relief of groaning as I did not want to give the guards the satisfaction of hearing me. The mental effect was almost as frightful as the physical. I felt I was going mad. That I should be stuck up on a pole suffering this frightful torture, a human scarecrow for men to stare at and wonder at, seemed part of some impossible nightmare that could not continue. At the very worst strength came to me and I knew I would not surrender. The battle was won, and though the suffering increased rather than decreased as the days wore on, I never had to fight it again . . .

Towards the end of the afternoon, in the small corner which was visible to me of the enclosure on the other side of the road, heads began to appear and disappear with great rapidity and much blowing of whistles and roars of 'Double, double!' resounded from the same quarter. After some time the sergeant came over and released me. I set out to walk to the tent without waiting, as I afterwards learned to, for the slow and painful return of the circulation to my numbed limbs, and immediately fell. I struggled on again, somehow and, stumbling and falling, managed to make my way to the tent . . .

A number of Anzac stories tell of a group of Australians and/ or New Zealanders who come across such a scene and are so horrified by its cruelty that they release the victim from his bonds and otherwise take matters into their own hands. One account appears in Aubrey Wade's 1936 memoir, *The War of the Guns*.

Close by the road where the crucifixion took place there ran a narrow road which led to a stream where it was usual for all the artillery in the area to water their horses. At evening stable-time the Australians rode through with their animals on their way to water, and it so happened on the third day of the wheel torture that the victim had been strung up on a wagon in full view of the road, which was an oversight, no doubt, on the part of the sergeant major.

The Aussies, coming along at the trot, pulled up dead and stared in blank amazement. They simply could not understand it. The corporal who appeared to be in charge of them (for so much as they were ever in anyone's charge) dismounted, handed over his horse and strode across to the scene of punishment while all of us watched him with the keenest anticipation. Then the Aussie spoke: 'Who in the hell's name tied you up like this, digger?' And without waiting for a reply he cut through the new brown straps with his jack-knife, releasing the prisoner who stood looking dazedly, while the guard discreetly found something urgently waiting to be done at the guard-room. 'Who tied you up, digger?' came a chorus from the watching Australians. 'Show us the b——d.' I prayed for the appearance of the sergeant-major. But no sergeant-major came. The corporal remounted. 'We'll be here again tomorrow,' he called, and with that he led his grinning troop away . . .

The next day, to the minute, the process was repeated. Again the victim was released in a jiffy by the Aussies, four more brand-new straps were ruined and the sergeant-major hid himself in fear of his life. But the crucifixion was not called off; the next afternoon the prisoner was led out and strapped tight, and we gleefully awaited the appearance of the Australians. This time they were a little later than usual, but they came right enough just as the sergeant-major emerged from the field in which the tents lay. He walked right into them before realizing that they were companions of the corporal who was busily engaged in cutting gun-straps to ribbons. Pushing between their horses he yelled at the corporal.

'Hello, b——d,' said the corporal pleasantly, looking round. 'Come down to watch the fun?' he continued, in a soft drawl which infuriated the sergeant-major. His hand flew to the riding crop tucked under his arm, but the Australian gazed at him steadily and contemptuously. The other rider drew closer. Then the corporal went up to the sergeant-major and told him that for two pins, more or less, he'd tie him to the tails of their horses and gallop him over half France. And for tying a poor digger up like that he ought to be strung up by an extremely susceptible part of his anatomy and flogged to death for a b——d. And every time they came that way they'd cut the prisoner down, and then they'd think about cutting the sergeant-major's throat. The rescuers formed a ring of horses round the two protagonists so that the sergeant-major should not miss one word for the good of his soul. It was a great day.

The walers

The waler is a type of horse bred for Australian conditions. It is a hardy animal with great stamina and can travel for considerable distance on little food and water. These characteristics made the waler valuable as a working horse in the bush and also as a mount for the Australian Light Horse during World War I, where it was well suited to the climate and terrain of Palestine and the Sinai Desert and to bearing the considerable weight of a fully equipped light horseman. The horses served with success and gallantry, winning the admiration and praise of many of the British cavalry who on several occasions observed them performing impressive feats of endurance and strength. One fabled performance was by Major Shanahan's difficult mount, known as 'Bill the Bastard'. Shanahan, an officer of the 2nd Light Horse Regiment, found four unhorsed Australians surrounded by Turks, and Bill carried all five men to safety through over a kilometre of soft sand. Such actions added to the reputation of the walers and also to the extensive mystique of the Light Horse units. When the war ended it is said that many light horsemen shot their beloved horses rather than see them left behind. Although historians can find little evidence, this belief persists.

There were roughly 10 000 horses—not all walers—remaining among the Australian forces in Syria, Egypt and Palestine when the war ended in November 1918. The cost of returning these beasts to Australia, together with the quarantine risks they would pose, meant that another solution was needed. Some were reassigned, some were sold. Those that were unhealthy or aged—between 2000 and 3000 horses (estimates vary)—were destroyed under veterinary supervision. Although the procedures for the disposal of the army horses were as humane and well organised as possible under the circumstances, many diggers who had served in the Middle East, light horsemen in particular, strongly resented what happened to their loyal mounts.

'The Horses Stay Behind', a poem published just after the war by journalist and soldier Oliver Hogue, who wrote under the pen name of 'Trooper Bluegum', was probably the most important initial inspiration for the notion that light horsemen shot their horses.

I don't think I could stand the thought of my old fancy hack
Just crawling around old Cairo with a Gyppo on his back.
Perhaps some English tourist out in Palestine may find
My broken-hearted waler with a wooden plough behind.
No: I think I'd better shoot him and tell a little lie
'He floundered in a wombat hole and then lay down to die.'
Maybe I'll get court-martialled; but I'm damned if I'm inclined
To go back to Australia and leave my horse behind.

Of the 136 000 horses used by Australian forces during World War I, only one returned home, 'Sandy', the mount of General Sir William Bridges. The general was killed on Gallipoli and Sandy was taken into army veterinary care and reposted to Egypt, France and finally back to England. Here the horse was quarantined for three months, found to be free of disease and shipped back to Australia in September–November 1919. He spent the rest of his days grazing at the Central Remount Depot in Maribyrnong, Victoria. In 1923 he was put down due to age and illness. His head was mounted and became a part of the collection of the Australian War Memorial. The head was displayed at the Memorial for many years as the only horse to return, and this perhaps contributed to the belief—although Sandy was not a waler—that these horses had indeed been shot by their riders. Regardless of the historical reality, the story has a firm hold on the Australian imagination. Together with the Light Horse units, the waler remains a powerfully romantic symbol of national identity and wartime pride.

ANZAC to Anzac

As most things connected with Anzac have more than one story attached to them, it would be surprising if the word itself was not the subject of a few. According to one of these tales, the abbreviation was chosen by General Birdwood, or 'Birdie', as the diggers knew him. By his own account:

When I took over the command of the Australian and New Zealand Army Corps in Egypt a year ago, I was asked to select a telegraphic code address for my Army Corps, and then adopted the word 'Anzac.' Later on, when we had effected our landing here in April last, I was asked by General Headquarters to suggest a name for the beach where we had made good our first precarious footing, and then asked that this might be recorded as 'Anzac Cove'—a name which the bravery of our men has now made historical, while it will remain a geographic landmark for all time.

Another claimant to the honour is General Sir Ian Hamilton, commander of the Gallipoli campaign. As he himself put it in the foreword to a book published in 1916:

As the man who first seeking to save himself the trouble, omitted the five full stops and brazenly coined the word 'ANZAC', I am glad to write a line or two in preface to sketches which may help to give currency to that token throughout the realms of glory.

According to the Australian war historian Charles Bean, a Lieutenant A. T. White, Royal Army Service Corps, of the British Regular Army was the originator.

O ne day early in 1915 Major C. M. Wagstaff, then a junior member of the 'operations' section of Birdwood's staff, walked into the General Staff office and mentioned to the clerks that a convenient word was wanted as a code name for the Corps. The clerks had noticed the big initials on the cases outside their room—A. & N. Z. A. C. and a rubber stamp for registering correspondence had also been cut with the same initials. When Wagstaff mentioned the need of a code word, one of the clerks (according to most accounts Lieutenant A.T. White) suggested: 'How about ANZAC?' Major Wagstaff proposed the word to the general who approved of it, and 'ANZAC' thereupon became the code name of the Australian and New Zealand Army Corps. It was however, some time before the code word came into everyday use, and at the Landing at Gallipoli many men in the divisions had not yet heard of it.

They soon did, though, and the term has well and truly stuck. The word has been controlled by Commonwealth and state legislation almost from the time it first appeared in wide usage. Controversy continues over whether it should be spelled as 'ANZAC' or 'Anzac'. One argument is that it is an acronym and so its original form should be preserved. Others insist that it has moved beyond the acronym stage to become a fully fledged word and so should appear as 'Anzac', unless referring to the original telegraphic address.

Anzac and the Rising Sun

The most recognisable symbol of Anzac is the Rising Sun badge. Use of a rising sun motif has a long history in Australia, where the concept of a young, growing colony, state or country has an obvious appeal. Rising sun motifs appeared quite frequently in colonial times on coins and also in trademarks and proprietary products such as 'Rising Sun Jam'.

But the famous 'Rising Sun' badge worn by members of the Australian military probably had its origins in South Australia. In 1893 the commander of the South Australian Permanent Artillery had a trophy made featuring bayonets radiating outwards from a central crown. According to legend, the trophy was the inspiration for the first Rising Sun badge, designed for the 1st Battalion, Australian Commonwealth Horse, during the Boer War. Modifications were made to this design when the first Commonwealth forces were formed, and the badge was worn by the First and Second AIF. Some further changes have been made since then, but the badge now worn by the Australian military forces is still the Rising Sun.

The first and the last

Two of the foundation legends of the Anzac tradition concern the identities of the first Australian to step ashore at Gallipoli on 25 April 1915 and of the last to leave eight months later. There have been and continue to be a number of competing claims for these honours. The passion with which the various first man to land and last man to leave stories are supported or refuted has been a constant theme, and reflects the important place that Anzac holds in the lives and hearts of large numbers of Australians.

An early contender for the title of first man ashore was 34-year-old cane cutter Joseph Stratford. Although he was a New South Wales man from the Lismore area, he had enlisted in the Queensland 9th Battalion. On the basis of some previous military training, he was promoted to sergeant. Stratford struggled ashore from the bow of a leading transport in the first wave. Like many from the boats, he jumped into fairly deep water and was dragged under by the weight of his pack and gun. Unlike many, he managed to get rid of the pack and, with a wet and therefore useless rifle, charged a Turkish machine gun with only a bayonet as a weapon. He stabbed two Turkish soldiers before being shot dead. Stratford's body was never found. It is said that an officer who witnessed Stratford's deed thought that he should have been awarded the Victoria Cross.

Research by family members has unearthed a number of eyewitness accounts from contemporary newspapers and letters that lend support to this story. One of his surviving mates, Private Gahan, wrote back to his parents: 'There was not a man amongst us who did not love and look up to him. He was fair and straight. I felt when he did not answer the roll call that I had lost an elder brother'.

Another 9th Battalion man, Lieutenant Duncan Chapman of Maryborough, Queensland, later claimed that his boat had been the first to land, and that, as he was in the bow, he was the first man to jump ashore. There was some corroboration of Chapman's claim from comrades who were with him at the time and from Charles Bean. Chapman was later promoted to major and was killed at Pozières in 1916. Despite Stratford's claim, most historians appear to accept that Chapman was the first man ashore at Gallipoli.

A claim has also been made for a Private James Bostock, also of the 9th Battalion. This has been given little credence by historians who have pointed out that in the chaos of the landings and in the dawn dimness it would have been difficult to determine exactly what happened at any particular moment.

As for the stories of the last Australian to leave Gallipoli in the early hours of 20 December 1915—there are even more contenders for this honour.

Victorian Lieutenant, later Brigadier, Leslie Maygar had fought in the Boer War, where he won the Victoria Cross. At Gallipoli he was in command of a group of 3rd Light Horse given the task of holding the trenches until 2.30 am on the morning of the evacuation, ensuring that everyone else had been safely taken off. An inspirational military leader, Maygar was killed at Beersheba in November 1917.

A different claim was made by Charles Bean for Fred Pollack of the 13th Battalion. Bean wrote that Pollack:

Had obtained permission for special reasons to have a rest in his dugout, having previously arranged with his mates to call him before they left. They, however, understood him to refer to a different dugout, and, having thoroughly searched the one in which he usually slept and found it empty, assumed that he had gone on to the beach. Pollack, waking later, found the area silent. He went along the trenches, but they were empty. Running to the shore, he found no sign of movement until at North Beach he came on men embarking on one of the last lighters and went with them.

The fortunate Pollack survived the war and lived until 1958.

Another bid is made for Lieutenant General Sir Frederick Stanley Maude, known as 'Joe Maude'. Maude's claim was supported by General Sir Ian Hamilton, and also celebrated in a lighthearted parody of the Victorian parlour piece 'Come Into the Garden, Maud' apparently composed by Maude's comrades. Allegedly 'Found on Helles on January 9th,' the poem refers to Maude's lateness in reaching the boat. He was carrying a large amount of equipment and, in the darkness, apparently became entangled in barbed wire, making him an hour late:

Come into the lighter, Maude,
For the fuse has long been lit,
Come into the lighter, Maude,
And never mind your kit,
I've waited here an hour or more,
For news that your march is o'er.
The sea runs high, but what care I,
It's better to be sick than blown sky high,
So jump into the lighter, Maude,
The allotted time is flown,
Come into the lighter, Maude,
I'm off in the launch alone,
I'm off in the lighter alone.

Private Edward Gornall thought he was the last man to leave in 1915, according to a report in a South Australian newspaper under the heading 'Last Man at Anzac'.

Private Edgar Gornall, son of Mr. W. Gornall, of Bathurst, Victoria, writing to his parents states that he was the last man to leave the Australian trenches during the evacuation of the Anzac positions. The officers hurried their men away, and Gornall and another man were given orders to make a bolt for it. At 3.20 they were the only two men on the post. The Turks failed to realise the truth and continued to hurl bombs and fire at the vacant loopholes.

Gornall further relates that while running his mate sprained an ankle. They suddenly discovered that the path along which they were to retire had been blocked by their own men with barbed wire. Neither of the men was able to scale the barrier, and there were thousands of suspicious Turks only a hundred yards away. On hunting round they luckily found another opening, and while making their way through this the mines in the trenches blew up. The Turks then opened a terrific infantry fire, but the two men successfully over took the last party as it was stepping aboard the last remaining motor barge.

All the next day the empty trenches lately occupied by the Fifth Division received the heaviest bombardment of the campaign; 36 hours after the evacuation the Turks charged the positions, but met with no opposition. The enemy speedily reached the beach, where the war ships, which had been on the lookout, badly cut them up.

Private Gornall explains that just before the withdrawal the troops were invited to help themselves to the stores on the beach, and, besides feeding on the best material available, each man helped himself to a new outfit. He saw ten thousand gallons of rum thrown on the rock on the beach, and in the depressions in the ground there were lakelets of wine and stout; thousands of hogsheads, barrels and bottles were smashed. Immense quantities of other goods were also destroyed, and two motor lorries and stacks of sawn timber were burnt.

Gornall's version is still accepted in and around Bathurst.

Other claims have been made for different people at different times. One was Tasmanian Captain Burford Sampson, a platoon commander who led troops at Quinn's Post and Courtney's Post. A Captain C. A. Littler of the 12th Battalion was in charge of beach movements and plausibly maintained he was the last to step aboard the last boat at 3.45 am. Lieutenant George Shaw, 28th Battalion, also laid claim to the honour of being the last man off, while Lieutenant Colonel (later Major-General) John Paton, who had temporary command of the 5th Brigade, was yet another claimant. Even General Birdwood was mistakenly given the glory by at least one writer, though he had left at 3 am.

Usually overlooked in disputes about the last man to leave is the vital role of the Royal Australian Navy. It was the Navy's Bridging Train that was the last unit to cast off from the shore at 4.30 am, about twenty minutes after the remaining troops had departed. The sailor who cast off the mooring line on that boat was actually the last man to leave Gallipoli. His name was not recorded.

Memories

As WELL AS fulfilling the need to memorialise the dead, acknowledge the wounded and allow the living to grieve for their loss, the concept of Anzac has always been a vehicle for the public expression of a sense of national identity. From the moment the news broke revealing what had happened on a small stretch of Turkish coast on the morning of 25 April 1915, Anzac has been bound up with the sense of what it means to be an Australian. At first, this involved patriotic speeches and protestations of loyalty to the British Empire and the motherland. Late in World War I as the enormous casualties mounted ever higher this began to give way to a less enthusiastic view of the 'crimson thread of kinship', as politician Henry Parkes, the 'father of Federation' and premier of New South Wales once described the Australian links with Britain.

By the time of World War II, these ties were still there but were growing weaker. The fall of Singapore to the Japanese in 1942, with the consequent reorientation of Australia's strategic and political alliances towards the USA, marked the fraying of any serious political connections between Australia and Britain. Through all these social, political and economic changes, the figure of the digger and his role as the hero of Anzac have continued to move many Australians deeply. In remembering, publically and privately, the deeds of those who have fought for Australia, at home and abroad, the country acknowledges its sense of self in the most powerful possible manner.

No. 008 Trooper J. Redgum

As a volunteer force, the AIF was full of colourful characters. One or two featured in *The Anzac Book*, including 'Wallaby Joe' in a tale related by W. R. C., 8th Australian Light Horse. Joe, or whatever his real name might have been, was, according to the story, one of the first to enlist when Australia went to war.

His real name matters little; suffice it that he was known among his comrades as 'Wallaby Joe.'

He came to Gallipoli via Egypt with the Light Horse. Incidentally, he has ridden nearly a thousand miles over sun-scorched, drought-stricken plains to join them.

Age about 38. In appearance the typical bushman. Tall and lean, but strong as a piece of hickory. A horseman from head to toe, and a dead shot. He possessed the usual beard of the lonely prospector of the extreme backblocks. Out of deference to a delicate hint from his squadron commander he shaved it off, but resolved to let it grow again when the exigencies of active service should discount such finicking niceties.

His conversation was laconic in the extreme. When the occasion demanded it he could swear profusely, and in a most picturesque vein. When a bursting shell from a '75' on one occasion blew away a chunk of prime Berkshire which he was cooking for breakfast, his remarks were intensely original and illuminative.

He could also drink beer for indefinite periods, but seldom committed the vulgar error of becoming 'tanked.' Not even that locality 'east of Suez,' where, as the song tells us, 'There ain't no Ten Commandments and a man can raise a thirst,' could make his steps erratic.

He was very shy in the presence of the softer sex. On one occasion his unwary footsteps caused him some embarrassment. Feeling thirsty he turned into one of those establishments, fairly common in Cairo, where the southern proprietors try to hide the villainous quality of their beer by bribing sundry young ladies of various nationalities and colours to give more high-class vaudeville turns. The aforementioned young ladies are aided and abetted by a coloured orchestra, one member of which manipulates the bagpipes.

A portly damsel had just concluded, amidst uproarious applause, the haunting strains of 'Ta-ra-ra- boom-de-ay.' She sidled up to Joe with a large-sized grin on her olive features.

'Gib it kiss,' she murmured, trying to look ravishing.

But Joe had fled.

Henceforth during his stay in Egypt he took his beer in a little Russian bar, the proprietor of which could speak English, and had been through the Russo-Japanese War.

When the Light Horse were ordered at last to the front, Joe took a sad farewell of his old bay mare. He was, as a rule, about as sentimental as a steamroller, but 'leaving the old nag behind hurt some.'

On the Peninsula and under fire his sterling qualities were not long in coming to the surface. Living all his life in an environment in which the pick and shovel plays an important part he proved himself an adept at sapping and mining. At this game he was worth four ordinary men. No matter how circuitous the maze of trenches, he could find his way with ease. He could turn out all sorts of dishes from his daily rations of flour, bacon, jam, and biscuits. An endless amount of initiative showed itself in everything he did. His mates learned quite a lot of things just by watching him potter about the trenches and bivouacs. His training at the military camps of Australia and, later, in Egypt, combined with the knowledge he had been imbibing from Nature all his life, made him an ideal soldier.

He was used extensively by his officers as a scout. As the Turkish trenches were often yards from our own, needless to say the scouting was done at night, the Turks' favourite time to attack being just before dawn. Often during these nocturnal excursions a slight rustle in the thick scrub would cause his mate to grasp his rifle with fixed bayonet and peer into the darkness, with strained eyes and ears and quickened pulse.

'A hare,' Joe would whisper, and probably advise him to take things easy while he himself watched.

This went on for some time until one night his mate came in alone, pale-faced and wild-eyed. Interrogated by the officer on duty, he informed him that Joe had been shot.

We brought the body in. He had been shot through the heart—a typical affair of outposts.

Tucked away in one of the innumerable gullies, a little grave, one among hundreds, contains a body of one of nature's grand men. On the wooden cross surmounting it is the following:

No.008 Trooper J. Redgum,

20th Australian Light Horse.

Killed in Action.

The first Anzac Days

In English tradition, 25 April is St Mark's Day, and the evening of 24 April—'St Mark's Eve'—is associated with 'porch watching'. In this old custom, villagers maintain a vigil in their local church in order to observe the shades of those who will die in the village during the coming year enter the church at midnight—and not come out again. The first Australian organisation to form in support of Anzac Day was well aware of this tradition and noted it in their deliberations about the best way to observe the new calendar event. In January 1916 the Anzac Day Commemoration Committee in Brisbane raised funds for building war memorials by selling lavender-coloured silk ribbons embossed with the lion of St Mark, who was one of Jesus' disciples and author of one of the gospels.

But the first Anzac Day observation in Australia had already taken place six months before 25 April 1916. It happened in South Australia on 13 October 1915. The Labor state government decided that the sacrifice of the troops still on Gallipoli was sufficient to justify re-christening the eight-hour holiday Anzac Day. When it came, the day had the flavour of a patriotic festival, with a procession headed by the Royal Australian Naval Brigade and band, followed by returned soldiers and new recruits. The usual trade union march followed on behind, featuring floats on patriotic themes. There were more festive activities, including air balloons, military kites, mock arrests of MPs and, the grand finale, a 'tram-car crash'. Two old trams were sent careering towards each other from opposite ends of a specially raised track. Together with some explosive additions, the resulting smash and fireball apparently satisfied the 15 000 spectators reported to have turned out for the show, 'watching two tramcars melt into a shapeless mass of twisted iron and splintered wood'. Not surprisingly, a lot of money was raised for the war effort and the idea was adopted in Victoria, where Melbourne had an Anzac Day on 17 December 1915 and Ballarat on 14 January 1916.

As these stories suggest, the first anniversary of the Gallipoli landings was immediately established as a popular day of national observance. But it was not celebrated in a broadly similar manner as it is today, nationwide. Instead, a variety of local customs, ideas and activities were tried out. In London there was a grand parade of Australian and New Zealand troops, making the streets ring with 'coo-ee' and 'kia-ora'. Most Anzacs, though, were still at the front line. Charles Bean recorded one observation on the western front:

Many of the Australian units marked the day by holding athletic and military sports meetings. The spectacle of five teams of enormous Victorians in a tug-of-war, on a corner of the Somme battlefield where old shell-holes had been filled in, and the whole brigade seated round as in an amphitheatre, was worth travelling leagues to see. Another brigade had a Hindenburg race, confined to men who lately reached and for some hours occupied the Hindenburg line . . . By a strange coincidence, this was won by a Western Australian who is reputed to have been the first man to reach the line in the fight.

In Egypt, the troops began the day with a religious service ending with 'The Last Post', then celebrated the day with a party. This was followed by 'a skit on the memorable landing by a freak destroyer manned by a lot of corked blackfellows hauling ashore a number of tiny tin boats full of tiny tin soldiers. It was screamingly funny', according to General Sir John Monash, who also said that 15 000 diggers swam naked in the Suez Canal. Monash concluded his account by describing the event as 'this famous day—OUR DAY'.

And while most cities and larger towns attempted some sort of acknowledgement of the day, most activities depended on community, veteran, religious and service groups rather than official government organisations. In fact, state and federal governments were curiously lukewarm about Anzac Day during the war and for a few years afterwards. For the 1917 Anzac Day, Prime Minister Billy Hughes did not even bother writing a new speech. He delivered the same one he had given the year before—in London. It was not until the community began to ask pointed questions in the press that officialdom finally joined in, from the early 1920s. From then, the day began to assume the more organised character that it has had since the 1930s, at which time the innovation of the Dawn Service began to be incorporated into most Anzac Day commemorations. Over the years following, the day has tended towards the more or less standard form that Australians know well, though local variations and developments are often featured, especially since the continuing popular rediscovery of the day from the 1990s onwards.

Return to Gallipoli

After the war ended in November 1918, it was not too many months before people began returning to the 'holy of holies', as one journalist called Gallipoli. In 1919 a ceremonial return of British troops took place under the terms of the war settlement. There were visits from the war graves representatives of the many nations who had taken part in the campaign, and the Australian war correspondent Charles Bean also returned seeking information for what was to become the official history of Australia's Great War experience. Bean had been at the initial landings and remained on Gallipoli for almost the whole campaign, so his return was a poignant event. He arrived in May 1919 and was interviewed by a journalist, his observations providing for the first time some insight into what it had been like for the Turks.

In compiling my history of the war, said Mr. Bean, the authorities in London thought it would be of advantage for me to visit Gallipoli, in order to ascertain what the real strength of the Turkish positions had been, and how far the Australians had penetrated on the first day of the landing, at Ari Burnu. I took with me several members of the Australian Historical Mission, including Captain Wilkins, M.C., photographer, Captain Lambert, the well-known Australian painter, and Lieut. Buchanan, in addition to a party of surveyors and draftsmen, and we worked continuously for three weeks. We did not land at the same place as we did when the famous landing was made at Anzac beach, but at Chanak, where the Turkish ports inside the Dardanelles are situated. From there, with a working party, I went through the ruins of Maidos, the town which was blown and burst by the guns of the *Queen Elizabeth* the day after the landing. There was nothing of it left. Some big shells evidently fell into the town, and set fire to the buildings; then the Turks pulled down the houses, using the material for making dug-outs. The Turks were great on salvage. We found the hillside for miles around the Turkish positions at Anzac littered with empty bully beef tins. The Turks took all the stores we left behind, and we were told that for months after the evacuation our beef was a common article of diet in Constantinople.

EARLY AUSTRALIAN SUCCESS.

We reached Anzac . . . from the Turkish side, from the district of Gun Ridge, the position which faced us for the whole eight months we spent at Anzac, and which had been our objective from the first day of landing, but which was never reached. Later we found traces of a few men having reached the lower, seaward side of Gun Ridge. We arrived at the certitude, from the traces we found, that a few Australian scouts reached this slope within a few hours of the landing. Little bits of kit were lying about, and on seeing spent cartridge cases, conviction stared us in the face that some Australians on their first day reached the farther slopes of Pine Ridge, which they never again approached. A few possibly reached Battleship Hill. All these positions have been marked on our survey plans, and if more perfect maps of the country had been available when we landed, or if the 'digger' had at that time possessed the wonderful experience which he achieved during the last six months of the campaign in France, we might have reached Gun Ridge and held it, or at least a part of it. As it was, the outstanding fact that struck us, as it must strike all beholders, was that it was marvellous that they went as far as they did.

THE TURKS' SIDE OF LONE PINE.

As soon as our party reached the top of Gun Ridge . . . we found ourselves looking into the Turkish side of Lone Pine. We were faced by the shelves on which the Turks had built their shelters and dug-outs. There was a little more green grass about than our minds pictured to exist at Anzac, as we knew the locality, except that every particle of timber or metal had been removed by the Turks. The place was otherwise unchanged. A road wound up the southern side of Lone Pine, and we rode along this road, but owing to there being trenches everywhere it was very difficult to get about, except on foot. Of course, we carefully examined the trenches, and they struck us as representing the most complicated and intricate maze of trench digging that we had ever seen. Our official photographer, who probably had visited more battlefields in France than any one else, agreed that he had never seen there anything approaching the work of the Turkish sappers. The trenches were all well conserved, and in such a state that if one got into them it was difficult to get out. On the top of the hill we came out on a square patch of grass, which we recognised at once as the 'daisy patch,' and which was some times known as 'dead men's field.' This position, over which the troops charged at Lone Pine, is unfortunately crowded with unidentified graves of our men, who were killed in the famous charge.

MARKING OF ANZAC GRAVES.

The work of marking the graves of those Australians who fell at Anzac is being extraordinarily well done by the small Australian party which is on the spot. Between 5000 and 6000 graves have already been identified, with absolute certainty, and when those of some of the 20,000 odd who lost their lives in No Man's Land have been placed with some accuracy one of our duties will be concluded.

FAMOUS BEACHY BILL BATTERY.

Mr. Bean was to look for Beachy Bill, the famous battery which used to enfilade the beach from the south. There were 50 theories that 'Bill' was dug back into the slope of the hill, in the olive grove behind Gaba Tepe. Some people said that 'he' was on rails, with a disappearing trap door, and others merely pictured 'him' in a deep cave, but . . . we found 'him' in the oak grove, south of the Aama Dere. It was exactly like any other German battery, the system of the ordinary open emplacement being fairly well camouflaged. There were about 30 gun positions, a dozen of which were new, and around every one of them there were marks of our own gun fire, and round some of the others, one especially, the ground was almost as much cut up as it would be round a battery in France. Beachy Bill certainly consisted of one battery of 5.9 howitzers, and two or three batteries of 4.2 guns and 75s. The only other place where Anzac was cut up by shell fire in a manner in any way comparable to the fields of France was on the slopes of Battleship Hill where the big guns of the *Queen Elizabeth, Bacchante* and other warships got onto the Turks on the first few days after the landing.

Another group of British, New Zealanders and Australians visited the Gallipoli battlefields in 1934 and were addressed by Mustafa Kemal Atatürk (1881–1938), Turkey's first president. Atatürk has an important role in the Anzac story. As a young military commander he was largely responsible for the success of the Turkish resistance to the Anzac attacks at Gallipoli (Gelibolu).

In a remarkably generous speech to the visitors, the president said of the Anzac dead:

Those heroes that shed their blood
And lost their lives.
You are now lying in the soil of a friendly country.
Therefore rest in peace.
There is no difference between the Johnnies
And the Mehmets to us where they lie side by side
Here in this country of ours.
You, the mothers,
Who sent their sons from far away countries
Wipe away your tears,
Your sons are now lying in our bosom
And are in peace
After having lost their lives on this land they have
Become our sons as well.

This text has been inscribed on the Ari Burnu Cemetery memorial and on memorials in New Zealand and Australia.

Visits to the Gallipoli battlefields in search of graves or other indications of the last resting place of loved ones began very soon after the war ended. These visits quickly became known as 'pilgrimages', an indication of the Australian and New Zealand attitude that this sparse area of rock and sand had become sacred ground.

After the war

During the war, diggers had often complained of the tendency of civilians to ask what the soldiers considered to be stupid questions about the front line. It seems that the same problem occurred after the war. 'The Silly Things Diggers Were Asked

After the War', or some version of it, appeared in more than one old soldiers' publication.

Jones: 'You're looking fine, old chap. I suppose if war started again you'd be anxious to have another go at them?'

Mother: 'I suppose you delighted in splashing about in the water in the trenches?'

The Flapper: 'It must have been great fun chasing the Germans with an eighteen-pounder, wasn't it?'

Tommy (aged five, longingly): 'Was there plenty of good mud over there, uncle?'

Aunt: 'I suppose those Germans are awfully ugly, aren't they?'

The Business Man: 'Now, what would be the number of tins, approximately, of course, of bully beef eaten per day?'

Maude: 'Wasn't it delightfully lovely living in those dear little dugouts?'

As the postwar years stretched out, so those who survived increasingly felt the need to relive their experiences. The 1920s and 1930s were thick with boozy reunions of old soldiers. These featured the telling of the old yarns yet again and the singing and reciting of song and verse from the trenches, the troopships and the estaminets. So powerful was the need to maintain or revive wartime memories that new items were composed and published long after the events to which they referred. 'The Digger's Alphabet' was written in 1931 by C. R. Collins, soldier, physical education trainer and avid writer on all matters digger. This particular 'Digger's Alphabet'—it was one of many similar poems—might well have been composed anytime between 1916 and 1918, but for one or two postwar references. It is full of digger lingo, old rumours and memories of long-ago transgressions. Such compositions, despite their anachronistic nature, were also a form of memorial.

THE DIGGER'S ALPHABET

A for the Adjutants, dashing young blades,
B for the Batmen who dodged all parades.
C for the Clink, aftermath of the spree,
The home of the birds who go making too free.
D for the Digger, the casual brute,
Who sauntered past 'Birdie' and didn't salute.
E for the 'Eggsers' who turned their hats down,
'The married man [sic] have to', we told the whole town.
F for the Furphies, related with zest,
Especially the one of the long-promised rest.
G for the Gunner, a decent old sport,
Except for his habit of dropping 'em short.
H stands for Hindenburg, sturdy and hale,
Till Monash and Co. put a twist in his tail.
I for intelligence, reigning serene,
The reason the blighters were tabbed out in green.
J stands for Jerry, and Jacko the Turk,
Who kept all the diggers in regular work.
K stands for Knighthoods that Generals got,
Except when the profiteers collared the lot.
L for the Legends we told all the flappers,
Of boomerang farms and the jackeroo-trappers.
M stand [sic] for Mademoiselle. It appears
That she lived in the town we pronounced 'Armenteers.'
N for the Nips that were seldom repaid,

Horseferry Road was the nub of this trade.

O for the O.B.E.s dished out in millions,

To actors and women and other civilians.

P for the Padre, the shifter of sin,

When you nipped him for gaspers you'd get the whole tin.

Q for the 'Quack' with his quick Number Nine,

And also the Quarter-bloke, dodging the line.

R for the Ration-state, figured and cinched,

Except for the Rum that the Quarter-bloke pinched.

S for the Sisters, the pride of the show,

But how they endured us, I'm hanged if I know.

T stands for 'Two-up' the national game;

When Princes have played it, are we much to blame?

U for the U-boats that scuttled in flight

Whene'er a destroyer would steam up in sight.

V for the 'vin blong' estaminets sold,

A potent prescription to keep out the cold.

W for War Books, so smutty in places,

All written by ladies or blokes from the bases.

X for the marks that they put upon casks,

To empty the same were our happiest tasks.

Y for the Y plus the M and C.A.,

The one little show that could make the war pay.

Z for the Zeppelins, purveyors of hate,

And also for Zero, the dread hour of fate.

The lonely Anzac

Will Longstaff's famous painting, 'Menin Gate at Midnight',
also known as 'The Ghosts of Menin', was painted in 1927.

Longstaff had been present at the unveiling ceremony of the Menin Gate Memorial at Ypres in Belgium and, according to one story, had been so affected by the experience that he walked along the Menin road and received the vision depicted in the painting, which he completed in a single marathon creative session after his return to London. He is also said to have been inspired by a woman he met on his walk. Mrs Mary Horsburgh had worked in a British canteen during the war, and she told him that she could feel 'her dead boys' all around her.

In the aftermath of World War I, the unprecedented immensity of grief on all sides produced an atmosphere of religious and spiritual emotion in which works like Longstaff's—if not as well known—were produced. Longstaff's powerfully symbolic representation of spectral soldiers hovering over a cornfield and moving towards the gate, with poppies in the background, evokes a general tone of mourning. It was immediately popular and remains so today.

The Menin Gate leading onto the road along which many Allied soldiers marched for the last time is known as 'the Memorial to the Missing' and has special significance for Australians and New Zealanders, as so many of their troops passed beneath it, never to return. The gate is specifically dedicated to those British and Commonwealth soldiers whose graves are unknown. Each night since 1928, with a break during World War II, there has been a memorial observance known as 'the Last Post Ceremony' at the gate, usually attended by thousands of tourists, local dignitaries and members of the armed and civic services.

But the spirits of Australian soldiers do not all lie on the battlefields of the Great War.

In July 1916 a wounded Australian soldier from the fighting at Pozières was travelling on a Red Cross train bound for a Yorkshire hospital. When the train reached Peterborough, Thomas Hunter was too ill to continue the journey. He was transferred to the Peterborough Infirmary where he died a few days later and was buried in the hospital grounds. This may have been simply another sad fatality during a war in which hundreds of thousands of Allied soldiers died but for the intense local reaction, then and since.

The death of Sergeant Hunter, a 36-year-old Gallipoli veteran, so far from Australia and from family, friends and comrades, drew the sympathy of Peterborough's wartime community. The mayor arranged for a civic funeral ceremony, which was attended by crowds of local people, many bearing wreaths. An appeal for funds to build a memorial was generously supported, generating income sufficient to build a substantial grave and to have a bronze plaque made and erected in Peterborough Cathedral. A desire to propagandise the war effort was probably the official inspiration for this reaction. It was a time of intense patriotism in which expressions of loyalty to king, country and the British Empire were regularly voiced in newspapers and pulpits and played out in public events. A poem published in the local newspaper summed up these ideas and the language used to express them.

Blood of our blood, son of our race,
Imperial and strong,
He came in all his youth's fair grace—
One of a glorious throng
Of heroes from the southern land
Linked in our empire's chain;

One of the famous Anzac band
From the far-distant main.

With British pride, in British soil,
Amidst our own dear dead
We laid him, freed from warrior's toil,
In a true warrior's bed.
His tomb, as long as it shall stand,
Shall keep alive his worth,
And link this spot of Motherland
With those who sent him forth.

But there was also genuine popular sympathy for the death of the 'Lone Anzac', as he was being called. Wreaths carried messages of sympathy from 'a soldier's mother' and 'for someone's darling boy'. Although he had migrated to Australia from his native County Durham in 1910, Hunter had an adopted family in Australia who wrote to a local family requesting that 'you will sometimes visit our darling's grave and think of his sorrowing father, mother and sister, fourteen thousand miles away, who seem to miss him more each day'. There was still considerable local interest two years after his death. The 1918 Anzac Day observance involved another subscription plea for further decorations to Hunter's grave and bronze memorial, while services were conducted in his memory at both these locations.

It seems that this local enthusiasm for the lonely Anzac faded away in the postwar years. But in September 1931 the first recorded manifestations of Thomas Hunter's ghost were reported in the Peterborough Museum, once the Peterborough Infirmary. The wife of the building's caretaker saw and heard a figure climbing the stairs. It was a man of about thirty with brown hair and wearing a green or grey suit. The figure walked through a closed door, down the corridor and then vanished. There were further sightings of the ghost over the next decades. These seem to have ceased in the 1970s, although unexplained cold spots and mysteriously moved furniture have been reported in the building.

Now, each Anzac Day since the 1980s, the Royal British Legion and the Peterborough community have commemorated the Lone Anzac. Members of the Australian High Commission or Australian military attend the event, together with hundreds of locals and civil dignitaries. During the ceremony, the stone cross that adorns his grave is covered with the Australian and British flags, and a special prayer is said.

The longest memorial

Who was Howard Hitchcock? He was a wealthy businessman who was also mayor of Geelong, Victoria, from 1917 to 1922 and the person whose vision, money and perseverance led to the building of the world's largest and longest constructed war memorial. As World War I dragged to an end, Hitchcock and a group of Geelong-based associates conceived the idea of building a road along the Victorian coast from Anglesea to Warrnambool. The road would open up land along the way, provide work for returned soldiers and also be a memorial to the sacrifices they and their comrades had made. Construction of the Great Ocean Road, as it would become known, began in 1919 and lasted for another thirteen years. The little-told story of the road is an epic of financial struggle, hard labour and controversy.

Officially, the Great Ocean Road runs for just over 240 kilometres (estimates vary) between Torquay and Allansford, though for most people it is the 75 kilometres of stunning sea and coast between Apollo Bay and Eastern View that constitutes the road. In 1917, this area was no more than a scattering of fishing villages accessible only by sea or a rough bridle track along the top of the cliffs. In partnership with the Victorian government, Hitchcock and others formed the Great Ocean Road Trust and surveying of the route began the next year.

To build the road it was necessary for the returned soldiers to live in camps. It was a hard and hazardous job and a number of workers died or were injured in accidents, mainly involving the explosives needed to push the road through the rocky terrain. A former worker on the road, Frank Fletcher, recollected that the men had to carry the detonators for the explosives on their knees as they bumped across the rough ground in carts, as this was the gentlest and least dangerous way to carry them. In the case of the returned soldiers who suffered from shell shock, the explosions brought back the trauma of war. Battlefield memories also played a role in the names the workers gave various parts of the road, including Shrapnel Gully and Sausage Gully.

Most of the work was done with pick and shovel and other hand tools, with very little mechanical assistance. The going was so hard that the labourers were only able to cut around three kilometres of road a month, and the workforce is said to have turned over twenty times during the thirteen years of building. This may have been related to the harshness of the supervision. According to folklore, if a man let a wheelbarrow fall down the steep cliffs he would be made to climb down and retrieve it.

Certainly much of the work depended on the labourers hanging from the dangerous cliffs on ropes.

Not only was the work dangerous, but there was also little opportunity for recreation after work, and appeals were made for donations of reading materials for the men. By the time the road was finished in 1932, around 3000 returned soldiers and depression 'sustenance' or 'dole' workers had laboured on the project. There were justified celebrations when it was over, though Hitchcock did not live to see his vision fulfilled, suffering a fatal heart attack in 1931. His chauffeur is said to have driven Hitchcock's car with his seat left empty in the cavalcade that drove along the road at the opening.

The Great Ocean Road has been progressively widened and improved, although landslides remain a danger. Today it is one of the world's great scenic drives, featuring a number of commemorative features, including a memorial to Hitchcock. The imposing Memorial Arch at Eastern View is a reminder to motorists that they are passing along a unique Anzac memorial.

The lone pines

Perhaps the most revered symbols of Gallipoli are the 'lone pines' and the many trees that have since been grown from their seeds. Today, trees grown from and descended from the seedlings brought back home can be found in parks, gardens, schools and in the vicinity of memorials all around Australia. The trees gain their powerful significance from their relationship to the battle that raged between 6 and 9 August 1915 around the single pine tree remaining on a plateau at the southern end of Anzac.

During this battle, the 1st Brigade AIF initially attacked the heavily fortified Turkish trenches, parts of which had been roofed with pine logs. Although the first attack succeeded very quickly, it took another four days of bloody hand-to-hand fighting before the Turks were finally routed, resulting in 2000 Australian casualties. Turkish dead or casualties were estimated at 6000 to 7000. Seven Victoria Crosses were won during the battle. One of the survivors, Hugh Anderson of the 1st Brigade, wrote home about his part in the battle a few months later. Like many young men, he had enlisted, as he wrote, 'for the adventure'.

We knew several days before that we were to charge the Lone Pine trenches. I was glad as I had come over for the adventure and this seemed what I was looking for.

We were issued with a white strip of calico to sew on to each arm and a big patch for the back, this was for the artillery to show where our men were, and also made a good mark for Johnnie as we soon found to our cost. We were then told what we were to take over with us and our officer gave us a rough sketch of the trenches and told us what was expected of us, and what we had to do.

On August 6th we paraded just after 3 o'clock in battle order and marched round to our trenches opposite the Lone Pine. The whole of the first division was to do the job, the 1st Battalion formed the first line and were in our advanced firing line, the 2nd Battalion were in the main firing line in the firing positions, and the 4th Battalion were in the bottom of the trench just behind them. The 3rd Battalion were the reserves and came over twenty minutes after we started. The brigade went in a little over 3000 strong and came out something over 400, so the casualties were very heavy.

We got to our positions about 4 pm and the artillery commenced bombarding the Turkish trenches and they returned the compliment and the crash and scream of shells was deafening for a little over an hour, the smell of explosives was very strong and the suspense of waiting tried our nerves. I was nervous I can tell you and put up many a prayer for courage. I bet others did also.

About 5 pm the officers were all there with watch in hand calling 3 minutes to go, 2 minutes to go, 1 minute to go half a minute to go and shut his watch and three shrill blasts of a whistle. Out scrambled the boys from advanced line up through holes in the ground, the trench being a tunnel. Over the parapet go the 2nd Battalion and we are close behind. I will never forget that picture, I was well up with the rest racing like mad, all nervousness gone now. The shrapnel falling as thick as hail, many a good man went down here although I never noticed it at the time.

We reached the Turkish lines and found the first trench covered in with logs and branches and dirt heaped on top. There was a partial check, some men fired in through the loop holes, others tried to pull the logs apart. Out runs our officer, old Dickie Seldon, waving a revolver, 'This won't do men! On! On! On!' and running over the top of the trench he came to the second trench and down into it the crowd followed.

I got alongside of Captain Milson of Milson's Point. I slid down into the trench, the Turks ran round a corner and got into a large cave place dug in the trench side as a bomb proof shelter. The first man to follow was shot dead, here we were checked. Captain Milson took command. A bomber came on the parapet and commenced throwing bombs round the corner among the

Turks. Very soon he was shot in the arm, and said he was useless and threw his bags of bombs down to us, several rolled away and out rushed a Turk to try and get them. I shot at him but never hit, and he got back quick.

Milson started throwing, and I was next to him lighting bombs for him. He then proposed getting a party the other side of this possie and bombing from both sides and asked if we would follow him. We all said 'yes' so he threw a bomb and dashed across. A dozen Turks shot him and he fell dead the other side. I was next and as I ran I threw my rifle into the possie and pulled the trigger. I suppose they had never got time to load as I never got hit, but no one followed and I was there alone with no bombs and only my rifle. I shouted to them to come on but they were not having any.

I felt a little dickie I can tell you, but I kept firing into the possie from where I was, some of the Turks were firing at me, and I knew it but I could not get away. Wack! Like a sledge hammer on the head and down I went across Milson's body and several Turks, some of whom were only wounded, and groaned and squirmed from time to time. I bled pretty freely and then I got a crack on the shoulder from a shrapnel pellet which hurt badly but did not do much damage.

Our men meanwhile were still bombing away and one bomb went off near my head, and I got bits of it in the hand and face and was knocked unconscious for a while. The next I remembered is a rush of feet and being trampled on. I lay very still and there was a big shooting and bombing match going on all round and back rushed the Turks over me leaving a heap of dead and wounded. I was very dry and tried to get Milson's water bottle, my own being empty, but could not. I tried to get my rifle but it was jammed between the bodies. Milson's revolver was handy, and I ought to have used that as I had a good view of the Turk's possie from where I was, but I did not have brains enough at the time.

Soon I heard someone call behind me 'Hullo Australia' and I crawled down the trench and found Seldon with one eye shot out, but still going, leading a party and I explained the position to him and he sent me away to a temporary dressing station while he went and fixed up the Turks. They captured 15 Turks and 1 German Officer for that position.

I got my head bandaged and a drink of rum and felt better, I picked up a rifle and was going round to the firing line when I came across Crichton's body with a frightful gash in it, further on our Corporal's with a bayonet hole through his back and chest. I went on and was set to dig in the now captured trench. There was only a man every 20 yards or so and we had to pass messages to head quarters for reinforcements and sandbags. They were still fighting on the flanks, the right most especially under Captain Scot, he got a DCM for this. I was taken off to collect arms and ammunition from the dead and it was heavy work.

As darkness come on reinforcements arrived, and I went into the firing line and stood on guard with them. While I was working and hot my head did not trouble me, but when it was cold it started to ache, and I had a bad time all night. I left the trenches on Saturday and how I was sent to Lemnos you already know.

Anderson was badly wounded during the fighting but recovered to fight on the western front. On 5 May 1917 he was killed in the second battle of Bullecourt. His grave is unknown.

It seems that the Turks may have used both native Turkish pines (*Pinus brutia*) and Aleppo pines (*Pinus halepensis*) to construct their fortifications. The two Australian soldiers said to have carried seeds from the battleground back to Australia brought different species. Lance Corporal Benjamin Smith brought a seed or seeds of the *Pinus halepensis*, which were eventually propagated at Inverell in New South Wales in 1931, while a Sergeant Keith McDowell brought a *Pinus brutia*, which was propagated at Warrnambool in Victoria in 1930. A lone pine also grows on the Paeroa Golf Course in New Zealand, thought to be descended from the Warrnambool *Pinus brutia* seed. Other New Zealand lone pines are said to grow at Te Mata in the North Island and in the South Island at Dunedin.

The significane of the 'lone pine' lies in its symbolic importance for Australians, New Zealanders and Turks. On Gallipoli itself, the large Lone Pine Cemetery contains the graves of 986 men. The memorial within the cemetery bears the dedication:

To the Glory of God and in lasting memory of 3,268 Australian soldiers who fought on Gallipoli in 1915 and who have no known graves, and 456 New Zealand soldiers whose names are not recorded in other graves on the Peninsula but who fell in the Anzac Area and have no known graves; and also of 960 Australians and 252 New Zealanders who, fighting on Gallipoli in 1915, incurred mortal wounds or sickness and found burial at Sea.

Mrs Kim's commemoration

The Korean War was fought between North and South Korea from 1950 to 1953. It was a hard and bitter war involving not only Koreans but also British, American and Australian troops.

Casualties were high, including 339 Australians. One of these, Sergeant Vince Healy of the 3rd Royal Australian Regiment, was killed in action during 'Operation Woodbine' on 7 March 1951. The 25 year old was buried in Tanggok War Cemetery at Pusan, South Korea, and became another statistic of another war.

Also a casualty of the fighting was a member of the South Korean forces. Lieutenant Kim In-Hyung was killed near Pusan on 18 September 1950. The night before, his wife dreamed she and her husband were walking together towards a pond. When they reached it, she went to the left and he went to the right. She called out to him but he did not answer. Mrs Kim later discovered that her husband had died the next day. With two children to support, she worked hard in the difficult years of South Korea's postwar reconstruction. In 1961 she chanced to read a newspaper report about an Australian woman who had saved for years so that she could visit her son's grave at Pusan. The woman had carried some Australian soil with her to place on the grave and had returned home with some Korean soil. She was the mother of Sergeant Vincent Healy.

Mrs Healy could never afford to return again to visit her son's last resting place, but her story so touched Mrs Kim that she began to visit Sergeant Healy's grave twice a year. She took fresh flowers and prayed for all young men killed in war, making an 800-kilometre round trip between her home and Pusan. Mrs Kim also made efforts to locate and contact Mrs Healy. These were eventually successful and the two grieving mothers wrote frequently to each other. In 1998, after seeing a documentary about the death in action of Lieutenant Colonel Charlie Green, commander of the Australian forces in Korea, Mrs Kim also began to visit his grave and started a correspondence with his widow.

This seemingly extraordinary story came to the attention of the Australian authorities. At the Australian War Memorial and in Sydney on Anzac Day, 1999, Mrs Kim was honoured as a special guest of the Australian government. She was officially thanked for her selfless devotion to the memories of two Korean War diggers who did not come home.

The long aftermath of Fromelles

One recent aftermath of the Battle of Fromelles in France (19–20 July 1916) is a reminder that wars do not end when the fighting stops. An unnamed 'Sergeant of machine guns' wrote down his experience of the attack and recorded his hope that the event would not be forgotten.

The general opinion of the boys was that we were attacking to relieve pressure on the Somme—that is, to make a demonstration and get the Huns to rush men and guns up and so weaken the other parts of the front. In this, I believe, we were very successful. Our bombardment opened at roughly II a.m. and gradually increased in violence until the air was filled with a tornado of flying missiles spreading death and destruction among the enemy opposite. Mind, we never had this our own way, for the enemy also opened out with a terrible fire on our line and communications. Of the next few hours, waiting in the front line, waiting for the word to go over, I will say little, but the boys lived a lifetime during those hours. Men endured, suffered, and died. God! shall one ever forget of the multitude of brave men?

Some were mere boys, some were older, but all faced death and mutilation, cheerfully singing favourite music-hall songs and 'Australia Will Be There'.

We received the order to go over about 6 p.m., and with a wild, ringing, hearty Australian cheer over the boys went. Personally I had to go over with the guns half an hour later to consolidate and hold ground won, and had the opportunity of watching the progress of the boys on my left. Two of our brigades made rapid progress across No Man's Land, and with fine dash soon captured the front line, but unfortunately, owing to the long distance across No Man's Land, and also a terrific barrage and enfilade machine-gun fire, my brigade was pressed back. Line after line went out into that land of death. What a thrill went through me to see them! Darkness set in and all night the battle ebbed and flowed. Our troops on the left did great work and captured three lines of trenches, and had established good communication, but owing to the reasons I gave our brigade was not so fortunate. The individual acts of bravery that night it would be impossible for me to relate, but I leave them to the reader's imagination.

Early next morning, owing to the Huns flooding one part of the captured line, our troops had to fall back to our original line, and thus ended one of the most daring and self-sacrificing demonstrations ever made during this war. When I say ended, I mean the offensive part of the action. For days brave men were going out into No Man's Land rescuing our wounded. I feel that in writing this I can only, in a small way, bring before our home folk the bravery of our boys on the glorious 19th of July, and I should like to assure those who lost loved ones during that action (and our casualties were heavy) that they can feel proud of their boys who so cheerfully and bravely laid their lives on the altar of sacrifice for the great fight for freedom which we are now waging. Australians, don't forget July 19, for on that day another great chapter was written in the glorious book of Australia's glorious history in the Great War. Of the success of the action I will say little. We captured some hundreds of prisoners and inflicted very heavy casualties on the enemy. We never held the ground won, but if it was for the purpose of drawing troops and guns from another part of the line, then the action was successful; but we probably shall never know. It was officially described as a raid on a large scale, but in reality it was a battle, in which, on both sides, there must have been 60,000 troops engaged. I trust July 19 will not be forgotten, but that it will be a day kept up in some way as a tribute to the fallen—lest we forget.

The sergeant and his comrades were right in their speculation that their role was a diversionary one. Although not forgotten, the action at Fromelles was often overlooked due to its location away from the main fighting at the Somme and the fact that it was quickly overshadowed by the fighting at Pozières. The bodies of the Allied soldiers killed at Fromelles were buried by the Germans in mass graves, which were discovered after the war. The bodies were exhumed and reinterred in cemeteries including the VC Corner Australian Cemetery and Memorial established close to Fromelles in the 1920s.

But in 2007 a previously unknown burial site was discovered through the research of Lambis Englezos and subsequently excavated in 2009. The remains included those of 203 Australians, many identified through DNA testing. A new cemetery was established in which the bodies were individually reinterred. The final digger, identity still unknown, was buried on 19 July 2010 with full military honours and in the presence of the governor-general, British dignitaries and clergy. Descendants of those soldiers who had been identified were hosted at the ceremony by the Commonwealth War Graves Commission, some of them reading letters sent by the soldiers before the battle. Many of these letters were heavy with foreboding about the outcome of the day.

The Unknown Sailor

Early in February 1942, a ship's life raft washed ashore on Christmas Island in the Indian Ocean. In the raft—known as a 'Carley float'—was the badly decomposed body of a white male in the remains of a boiler suit. The body was examined by the local doctor and then buried with military honours in the old European cemetery. An inquest was arranged, though the findings were apparently lost when Japanese forces occupied the island at the end of March that year. Over the succeeding years the rough grave itself also disappeared.

But a question remained unanswered—where did the raft and its grim cargo come from?

There has been a strong belief that the body was that of a sailor from HMAS *Sydney* (II), sunk with all hands by the German raider *Kormoran* in one of the great mysteries of Australia's wartime experience.

On 19 November 1941, *Sydney* apparently approached the auxiliary cruiser HSK *Kormoran*, which was disguised as a Dutch merchant vessel. Before the true identity of *Kormoran* could be determined, the German ship fired on *Sydney* at close quarters. The Australian ship, badly damaged, fired back, disabling the raider. The ships drifted apart. *Sydney* went to a long-unknown grave and *Kormoran* was scuttled, her surviving crew escaping in lifeboats. No survivors or even evidence of the *Sydney* were ever found, unless the Christmas Island sailor was one of them.

The seemingly inexplicable elements of this tragedy were many. Did the Australian commander, an experienced sailor, bring the *Sydney* too close to the disguised raider? How was it possible that all hands were lost without trace? Was the crew of the *Kormoran* covering up a wartime atrocity? Where did the stricken ships finally sink to their last resting places? And was the body on Christmas Island the only remnant of the tragic event?

These questions, and the many different answers to them, echoed through the national community for decades. Numerous searches for the *Sydney* were mounted by military and private groups, research was undertaken and conspiracy theories developed. In the meantime, the families of the *Sydney*'s sailors continued to grieve and to wonder where their loved ones lay.

In 2008, a Royal Commission was established to inquire into the fate of the *Sydney* and the ongoing mystery of the unknown sailor. The commission considered all the aspects of the case, surveyed the records, publications and other relevant documents, and made the most intensive efforts possible to establish the facts, publishing a weighty volume of its deliberations and findings in 2009.

Even as the Royal Commission deliberated, the wreck of HMAS *Sydney II* was finally found in March 2008. The news was announced shortly after notification that *Kormoran* had also been found. There are numerous memorials to the *Sydney* and her crew around Australia, the most impressive at Geraldton in Western Australia, where there is also a memorial to the Unknown Sailor. In 2006 the remains of the Christmas Island sailor were rediscovered and reinterred with full military honours on the mainland in the Geraldton War Cemetery, beneath a gravestone inscribed:

A Serviceman

of the

1939–1945

War

HMAS Sydney

The original Christmas Island gravesite has also been marked with a plaque. Efforts are being made to determine whether the unknown sailor was from the *Sydney* using DNA testing. At the time of writing no results have been announced.

The Long Tan cross

The story of the Long Tan cross is rich with the ironies of war, peace and memory. It began in the heat of the fiercest fighting of the Vietnam War during the 'Tet offensive', in which Communist North Vietnamese forces mounted large-scale attacks on American, Australian and South Vietnamese positions.

On 18 August 1966, members of D Company 6th Royal Australian Regiment engaged a much larger force of approximately 2500 in the Long Tan rubber plantation in South Vietnam's Phuoc Tuy province. Many D Company soldiers were National Servicemen, led mainly by professional soldiers. Rain fell throughout the three hours of the savage battle. It ended when the North Vietnamese forces withdrew, leaving 260 dead, with many wounded. Australian casualties were eighteen dead, with twenty-one wounded. D Company was awarded a US Presidential Unit Citation for 'extraordinary heroism while engaged in military operations against an opposing armed force'.

On the third anniversary of the battle, members of the regiment erected a white cross at the site. Designed by Regimental Sergeant Major (RSM) WO1 James 'Jimmy' Cruickshank, the distinctive cross with its central lozenge was built by the unit's Pioneer Platoon. After the war, it seems that the cross fell into decay and was removed to the Bien Hoa museum. But in 2002, as a result of ongoing efforts by the Australian Veterans Vietnam Reconstruction Group (AVVRG) and other bodies, a new cross was erected and unveiled at the same site, recognition by the Vietnamese people of the significance of the memorial for many Australians.

Long Tan has increasingly become the focus of commemorative visits by Vietnam veterans, their families and other Australians, both on Anzac Day and on Vietnam Veterans' Day (18 August), also known as Long Tan Day. Other Long Tan crosses have been erected in various locations throughout Australia. One can be found in 80 Mile Beach Caravan Park, near Broome, in Western Australia, which was unveiled on Vietnam Veterans' Day 2009. The impressively simple structure is in the form of a white wooden Long Tan cross, memorial plaques, military insignia and a flagpole set in a grassed garden, all enclosed in a white picket fence. The inscriptions on the cross is 'Lest We Forget'. The plaque at the bottom of the memorial reads:

THIS MEMORIAL WAS BUILT BY
THE VIETNAM VETERANS OF
80 MILE BEACH TO HONOUR
THOSE MEN AND WOMEN WHO
PAID THE SUPREME SACRIFICE
IN ALL THE WARS AND CONFLICTS

This memorial was instigated by regular holiday-makers Ray and Coral Miles and further developed by holidaying volunteers so that they would have somewhere local to observe Anzac Day and Vietnam Veterans' Day. Some materials were donated by local businesses. Up to 300 people now attend the Dawn Service there on 25 April, with large numbers attending on Vietnam Veterans' Day.

While built by and for Vietnam veterans, the memorial honours Australians who have died in all conflicts.

Flowers of remembrance

Certain plants and flowers have long been associated with mourning and remembrance, including the violet and the aromatic herb rosemary. These may be worn at funerals and at ceremonies commemorating the dead, or they may also be woven into commemorative wreaths together with other plants and placed at graves, or other markers of memory. In the Anzac tradition, some flowers have become powerful symbols for remembering the war dead.

Although rosemary has long been associated with remembrance, a specifically Australian and New Zealand floral custom is the wearing of a sprig of rosemary on Anzac Day. The hillsides of Gallipoli were covered with this herb, and for those who were there its pungent aroma became associated with the wartime experience itself. Rosemary subsequently became a commemorative emblem. Those who display medals—their own or a forebear's—on Anzac Day may wear rosemary beneath them. In recent years, the wearing of rosemary on Anzac Day has become a very widespread custom, necessitating the growth of a small cottage industry engaged in preparing wearable sprigs.

Arrangements of symbolic flowers and/or leaves have a long history and are particularly associated in Western societies with death and mourning. Wreath laying at memorials, graves and plaques was one of the earliest components of Anzac Day observances and remains a central element. Wreaths have often consisted of native flowers, although, in recent years, wreaths consisting of red poppies—previously more closely associated with Remembrance Day—have become popular at Anzac Day ceremonies. Simple bunches of flowers may also be placed at wreath-laying ceremonies, particularly by children.

Perhaps the most potent symbol of the Great War, the poppy is used for commemorative purposes around the world. Soldiers in France and in Belgium (often referred to as 'Flanders Fields') were impressed by the springtime blooming of these flowers in the devastated wasteland of the battlefields. It was not hard to make a connection between the blood red petals of the poppy and the blood-soaked ground on which millions had fought and been killed. The significance of the poppy was captured by a Canadian army doctor, John McCrae, who scribbled a few hurried verses after seeing a good friend die in the Second Battle of Ypres, Belgium, in spring 1915, and sent them off to the English magazine *Punch*. On its publication in December 1915,

McCrae's 'In Flanders Fields' caused a sensation throughout the English-speaking forces and home fronts, so simply but powerfully did the verses capture the sentiments of the moment.

In Flanders fields the poppies blow ['grow' in some versions]
Between the crosses, row on row,
That mark our place; and in the sky
The larks, still bravely singing, fly
Scarce heard amid the guns below.

We are the Dead. Short days ago
We lived, felt dawn, saw sunset glow,
Loved and were loved, and now we lie,
In Flanders fields.

Take up our quarrel with the foe:
To you from failing hands we throw
The torch; be yours to hold it high.
If ye break faith with us who die
We shall not sleep, though poppies grow
In Flanders fields.

McCrae died in 1918, worn out from his unremitting labours as an army doctor. But his unpretentious poem lived on and is the basis for much of the meaning attached to the poppy. In Australia, the poppy (usually made of paper or plastic) is worn or displayed on Remembrance (originally Armistice) Day, 11 November. An Australian custom had evolved in which a poppy is placed next to the name of a relation on the Wall of Memory at the Australian War Memorial in Canberra, forming an unofficial but moving visual commemoration.

In the gardens around Melbourne's Shrine of Remembrance, a custom combining the symbolism of both the poppy and rosemary can be seen. The wire 'stalks' of artificial poppies are wound around the tips of rosemary bushes growing in beds surrounding the memorial and its Eternal Flame of commemoration.

The lady of violets

Through two World Wars the Cheer-Up Society of South Australia brought comfort and practical assistance to soldiers and their families. The society was formed in November 1914 by businesswoman Alexandrine Seager (1870–1950). Mrs Seager had recently visited her son George in camp with the AIF at Morphettville, South Australia, and came away determined to play her part in the war effort. She appealed to the women of South Australia to support her, and rapidly established a large and expanding network of 'the highest type of womanhood' who would provide food, conversation and companionship to often lonely young recruits awaiting shipment to the front. Her stated aim was straightforward: 'to make life brighter for the gallant men'.

One of the society's first activities was to establish 'The Cheer-Up Hut'. At the beginning this was simply a tent, but it was soon replaced by a wooden structure located behind Adelaide Railway Station; from here the 'hut' later moved to Elder Park on the banks of the River Torrens. As the war progressed, society members also greeted soldiers returning from Gallipoli, the Middle East and the western front. By 1919, an extraordinary 200 000 soldiers would be fed and entertained in these makeshift premises by volunteer women from the society dressed in their bright white uniforms.

The Cheer-Up Society quickly became involved in fund-raising to pay for these practical measures, as well as with recruiting for the war. Mrs Seager's husband, Clarendon, was a recruiting officer and all her three sons fought with the AIF. On 2 July 1915 the Violet Day appeal was established, with the aim of obtaining funds to build a permanent clubhouse for the Cheer-Up Society. Violet flowers have long been associated with death, and this symbolism was adopted by the society as a fitting floral tribute for eternal remembrance of the war dead. Violet bouquets set in purple ribbons printed with the phrase 'In Memory' were sold in the streets of Adelaide, together with memorial buttons.

The day was launched with great fanfare and ceremony. Eminent members of the community spoke, bands played and the event concluded with the strains of 'The Last Post'. Violet Day was a success and became an annual observance throughout the war and long after. A collection of verse written specifically for the day was sold under the title Violet Verses. Alexandrine, herself a keen amateur poet, contributed a memorial poem:

Today we wear the clinging violet
In memory of the brave,
While ever thoughts of fond but proud regret,
Come surging wave on wave.

All proceeds went towards the work of the society, to which Mrs Seager devoted all her considerable energy and organising ability. The Cheer-Up Society also received funding from various other community groups, including the Country Women's Association. Later in the war, the society entered show business, sending troupes of professional performers to tour the battlefields and entertain the troops.

Not content with these considerable good works, Mrs Seager was primarily responsible for the foundation of the South Australian Returned Soldiers' Association, funded initially by funds from the Cheer-Up Society. She served as vice-president of the RSA from 1915 to 1919, when she resigned the office to a returned soldier.

In 1920, the work of the Cheer-Up Society was deemed to be no longer necessary and it was dissolved, although Violet Day continued, the date moving in 1928 from July to August. Alexandrine Seager returned to community work again during the Great Depression of the 1930s, although arthritis forced her to retire in 1937.

But only two years later the Cheer-Up Society was re-established, as a new generation faced up to the challenges of all-in war. The gleaming white ladies of the Great War now became 'Cheer-Up Girls' in uniforms similar to those of nurses. Like their predecessors, they volunteered to provide soldiers—including visiting Americans—with company, dance partners and a meal. After the war, the Cheer-Up Society carried on until 1964. Violet Day was held for the last time in 1970.

The energetic and dedicated founder of the Cheer-Up Society and Violet Day had no involvement with the new organisation. Alexandrine Seager died on Kangaroo Island in 1950 and was buried at Kingscote. Her husband had already passed away, but their three daughters attended the funeral, along with two of their sons. George had been killed at Gallipoli.

Sound and silence

Ceremonies of commemoration—religious or secular—usually feature songs, poetry and speeches. These may take the form of hymns or other sacred songs, and appropriate verse and fitting words, whether delivered as sermons or addresses. Instrumental music is often an important element of such events, together with silence in the form of personal prayer or reflection. Certain combinations of these elements have become characteristic of all Anzac commemorations.

A 'gunfire breakfast' is said to have been a basic meal taken by British soldiers when under fire, often featuring a tot of rum to instil bravery in the men. When the Dawn Service became a popular feature of Anzac Day observances during the 1930s, Returned Services Clubs instituted the custom of taking a light meal and glass of alcohol before attending the service. It was regarded as being symbolic of the meal that the first Anzacs took while waiting to leave the troopships and land on the beaches of Gallipoli.

While this ritual began as a private returned soldiers' observance, the gunfire breakfast or similar event is now a frequent feature of pre– or post–Dawn Service events on Anzac Day. As the day has increased in popularity over the last decade or more, so the late gunfire breakfast tradition has spread, being used to fill the time between the ending of the Dawn Service and the start of the morning march that takes place in many cities and towns. As many families now attend, the gunfire breakfast may often take the form of a sausage sizzle or similar non-alcoholic alternative.

The 'Ode' that is recited at the Dawn Service is derived from the Laurence Binyon poem 'For the Fallen' (1914).

Age shall not weary them, nor the years condemn.
At the going down of the sun and in the morning
We will remember them.

These lines gradually became the orthodox form from at least 1921, with the addition of 'Lest We Forget' from Kipling's 'Recessional' (1897), a poem popular in the Boer War period and after, particularly as a hymn. These lines are recited at Anzac Day ceremonies, with the participants repeating 'We will remember them' and, after a pause, usually intoning 'Lest we forget' in the manner of the 'amen' at the end of 'The Lord's Prayer'.

Although moments of silence had long been a feature of memorialisation for tragedies such as mining accidents, they were not a feature of wartime commemoration until World War I, the first conflict in which the sacrifice of the many had been recognised. The one- or two-minute silence that is a feature of most Anzac observations is thought to have evolved from a suggestion for five minutes of silence to mark the end of the war, made in the London *Evening News* of 8 May 1919 by Australian journalist Edward George Honey (1885–1922), using the pen name Warren Foster.

Nothing resulted from this, but some months later a South African politician, Sir Percy Fitzpatrick, suggested to the king's secretary that a few moments of silence be observed by British Empire countries each Armistice Day. According to tradition, the king used the Grenadier Guards to experiment with a commemorative silence and discovered that five minutes was too long a period. Just before Armistice Day 1919, the king proclaimed a two-minute silence so that 'the thoughts of everyone may be concentrated on reverent remembrance of the glorious dead'. Since then, the silence has also become part of the Returned Services League clubs' nightly 9 o'clock remembrance ritual and of Anzac Day ceremonies.

'The Last Post' is a simple but evocative military bugle call signifying the end of the day. It has become an aural symbol of Anzac Day commemoration, and is usually followed by a one- or two-minute period of silence, which is then concluded with the bugle call 'Rouse'—usually referred to, incorrectly, as 'Reveille', which is a different call.

Other customs derived from military tradition may feature in Anzac Day events, including the all-night 'vigil' over a war memorial that is to be the focus of the Dawn Service. The 'march' or 'parade' is also of military origin.

Hugo Throssell's VC

On 19 November 1933, Hugo Throssell VC took out his old service pistol and shot himself dead. He had come to loathe the war in which he had fought so gallantly and was an outspoken pacifist. This, together with financial problems, made him an outcast among those who had previously been his friends and acquaintances. Throssell's journey from idealistic young man and VC winner to such a bitter end was one of many tragedies in the difficult postwar decades of the 1920s and 1930s.

Born at Northam, Western Australia, in 1894, Throssell— together with his brother Frank, known as 'Ric'—joined the 10th Light Horse at the outbreak of war. As a Second Lieutenant, Hugo Throssell arrived on Anzac in time for the disastrous attack at the Nek in early August 1915. He was one of the few survivors, and resolved to revenge the 10th Light Horse. His opportunity came a few weeks later at Hill 60.

Less than a kilometre from the beach, the low, scrubby bump had been held by the Turks against all previous attacks. It effectively divided the British forces and the Anzacs. The commanders believed that taking the hill would allow the Allies to merge into a more effective force against the Turks. Late on the night of 29 August, Throssell led his men into a long trench, most of which was held by the enemy. While his men built a barricade, Throssell acted as guard and killed five Turks. A bomb fight began in which over 3000 missiles were hurled by both sides. The Australians kept their bombs on short fuses to make sure the Turks would not throw them back before they exploded, in 'a kind of tennis'. The deadly game went on until dawn, when the Turks launched three unsuccessful charges. Throssell was wounded twice but continued to fight, yelling encouragement to his men despite the blood covering his face, caused by shell splinter wounds. After finally seeking medical assistance, he returned to the fighting as soon as he was treated—until ordered out by a medical officer.

The battle for Hill 60 is one of the lesser-known disasters of Gallipoli, largely forgotten in comparison to chilling stories like those of the Nek and Lone Pine. By the time Throssell and his light horsemen arrived at the Hill 60 engagement, the 4th Brigade had lost almost three-quarters of its strength, the 9th and 10th Light Horse units had suffered almost total casualties, and only 365 men survived from the four regiments of the New Zealand Mounted Rifles who had already tried to take the position. The actions of Throssell and his men, while only one part of a larger attack, succeeded in holding their section of the trench against greatly superior forces. Throssell was awarded the only VC ever to be won by a light horseman, but Hill 60 remained firmly in Turkish control at the cost of 2400 casualties. The Anzacs were depleted and exhausted.

A British historian of Gallipoli, Robert Rhodes James, wrote that 'For connoisseurs of military futility, valour, incompetence and determination, the attacks on Hill 60 are in a class of their own'. The pointless slaughter made plain to any but the most pig-headed that the Gallipoli campaign could not succeed. General Hamilton was relieved of his command of the campaign and replaced by General Charles Monro. Monro immediately understood the hopelessness of the situation, a view backed by Lord Kitchener, British supreme commander, when he came to see for himself in November. A little over a month later, the Anzacs had left Gallipoli.

Throssell recovered from his wounds in Egypt, during which time he contracted meningitis, an affliction that would trouble him physically and mentally for the rest of his life. Promoted to captain, he was again wounded in the second battle of Gaza in April 1917. His brother went missing in the same battle and Throssell crawled out into no man's land, whistling their boyhood signal in a hopeless attempt to find him. Hugo Throssell continued fighting in Palestine and was at the head of the 10th Light Horse guard of honour when Jerusalem fell to the British and Australian forces in 1917.

After the war, Throssell married the radical Australian writer Katharine Susannah Prichard in London. They returned to Australia to farm and engage in political activism. The war hero and the Communist author had an exotic appeal in the politically troubled 1920s. But with the onset of economic Depression in the following decade, Throssell failed in a number of business ventures and the family went heavily into debt. While Prichard was pursuing her political convictions in the Soviet Union in 1933, Hugo Throssell shot himself, believing that his war service pension would benefit his wife and son. He left a note on the back of the will he had written a day earlier: 'I have never recovered from my 1914–18 experiences, and with this in view I appeal to the State to see that my wife and child get the usual war pension. No one could have a truer mate'. Captain Throssell was buried with full military honours.

The Victoria Cross remained in the family until 1983 when Hugo and Katharine's son, Ric, presented it to the Campaign for Nuclear Disarmament. The RSL subsequently purchased the medal and donated it to the Australian War Memorial, where it rests today, as part of an extensive collection of Australian VCs.

Hugo Throssell, VC is commemorated in a number of road names in the southwest and in a memorial outside Fitzgerald's Hotel in Northam. In the 1950s, local Greenmount residents raised funds for a playground dedicated to Throssell in the park opposite the home he and his family had occupied. At the same time, a memorial bus shelter was erected outside the park. The shelter is in the form of a small granite rotunda with a tiled roof. The dedication reads simply:

To the Memory of
Captain Hugo Throssell V.C.
1914–1918

Why build such a memorial, particularly so many years after the Great War and Hugo's suicide? No-one now seems to know.

But it is perhaps significant that it commemorates only his war service, rather than his life. This tragic story of one Anzac and his medal connects the national and the local, highlighting the continuing complexities of war, heroism, peace and memory.

Do you remember?

An anonymous reflection on the Great War by someone who must have been there captures the mixed emotions of nostalgia, regret and sorrow that characterise the aftermath of every war. It is titled simply, 'Do You Remember?'

. . . the day you enlisted, when you waited in a queue
(They called it a 'line' in those days). The first visit to the QM store,
Trying on your first digger hat and your army boots,
Your first night in camp between army blankets,
Your first leave in uniform—feeling a little self-conscious.
Our first long route-march, when you grumbled because the others grumbled.
But thought it was not so bad, really.
The soft-drink merchants on the road and the ten minute halts.
Your first resentment at being put on menial fatigue.
The bloke who kept the troops in good humour on the march.
The bloke who always had a yarn about 'a bloke and a tart'.
The bird who'd never close the door or a tent flap
And who'd step all over you with muddy boots coming in.
The first march through town and the friends on the footpath.
Your last glimpse of the Australian shore before 'going below'.
The flying fishes in the spray at the stern.

The crown and anchor on the hatch.

The cry of 'mess orderlies'.

The blue of the Indian Ocean—the heat of the Canal.

Your first morning on Egyptian soil—'Gibbit piastre, Mister?'

Your first trip to Cairo or Alexandria—'Clean boots, Mr
McKenzie?'

The route-marches in the sand, and all-night manoeuvres.

The cart-wheels of figs and the lovely-complexioned women of
Lemnos.

Your days on Anzac—the beach and the steep climbs, with the
queues for chlorinated water.

Beachy Bill—the Turkish Howitzer at tea-time—'his' snipers.

Your first look at France and your first feed of 'deux oeufs'.

Your first 'ride-up' in cattle trucks—'Eight chevaux, forty
hommes'.

The Froggies and the cess-pit in the farmhouse yard.

The whine of the bullets and the splatter of machine guns.

The raiding parties, wiring and digging, and the saps.

The duckboards going up the line.

The first night spent within easy reach of Fritz.

The first raiding party, and the 'hop-over'.

The minutes leading up to zero-hour at dawn.

The cry of 'stretcher-bearer wanted on the right'.

The winter of 1916–17 and the mud of the Somme.

The trench with the hand of a Fritzy sticking out.

The trench with the floor of 'ballooned' dead Fritzes.

The first gas masks and the sinister 'plop' of the gas shells.

The rum issue and the occasional strawberry jam amongst all
the apricot tins.

The swagger breeches bought from Tommies for twenty francs.

The coffee-stall halfway up, with its empty tins for cups.

The day you were hit (secretly glad to be out of it for a while).

Your first day with an army nurse taking care of you.

Blighty, the theatre and the music hall stars, to say nothing of Leicester Square.

Trips to the places you always wanted to see; the Beefeaters at the Tower.

Armistice Day, 1918, La Guerre fini.

Do you remember? Can you ever forget?

Select sources and references

Contemporary sources of significant direct quotations and excerpts are given here, together with selected secondary works relevant to the themes of each chapter.

Foundations of Anzac

Salt, 24 April 1944; 5 June 1944.

The Capricornian (Rockhampton, Qld), 28 November 1914.

A. H. Edmonds, 'The Anzacs at Lemnos', *Reveille*, 1 April 1935.

Archie Albert Barwick diaries, 1915–16.

Albert Knaggs diary, 1915–16.

Sydney Morning Herald (NSW), 8 May 1915.

Sydney Morning Herald (NSW), 15 May 1915. A re-edited version was published in the *Commonwealth of Australia Gazette*, no. 39, 17 May 1915.

The Advertiser (Adelaide, SA), 7 July 1915.

C. E. W. Bean (ed.), *The Anzac Book*, Cassell, London, 1916.

Aubrey Herbert, *Ben Kendim: A Record of Eastern Travels*, Hutchinson, London, 1924.

Albany Advertiser (WA), 8 March 1916.

The Register (Adelaide, SA), 23 December 1918.
Camperdown Chronicle (Vic.), 26 September 1916.
The West Australian (Perth, WA), 2 January 1918.
Queanbeyan Age and Queanbeyan Observer (NSW), 8 March 1918.
John Robertson, *ANZAC and Empire*, Hamlyn, Melbourne, 1990.

Heroes of Anzac

Yea Chronicle (Vic.), 25 November 1915.
The West Australian (Perth, WA), 13 July 1915.
Reveille, 31 August 1931.
Michael McKernan, 'McKenzie, William (1869–1947)', *Australian Dictionary of Biography*, National Centre of Biography, Australian National University, vol. 10, Melbourne University Press, Melbourne, 1986.
The Argus (Melbourne, Vic.), 10 April 1920.
Albert Horace Cooper, *Character Glimpses: Australians on the Somme*, Waverley Press, Sydney (192_?).
The Daily News (Perth, WA), 17 December 1918 (third edition).
The Horsham Times (Vic.), 2 May 1919.
The Mercury (Hobart, Tas.), 14 January 1918.
Albany Advertiser (WA), 27 October 1941.
Alan Stephens, 'Truscott, Keith William (Bluey) (1916–1943)', *Australian Dictionary of Biography*, National Centre of Biography, Australian National University, vol. 16, Melbourne University Press, Melbourne, 2002.
The Australian Women's Weekly, 9 January 1943.
Courier Mail (Brisbane, Qld), 31 October 1942.
http://www.ww2australia.gov.au/farflung/cuttingcables.html
http://www.museum.wa.gov.au/collections/maritime/submarine/xcraft.asp
W. Gammage, *The Broken Years: Australian Soldiers in the Great War*, Penguin, Ringwood, Vic. 1975.

The home front

The Bulletin, 24 May 1917.
The Mercury (Hobart, Tas.), 3 May 1954.

The North Western Advocate and the Emu Bay Times (Tas.), 3 December 1918.

The Codford Wheeze, no. 3, 25 December 1918.

Hugh Garland, *Vignettes of War: from the notebook of a journalist in arms*, W. K. Thomas, Adelaide, 1918.

W. G. Millard diary (author's collection).

The Advertiser (Adelaide, SA), 4 August 1915.

'A. Tiveychoc' (Rowland Edward Lording), *There and Back*, Returned Sailors and Soldiers' Imperial League of Australia, Sydney, 1935.

Anonymous, *Instructions for American servicemen in Australia*, War and Navy Departments Washington, D.C., 1942.

Grace Luckman diary (author's collection).

Michael McKernan, *All in!: fighting the war at home*, St Leonards, 1995.

Laughter

www.greatwar.nl/

C. E. W. Bean (ed.), *The Anzac Book*, Cassell, London, 1916.

Anon., *Lest We Forget: Digger Tales 1914–1918, 1939–1941*, Melbourne (1941?).

Australian Corps News Sheet, 6 November 1918.

Anzac Records Gazette, November 1915.

Australasian Post, 26 April 1956.

Anon., *Digger Doings*, Geo Nye, Petersham (c. 1943).

Anon., *Marching On: Tales of the Diggers*, Geo Nye, Petersham (c. 1942).

League Post, 1 October 1932.

'The Twinkler' (F. J. Mills), *Square Dinkum*, Melville & Mullen, Melbourne, 1917.

'Semaphore', *Digger Yarns (and some others) to Laugh At*, E H Gibbs & Son, Melbourne, 1936.

Anon., *Digger Aussiosities*, Sydney, 1927.

G. Cuttriss, *Over the Top with the 3rd Australian Division*, London (1918?).

Smith's Weekly, Christmas 1942.

Mud and Blood, 2/23 Australian Infantry Battalion newsletter, 25 June 1941. Author's collection.

G. Seal, *Inventing Anzac: The Digger and National Mythology*, University of Queensland Press, St Lucia, 2004.

Legends of Anzac

Truth, February 1915.

F. Loraine Petre, *The History of the Norfolk Regiment 1685–1918*, vol. 2, Jarrold & Sons, The Empire Press, Norwich, 1922.

Sunday Times (Perth, WA), 16 April 1916, Second Section.

C. E. W. Bean (ed.), *The Anzac Book*, Cassell, London, 1916.

Australasian Post, 26 October 1967.

The Times, 10 May 1915.

Archibald Baxter, *We Will Not Cease*, Victor Gollancz, London, 1939.

Aubrey Wade, *The War of the Guns*, Batsford, London, 1936.

H. S. Gullett and C. Barrett (eds), *Australia in Palestine*, Angus & Robertson, Sydney, 1919.

C. E. W. Bean, *The Story of ANZAC: Official History of Australia in the War of 1914–1918*, vols I and II, Angus & Robertson, Sydney, 1936.

Burra Record (SA), 5 April 1916.

Peter Stanley, *Bad Characters: Sex, Crime, Mutiny, Murder and the Australian Imperial Force*, Pier 9, Sydney, 2010.

Memories

C. E. W. Bean (ed), *The Anzac Book*, Cassell, London, 1916.

Morning Bulletin (Rockhampton, Qld), 10 May 1919.

The Listening Post, 24 April 1931.

www.australiansatwar.gov.au

Sunday Times (Perth, WA), 22 July 1917, First Section.

Evening News (London), 8 May 1919.

C. Longmore (ed), *Carry On! The Traditions of the AIF*, Imperial Printing Company, Perth, 1940.

W. G. Millard papers (author's collection).

Bruce Scates, *Return to Gallipoli*, Cambridge University Press, Melbourne, 2006.

Picture credits

Foundations of Anzac
Gallipoli Peninsula, Turkey. Australian troops relax inside a captured Turkish trench at Lone Pine. Photo taken by C. E. W. Bean, 12 August 1915. Australian War Memorial no. G01126

Heroes of Anzac
Photo taken by George Silk, Buna, Papua, 25 December 1942. Private George C. 'Dick' Whittington being helped along a track through the kunai grass towards a field hospital at Dobodura. The Papuan native helping him is Raphael Oimbari. Australian War Memorial no. 014028

The home front
Christmas, 1918. Patients and nursing staff prepared to celebrate at No. 3 Australian Army Auxiliary Hospital at Dartford, England. Australian War Memorial no. H03905

Laughter
Vaire-sur-Somme, France. 5 May 1918. Australian soldiers resting at the ferry landing on the bank of the River Somme. Note 'Circular Quay' painted on the wall, a reference to the famous large ferry terminal in Sydney. Australian War Memorial no. E04795

Legends of Anzac
Photo taken by C. E. W. Bean of troops landing in Anzac Cove at about 10 am on 25 April 1915. The horse boats (with the ends down) had landed mules. Troops can also be seen landing at the southern end of the beach. In the background is the light cruiser HMS *Bacchante*. Australian War Memorial no. G00905

Memories
Photo taken by George Wilkins of Lt Herbert Buchanan standing beside a flowering fruit tree on Silt Spur. The tree probably originated from an apricot or plum seed discarded by a soldier in 1915. One of a series of photographs taken on the Gallipoli Peninsula under the direction of Captain C. E. W. Bean of the Australian Historical Mission, during the months of February and March, 1919. Australian War Memorial no. G01951

Index